Dispersed but Not Destroyed

Dispersed but Not Destroyed

A History of the Seventeenth-Century Wendat People

Kathryn Magee Labelle

UBCPress · Vancouver · Toronto

21 20 19 18 17 16 15 14 13   5 4 3 2 1

Printed in Canada on FSC-certified ancient-forest-free paper (100% post-consumer recycled) that is processed chlorine- and acid-free.

Library and Archives Canada Cataloguing in Publication

Labelle, Kathryn Magee, 1983-
  Dispersed but not destroyed : a history of the seventeenth-century Wendat people / Kathryn Magee Labelle.

Includes bibliographical references and index.
Also issued in electronic format.
ISBN 978-0-7748-2555-9 (bound); ISBN 978-0-7748-2556-6 (pbk.)

  1. Wyandot Indians – History – 17th century. 2. Huron Indians – History – 17th century. I. Title.

E99.H9L32 2013   971.004'97555   C2012-907138-2

Canadä

UBC Press gratefully acknowledges the financial support for our publishing program of the Government of Canada (through the Canada Book Fund), the Canada Council for the Arts, and the British Columbia Arts Council.

This book has been published with the help of a grant from the Canadian Federation for the Humanities and Social Sciences, through the Awards to Scholarly Publications Program, using funds provided by the Social Sciences and Humanities Research Council of Canada.

Printed in Canada
Set in Galliard and New Baskerville by Artegraphica Design Co. Ltd.
Copy editor: Stephanie VanderMeulen
Proofreader: Helen Godolphin
Indexer: Cheryl Lemmens
Cartographer: Eric Leinberger

UBC Press
The University of British Columbia
2029 West Mall
Vancouver, BC V6T 1Z2
www.ubcpress.ca

For Grandpa: Robert Stanley Magee (1924-2012)

Contents

Acknowledgments

THIS BOOK WOULD NOT have been possible without the help and support of several people and institutions. This work stems in large part from my doctoral research. I am sincerely indebted to the guidance and support of Margaret Newell, Lucy Murphy, John Brooke, and Alan Gallay. Along the way I was lucky enough to gain additional professional insight from Carolyn Podruchny, Brenda Macdougall, Nicole St-Onge, Christine Belangée-Morris, Daniel Richter, Susan Sleeper-Smith, Geoffrey Parker, Roger Carpenter, Charles Garrad, John Steckley, Thomas Peace, Joseph Genetin-Pilawa, Megan McMullen, Melissah Pawlikowski, Michael Cox, Andrew Sturtevant, Guillaume Teasdale, Robert Englebert, Omeasoo Butt, Kit Bevan, Rebecca Dirflinger, and Triet Nguyen. Special appreciation goes to Elizabeth Mancke for endless hours of "porch" discussion on North American alliances and systems of power. Members of the modern Wendat diaspora also gave essential support. I am eternally grateful to archivists Jonathan Lainey at Library and Archives Canada and Stéphane Picard at the Wendake Archives, with special appreciation and gratitude to my Wendat aunt, Chief Janith English and my Wendat uncle, Georges E. Sioui.

My research would not have been possible without the generous assistance provided by the following: the Ohio State University, the University of Ottawa, the University of Saskatchewan, the Lynde and Harry Bradley Foundation Fellowship, CIC-American Indian Studies Consortium, Carl J. Ekberg Research Grant from the Center for French Colonial Studies, Social Science and Humanities Research Council of Canada, American Association of University Women, the Mershon Center For International Security Studies, the D'arcy McNickle Center for American Indian and Indigenous Studies, and the Voyageur Project.

Finally, I am thankful for the years of unwavering encouragement from family and friends. Thank you to Kayla Scott, Lindsay Bolton, Alison Dickey, Jennifer Fair, Sean Magee, Kim Magee, Chris Tait, Dorothy Doyle,

Don Doyle, Joyce Magee, Bob Magee, Sylvie Vaillancourt, Julie Lalonde, Rachelle Labelle, and Yvonne Vaillancourt. Of course, none of this would have been achieved without my parents Steve and Diane Magee, and their persistent dedication to my work and success – this project is due in large part to them. Last, but not least, I am forever grateful for the devotion and love of my husband, Maurice JR Labelle. He inspired me to go above and beyond traditional sources and interpretations, pushing me to continue in moments of uncertainty and doubt. I look forward to many more projects (professionally and personally) with him by my side.

A Brief Chronology

Selected Wendat Events and Migration, 1400-1701

Wendake

ca. 1400	The Bear and Cord join to create the Wendat Confederacy
ca. 1570	The People of the Deer join the Confederacy
1609	Samuel de Champlain meets the Wendat in Wendake for the first time
ca. 1610	The People of the Rock join the Confederacy
1634	The Jesuits establish residence in Wendake; first epidemic
1636	The Feast of Souls at the village of Ossossane
1637	The headmen Taretande and Aenon die
1648-49	The Wendat are attacked by the Iroquois and their villages are abandoned
1649-51	The Wendat seek refuge at Gahoendoe Island

Wendat Migration and Settlement in the East

1651	Île d'Orléans
1656	Quebec City
1657	Some Wendat decide to join various Iroquois communities
1660	Fort of the Huron
1668	Beauport
1669	Notre-Dame-de-Foy
1673	Ancienne Lorette
1697	Jeune Lorette

Wendat Migration and Settlement in the West

1651	Mackinac Island
1653	Green Bay
1659	Chippewa River
1661	Chequamegon
1671	Michilimackinac
1701	Fort Pontchartrain/Detroit

Dispersed but Not Destroyed

Introduction

THIS BOOK BEGINS WHERE the Wendat world begins, with the Legend of Sky Woman.[1] In 1912, Catherine Johnson, a descendant of the seventeenth-century Wendat Confederacy, shared her people's Creation story, which she called "The Young Woman Fallen From Above." According to Johnson, Sky Woman, or Aataentsic, fell from her home in the clouds at a time when the world was a vast ocean inhabited only by sea animals. These animals gathered together in council upon witnessing the falling woman. In order to save her life, they agreed to create a landmass on the back of a giant turtle. Toad led the initiative by diving to the bottom of the ocean, retrieving mud and placing it on the back of Turtle. By the time Sky Woman reached the water, they had formed an earthly continent. Wild geese grabbed hold of Aataentsic's feet and arms to cushion the fall, guiding her to her new home, which we now call North America. The Wendat believe themselves to be the descendants of Aataentsic and they have structured their society in relation to these cosmological origins.[2] In many ways, the Legend of Sky Woman highlights some of the most significant features of early modern Wendat society; it emphasizes the important roles of leaders (Toad), women (Aataentsic), and communal systems of power (the council). By the 1600s, the Children of Aataentsic had formed one of the most important polities in seventeenth-century North America.[3]

Situated within the territory stretching from Georgian Bay in the north to Lake Simcoe in the east (also known as Wendake), the Wendat Confederacy flourished for two hundred years by the time of European contact.[4] The Confederacy consisted of four or five autonomous nations: the Bear Nation (Attignawantan), the Nation of the Rock (Arendaeronnon), the People of the Cord (Attigneenongnahac), the People of the Deer (Tahontaenrat), and perhaps a fifth group, the People of the Marsh (Ataronchronon).[5] Every nation included several villages, organized around twelve matrilineal clans – Big Turtle, Little Turtle, Mud Turtle,

Wolf, Bear, Beaver, Deer, Porcupine, Striped Turtle, Highland Turtle, Snake, and Hawk. While politics remained a predominantly local affair, with decisions reflecting village-level interests, village representatives frequently came together for general meetings of their nation, and at least once a year delegates joined to discuss matters concerning the Confederacy at large. Within this multifaceted association, each village and nation remained free to create separate agreements in terms of trade, military, and diplomatic policies, although they often made collective decisions concerning these aspects as well. At most, the Confederacy consisted of an estimated 30,000 people, occupying roughly twenty to thirty palisaded longhouse villages that changed location about every ten to thirty years.[6]

The Wendat were part of a larger Nadowekian ethnic heritage.[7] They shared a common Nadowekian language, matricentric social order, and agricultural tradition with other groups, such as the Iroquois, Mingo, Cherokee, Erie, Neutral, Petun, and Susquehannock. The Nadowek were matrilineal and matriarchal; thus, they structured clans around the female line, and women controlled community fields, activities around the home, and domestic life. Clan mothers also exercised significant influence concerning the selection of leaders and their community's participation in warfare. By the sixth century A.D., most Nadowek had transitioned to maize agriculture, supporting relatively large and sedentary villages in comparison to Native societies centred on hunting and gathering.

Although one might suspect that the similarities between the seventeenth-century Nadowek would foster close relations, the Wendat often chose alliances with groups outside this cultural category. From the thirteenth century on, the Wendat maintained robust trading networks with their Anishinaabe neighbours through the exchange of corn for furs.[8] This system extended beyond economic and subsistence partnership, developing into an official alliance that connected the Wendat and Anishinaabeg through marriage, diplomacy, and cultural rituals. The so-called Coalition dominated the geopolitics of the Great Lakes and St. Lawrence corridor for centuries.

The Wendat expanded their alliance system with the arrival of French colonists and missionaries. Beginning with Samuel de Champlain's expedition in 1603, and later the establishment of Quebec City (1608), Trois-Rivières (1634), and Montreal (1642), the founding of New France presented innovative opportunities for Wendat confederates. These sites became not only seventeenth-century hubs for French commerce, culture, and colonial political power but also points of interest for the Wendat concerned in extending trade and diplomatic initiatives. Missionaries were a key component to the French–Wendat alliance. Jesuits became permanent residents of Wendake by the 1630s. Through their Christian faith and a desire to convert Natives, these men dedicated years, if not their lives, to the Wendat people. Missionaries and the Wendat exchanged intellectual capital, discussing not only spiritual beliefs but also secular policies connected to trade and politics. Often the Jesuits acted as interpreters and middlemen between French administrators and Wendat headmen, facilitating treaty negotiations between the two. In addition, French citizens such as lay workers for the missionaries, fur traders, judges, and notaries, as well as colonial administrators including governors, intendants, and soldiers, became well-known figures to the Wendat community. In many cases, French colonists forged intimate ties with the Wendat, becoming their husbands, landlords, and godparents. Governors in particular engaged in face-to-face meetings with Wendat diplomats and traders, and forged long-lasting and personal relationships with them. This type of intricate association remained an important component to Wendat foreign policy and alliance making for over a century.

If the Wendat viewed the Anishinaabeg and French as their foremost allies, then unequivocally the Nadowek nations comprising the Iroquois Confederacy (Mohawk, Seneca, Onondaga, Oneida, and Cayuga) were their principal enemies. Iroquois territory included most of present-day central and upstate New York, which led to frequent encounters with the Wendat along the Ottawa and St. Lawrence rivers. Much like their Wendat foes, each Iroquois nation remained autonomous while still loyal to their overall alliance. The Iroquois frequently campaigned (both independently from each other as well as in unified fronts) against the Wendat to avenge blood feuds and because of a desire to repopulate communities by adopting captives. The central location of Wendake in respect to river systems and commercial depots of the northeast, along with the regular trade of the Wendat with the Anishinaabeg, further motivated Iroquois aggression. During the seventeenth century, the Wendat orchestrated an elaborate geopolitical strategy, making them powerful diplomats and traders and thereby the targets of envious Iroquois adversaries.

By the mid-seventeenth century, many customary features of Wendat society, including leadership roles, women's status, and power dynamics, were under attack. Within the span of only a few decades, European encounters set in motion a series of deadly epidemics throughout Wendake that killed many of its leaders. The combination of Christian patriarchal influences, as well as a lack of choice in community headmen, destabilized women's authority, and incessant warfare threatened their ability to maintain trade and an agricultural surplus. Then, in 1649, the Iroquois executed a number of successful attacks on Wendat villages. Despite concerted efforts by Wendat warriors, many lost their lives in battle, while others became Iroquois captives destined for torture or forced adoption. Those left behind witnessed the ruin of Wendat homes and fields, as well as widespread expressions of panic and despair. As a result, survivors reconsidered the security of Wendake. After much deliberation, they resolved to evacuate their homeland and recreate their communities in new territories. The Wendat packed up their belongings, dismantled their villages, and tried to avoid any further Iroquois encounters as they set out to start anew. This Wendat dispersal, according to conventional accounts, marks the "destruction" of the Confederacy.[9]

Scholars have contributed greatly to our knowledge of Wendat society and in particular their history before 1650. In fact, the most influential studies focus on the pre-dispersal period.[10] Notwithstanding their importance, this temporal framework tends to constrict Wendat history and implies a declension model typically used to describe the experiences of Native Americans in the post-contact period. This model portrays Native peoples as passive casualties (in this case, the victims of Iroquois aggression and European disease), which leads to the assumption that the Wendat experienced destruction as a people. With the Iroquois conquest of 1649 as the climax, Wendat history beyond the dispersal becomes an epilogue perpetuating the belief that whatever happened afterwards is marginal to the overall understanding of the early modern Wendat. As a result, the extermination of one of the most powerful polities of seventeenth-century North America remains an emblematic conclusion – or allusion – to the story of first encounters.

By refocusing the historical lens on the dispersal and its aftermath, this book is an attempt to extend the seventeenth-century Wendat narrative. The Wendat re-emerge in the historiography as important leaders, interpreters, and signatories during the negotiations of the famous Great Peace of Montreal in 1701 – fifty years after their evacuation from Wendake. Their presence indicates that they retained their status as influential diplomats and traders despite the dispersal, and complicates the notion of a destroyed people. The following chapters trace Wendat resistance, evacuation, and relocation from 1630 to 1701.[11] Through this framework, notions of identity, cultural continuity, and diaspora formation unique to Wendat society after 1650 are explored. Overall, I contend that the Wendat remained culturally and politically "Wendat" throughout the seventeenth century. By extension, I counter the declension model in terms of Native political organization, women's power, and cultural assimilation after European encounters. The power of the Confederacy did not cease to exist in the latter half of the century; Wendat leaders continued to present themselves collectively at councils, trade negotiations, and diplomatic ventures, relying on old, established customs of accountability and consensus. Similarly, despite the fact that women may have lost ground in terms of political influence due to Jesuit persuasion towards a patriarchal society, they nonetheless found solace and strength as Christians, which gave them a powerful place within their new communities as lay ministers, seminarians, and nuns. Last but not least, the Wendat retained cultural traits that maintained their unique "Wendat" identity after 1650. For the most part, they did not become French, Anishinaabeg, or Iroquois, as scholars have suggested.

Although situated in the seventeenth-century Great Lakes region, a time and space often framed by European–Native American encounters, this is not a typical "contact" narrative. Clearly focused on the Wendat experience, Europeans, particularly the French, are present but are given no more weight than the Anishinaabeg or Iroquois. Through this approach I dissect Wendat foreign relations in terms of multiple systems of power and within a North American rather than Eurocentric context.[12] It is my hope that this type of research will contribute to several scholarly discussions beyond the Wendat and with broader scope.

First, this research demonstrates that Europeans were not the only ones who transplanted their societies in seventeenth-century North America in an attempt to recreate and impose familiar structures within a new homeland. Native Americans did this as well. The Wendat uprooted their population, packed up their material and cultural capital, and re-established themselves in far-off lands according to Wendat customs. While important research has been done on the ability of Native refugees to create new worlds and cultural matrix, the Wendat experience highlights how Natives based additional removal strategies on old systems and traditions.[13]

The Wendat dispersal also contributes to our knowledge of indigenous forced migrations. The most comprehensive studies of North American Native removals and relocations focus on the infamous Trail of Tears and the American Indian Removal Act of 1830.[14] Yet, many Native Americans underwent similar situations of relocation two hundred years earlier. In the northeast alone, the Wendat joined many other groups, such as the Ottawa, Erie, Neutral, Potawatomi, and Miami, who fled Iroquois violence and European disease. The Wendat experience is, therefore, an investigation into Native diasporas of the colonial period, offering a detailed portrait of the strategies, tactics, and cost of removal within a seventeenth-century context.

A third aim of this book is to redefine early North American societies into systems of power. These systems were based on multifunctional networks rather than static organizational frameworks rooted in ethnic, tribal, or regional similarities.[15] Understandably, politics, military defence, ethnicity, trade, and religion fundamentally shaped European political organizations in the seventeenth century, thus making them logical points of reference for historians engaging with European and Euro-American sources.[16] In reality, Native systems looked very different from European ones, as the contrast between metropoles in Europe and the lack of identifiable centres in North America demonstrates.[17] The prevalence of these seemingly ambiguous Native networks, often functioning outside the realm of the popular Wendat or Iroquois Confederacy framework, suggests that they were some of the most prevailing systems of alliances within the North American context. A "system" paradigm, therefore, questions the validity of confederacies as an appropriate analytical tool for Native North America, offering diasporic polities as an alternative.[18]

Finally, in writing this history, I give considerable weight to the personal biographies of Wendat individuals as a means to offset the widespread "faceless" history of Native North America. Historian Daniel Richter attributes the lack of research on Native individuals to evidentiary problems, noting, "It is much easier to reconstruct the abstract forces that constrained the seventeenth-century Native world than it is to recover the personal experiences of the people who struggled to give the world human shape."[19] Like the European imperial sources they draw upon, historians privilege group actions and pan-Indian policies rather than individual agency. By including biographical accounts of Wendat people, this work gives voice to the individuals who influenced this period of Wendat history. The initiatives of particular male and female Wendat leaders allowed them to survive their dispersal; whether relocating to Anishinaabe territory, sending daughters to convents, or replacing civil headmen with war chiefs, Wendat strategies rested on the ideas and actions of specific people.

This book is organized into three sections. In Part 1: Resistance, I offer a thematic analysis of disease, diplomacy, and warfare before the dispersal, emphasizing the factors that led to the Iroquois victory. Chapter 1 begins in the 1630s with the introduction of European disease in Wendake, and examines Wendat civil leaders and their policies to address the loss of life and social unrest before the dispersal. The actions of influential Wendat leaders such as Taretande and Aenon illustrate the diplomatic successes, political divisions, failed military strategies, and secret meetings that reveal Wendat responses to the crises they faced. This chapter also assesses the impact that the deaths of key leaders had on the community during an era of epidemic disease, and explores the ways in which leadership changes affected Wendat decision making. Ultimately, in contrast to accounts that stress Wendat disorganization and cultural decline, I argue that the 1630s was simultaneously a time of collaboration and renewal.

Chapter 2 explores Nadowek warfare in the 1640s and charts the emergence of what I term "a culture of war" during the heightened conflict with the Iroquois. The Wendat military defeat in 1649 did not result from a single decisive attack by the Iroquois, but rather was the culmination of a decade of battles between the two groups. Military strategy and leadership changed during this period. Most strikingly, war chiefs replaced the civil headmen who had traditionally led the Confederacy. This shift in political power, from civil leaders to those charged to lead in times of war, helps to explain some of the more frequent violence of the 1640s. Although the Wendat experienced extreme levels of conflict and captivity, they won notable battles as well, presenting a strong opposition to the Iroquois throughout the period despite their loss in 1649.

Part 2: Evacuation and Relocation, explores the people, ideas, and motivations behind the community's decision to abandon the Wendat homeland in 1649, as well as the experience of migration itself. Each of the five chapters – "Wendat Country," "Anishinaabe Neighbours," "The West," "The East," and "Iroquois Country" – focuses on destinations the Wendat chose for relocation. Chapter 3 examines the decision to leave Wendat villages and take refuge in other parts of Wendat country – most notably the relocation of thousands to Gahoendoe. During the interim settlement of this island, many Wendat experienced famine, fear, and death. Out of an estimated six thousand initial residents, only one thousand survived. Ultimately, this chapter looks at the internal decision-making process that preceded the move to Gahoendoe in 1649, and the circumstances that pushed the Wendat to reconsider their choice a year later. The island relocation formed an integral part of a calculated plan to overcome the military defeat by the Iroquois and keep a foothold in the geopolitical world of the northeast. Indeed, while disease and the Iroquois factored into the Wendat resolution to leave their homeland, the food crisis on Gahoendoe in 1649-50 was the most important issue shaping the future of the Wendat and their subsequent exodus from Wendat country.

Chapters 4 to 7 examine the processes and experiences of the Wendat survivors who relocated outside traditional Wendat territory. Many Wendat chose to move east towards Quebec City, while others went west, travelling towards Lake Michigan and settling near Michilimackinac. Still, the majority of the Wendat chose to relocate within existing Native societies, ranging from their rivals, the Iroquois, to their allies such as the Petun and Ojibwe. One of the surprising elements of this story is that as a survival tactic, the Wendat consciously decided to become geographically divided. This strategy expanded Wendat geopolitical boundaries; spreading themselves throughout the Great Lakes allowed the Wendat to re-establish their regional position as influential diplomats and traders. In contrast to the central and confined parameters of Wendake, the diaspora extended Wendat spatial power from Quebec City to Michilimackinac. Despite the changed geopolitical realities and Iroquois ascendancy, Wendat acceptance of Christian conversion and continued economic activity helped them maintain crucial ties with the French, which in turn gave the Children of Aataentsic leverage with both their allies and enemies.

The third and final section of this book, Part 3: Diaspora, outlines the societies that the Wendat created in exile by exploring key themes in diaspora Wendat culture. It revisits the communities discussed in Part 2, and offers an extended analysis and concluding remarks on the persistent Wendat concepts of leadership, women, and power. In Chapter 8, "Leadership," I contend that despite the dispersal, with its various migrations and resettlement strategies, as well as changes in geography, demography, and community, the nature of Wendat leadership remained intact. Continuing the emphasis on individual Native stories, this chapter includes biographical sketches of Wendat leaders in the post-dispersal period. Leadership provides a prism for understanding how the Wendat maintained their polity, because headmen exercised their duties in relation to their community and formal alliances. The cults of personality that emerged around certain exemplary leaders also offered the Wendat a means of maintaining cultural values across generations.

Chapter 9 examines another important leadership class – women. Many accounts insist that Wendat women lost political and social status due to the dispersal. Although this might be true in the long run, it was not immediate; also, this teleological argument does not reflect the numerous ways women continued to project their influence in the post-dispersal period. Women instigated relocations and shaped the early stages of diaspora formation. At the same time, the dispersal created unique new opportunities for women to assume leadership roles, enter trade, and acquire formal education. On the whole, Christianity did not constrain women as in the pre-dispersal period, but provided a vehicle for unity, spirituality, and social mobility.

Concluding this section is a chapter called "Power," in which I analyze the sources and systems of power made available to the Wendat after their dispersal. Power can be used as an indication of strength and prosperity as well as a sign of societal struggle and disadvantage. The ways in which people gain, use, and lose power often reflects their social, economic, and political standing. The Wendat drew from a range of sources to survive their plan of resettlement. In turn, these sources translated into multidimensional systems of power based on long-standing relationships, reformulated to meet the needs of the Wendat post-1650. Overall, Wendat power did not wane during this period, but grew in terms of regional reputation for economic and diplomatic skill.

This book ends with an epilogue, "Reconnecting the Modern Diaspora, 1999," centred on a gathering of the modern Wendat diaspora in their ancestral homeland of Wendake in 1999. The meeting signified a renewal of the Wendat Confederacy among contemporary Wendat groups residing in Quebec, Ontario/Michigan, Kansas, and Oklahoma. Notwithstanding the important and complex history of these separate nations throughout the eighteenth, nineteenth, and twentieth centuries, one may argue that these people, along with their connection to Wendake, and their ability to identify and unite as "Wendat," originated during the period immediately after their ancestors' dispersal in 1649. Within the span of fifty years, generations of Wendat came to understand their place as both individuals living within the physical territory of the French, Iroquois, or Anishinaabeg while preserving a connection to a larger community connected by a common heritage. The modern Wendat, like many other Native groups, exist within a flexible system of citizenry. Based on seventeenth-century notions of alliances, the present-day Wendat root the contours of their ethnic identity in relation to their homeland of Wendake; even as most reside outside those geographic boundaries.

Several key terms used extensively throughout this study require clarification. Although there is some ambiguity to the meaning of Wendat, as scholars debate whether it translates into "the islanders" or "the people of the peninsula," the seventeenth-century Wendat used this word to describe themselves, and therefore I use it to designate the people of the seventeenth-century Wendat Confederacy and their descendants.[20] The territory occupied by the Wendat before their dispersal was referred to by the Wendat as "Wendake" and is identified as such throughout this study. The popularized term "Huron" has also been used to describe the Wendat and "Huronia," their country. Huron is a European-derived label. For this reason, I use Wendat instead of Huron, unless quoted in an original source.

PART 1

Resistance

THIS SECTION IS A THEMATIC analysis of the years leading up to the Iroquois invasion of Wendake. It builds upon previous work on the pre-dispersal years, expanding on the two most important factors shaping Wendat society during this period – disease and warfare. Epidemics in the 1630s, brought on by an increased interaction with Europeans (and specifically the French), devastated the Wendat population on many different levels. Despite concerted efforts made by Wendat healers, traditional practices fell short in addressing the physical ailments of these diseases. Consequently, death ensued at a catastrophic rate, leaving leaders to guide survivors through the psychological torments of loss and despair. This was not the end of Wendat ordeals, however. By the 1640s the Wendat were making considerable attempts to replenish their dwindling population by taking war captives, while at the same time reasserting their geopolitical stronghold in the Great Lakes region. Military campaigns against the Iroquois nations were the main focus of this strategy, and resulted in additional deaths and constant social insecurity. The following chapters trace Wendat resistance against a pending societal collapse through their experience with disease and warfare during the tumultuous twenty years before the dispersal. It concludes just before the Iroquois victory, when resistance gave way to a new strategy of dispersal and relocation.

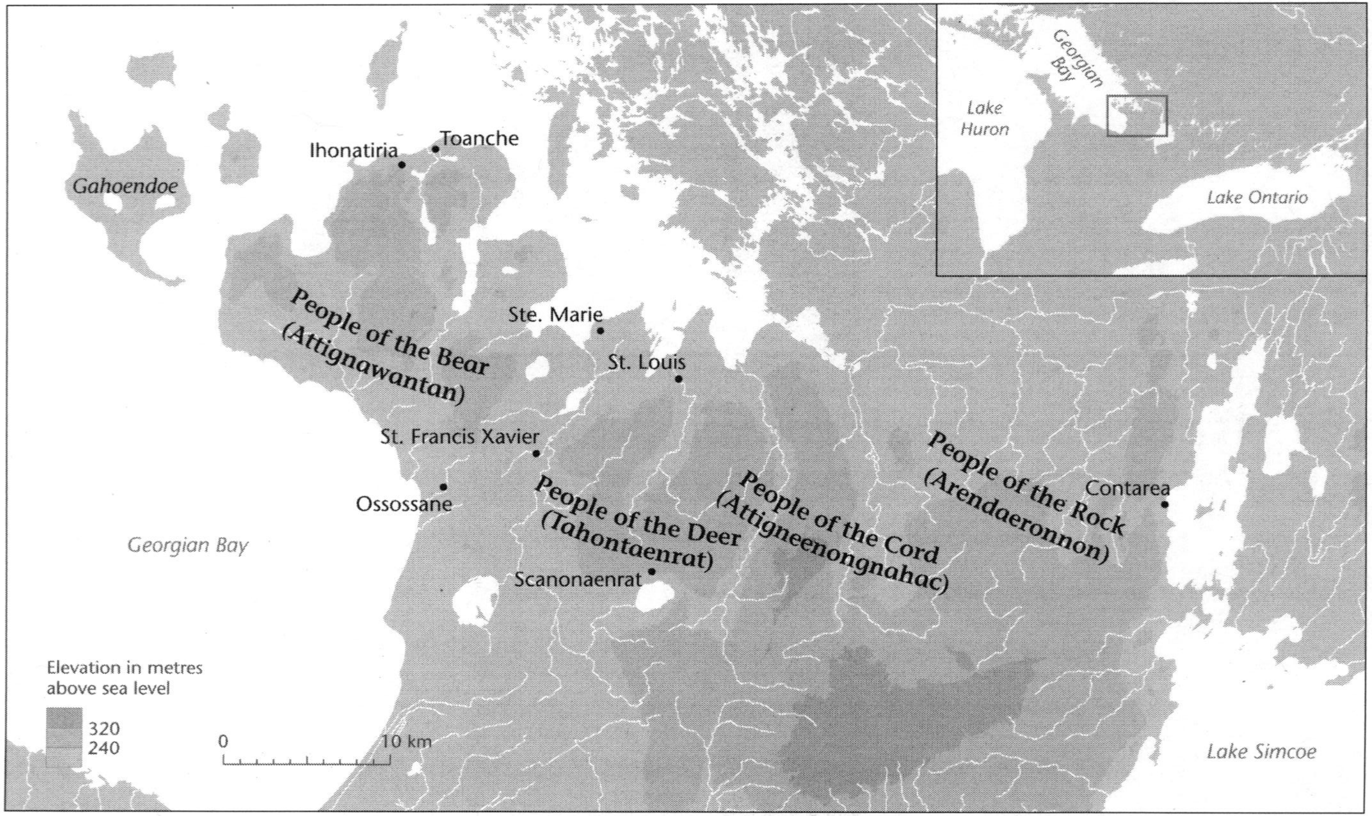

Wendake pre-dispersal, ca. 1634

1
Disease and Diplomacy
The Loss of Leadership and Life in Wendake

ON THE EVENING OF 4 AUGUST 1638, the Wendat Confederacy called a general council to order. A number of French Jesuit priests attended; the atmosphere was solemn and serious. Father Paul Le Jeune described the council in the following way:

> I do not know that I have seen anything more lugubrious than this assembly. In the beginning, they looked at one another like corpses, or rather like men who already feel the terrors of death; they spoke only in sighs, each one understanding the enumeration of the dead and sick in his family. All that was only to incite them to vomit more bitterly upon us the venom which they concealed within.[1]

This seemingly traditional council symbolized immense social change; the Wendat faced a devastating new reality. As a result of their encounters with European traders and missionaries, epidemic disease waged crippling attacks on this community not once but three times during the 1630s, killing up to 60 percent of the population.[2] Men were lost; leaders were sick; councils were disillusioned. Thus, the "lugubrious" state of the delegates at the August assembly highlighted the experience of disease across the Wendat Confederacy.

Many scholars have discussed the impact of disease on Native American communities. Demographic depopulation, European conquest, warfare, religious conversion, and economy, as well as Native perspectives and reactions to disease, have attracted much attention.[3] Studies focused on the Wendat experience generally point to disease as the Wendat's weakness in the face of Iroquois attacks, arguing it is a key factor in their "destruction."[4] Yet although these studies stress the importance of Native American population loss and demographics, there is almost nothing pertaining to the Native person. Current scholarship focuses on overall reactions, universal perceptions, and general dynamics of disease-ridden societies; the stories of the individuals who lost their lives are overlooked and relegated to numerical statistics or faceless accounts. The personal and historical narratives of Wendat civil headmen who died as a result of the epidemics of the 1630s indicate that Native Americans experienced disease not only as a collective disaster but also as a deeply personal tragedy. Shifting from a general to a particular focus reveals the important political and cultural dynamics of a society in crisis. In reaction to disease, Wendat leaders instigated policies to address the precarious cultural disruptions brought on by these circumstances.

In his seminal work, *The Children of Aataentsic,* renowned scholar of the Wendat Bruce Trigger speculates that the Wendat lost experienced headmen throughout the 1630s. It is also likely, according to Trigger, that many of them died before they could transmit any of their knowledge to their heirs.[5] Although this is the most comprehensive study of Wendat society, Trigger's analysis remains hypothetical, since his interest is much broader in scope, thus allowing little time for the intricate details of individual lives. The headmen described in this chapter both confirm Trigger's analysis and help reveal the complex and intense atmosphere of the 1630s in a concrete way. During this period, the Wendat faced severe demographic and military pressures. They confronted new geopolitical realities in the form of a potential French alliance and Iroquois aggression. Christianity offered an attractive new spiritual and political path for some members of the community, but elicited angry rejection from others. All of these factors created conflict within the Confederacy; yet death and disease meant constant turnovers in leadership and policy, often removing the very individuals best suited to generate consensus. Through an examination of these leaders, one may come to understand that *60 percent* mortality is not simply a statistic but also a symbolic reference to thousands of potential agents of change whose loss shaped the future of Wendat society.

The Atmosphere of Disease

Disease was a major concern for the Wendat throughout the 1630s. In the autumn of 1633 smallpox made its first decisive attack on the Confederacy, and by 1640 the total population was reduced by half.[6] Following the introduction of smallpox in 1633, the Wendat experienced a major epidemic in 1634. This epidemic began in the summer and continued to debilitate the population throughout the winter months.[7] The Jesuits observed it first-hand and made notes on the symptoms of the disease, describing it as a "sort of measles and an oppression of the stomach."[8] According to Jesuit Jean de Brébeuf, it usually began with a high fever and ended with a bout of diarrhea followed by a rash that looked like "a sort of measles or smallpox, but different from that common in France." Some victims also suffered blindness or blurred vision for several days. This particular epidemic was so severe that communities were unable to harvest food for sustenance during the winter.[9] The exact number of people affected by this disease is uncertain, but one scholar argues that "there can be no doubt that many Huron were stricken by this epidemic."[10] Commenting on the loss of Wendat life throughout this period due to disease, Father Brébeuf stated, "It has been so universal among the savages of our acquaintance that I do not know if one has escaped its attacks."[11]

While the epidemic subsided after the winter and during the early months of 1635, Jesuit records indicate that death rates within Wendake remained uncharacteristically high in comparison to previous years. Another epidemic, more devastating than the last, attacked Wendat villages in the spring of 1636. It began in May and persisted for the next six months.[12] This time symptoms were much more drawn out than those of 1634, and victims were often bedridden for long periods of time before they either began to recover or passed away. This inhibited other sorts of crucial activities, such as planting corn, gathering food, and trade.[13] Death rates were unprecedented. In the span of eight days, the village of Ossossane lost ten individuals.[14] By the end of the epidemic, this same village lost fifty people in total, or 20 percent of the village's total population.[15] Based on the total deaths from Ossossane, it is estimated that roughly five hundred Wendat died during the 1636 epidemic.[16] A third epidemic, which may have been scarlet fever, hit the Wendat in the summer of 1637.[17] It lasted well into the fall; Jesuit accounts depict the disease being the most extreme during mid-November. Missionaries were anxious about the illness, writing often of how they were constantly surrounded by the sick and dying during this period.[18]

The personal experiences of those caught in this traumatic event best illustrate the devastation of the epidemics. Father Le Jeune was particularly struck by the loss of an eleven-year-old boy named Arakhie. He grieved the child's death to such an extent that the priest omitted his account of this subject in his original records, and included it only after he "was ready to write about it, [feeling] its strong hold upon [his] heart ... [hardly able to] keep the tears from falling from [his] eyes."[19]

Arakhie, which means "closing day," was a young boy who was like "a little Sun which arose before the eyes." Le Jeune stressed the child's physical appearance, both taller and stronger than any of the boys his age. He was also intelligent beyond his years, described as an equal to the adults of his community. Contemporaries characterized Arakhie as "sedate, grave, obliging and of agreeable conversation. He was polite, and took pride in appearing serious in the midst of the insolence of his companions ... He was wonderfully docile, and he had a very happy memory."[20]

Despite his exceptional qualities, Arakhie could not escape disease. He was the first to fall ill in his family, followed quickly by his grandmother, mother, and four or five others within his household. Eventually, disease immobilized this boy and his family; they isolated themselves from their community, fearing that they might spread their illness to others. Arakhie lost his will to speak, refusing to maintain conversation with anyone, transforming from an exuberant and articulate boy into a sorrowful, weak soul. After several weeks of seclusion, Arakhie's family members began to recover, but the young boy was not as lucky. Hours before his death, this boy, who was known for his stimulating conversation and superior intelligence, mumbled his last word: "*chieske.*" The translation reads: "What do I know?"[21]

Arakhie's story is significant for several reasons. First, the sense of loss and sadness felt by those around this young boy demonstrates the severe psychological devastation experienced by those dealing with disease. This kind of despair impaired the ability of the survivors to organize and maintain a functioning society in light of their personal grief. In addition, Arakhie was not only loved but also respected by his community. Already, at the age of eleven, this young Wendat possessed the qualities associated with the leadership of a talented headman. He is, then, a prime example of a future Wendat leader who never had the chance to reach his potential. Finally, Arakhie was not an isolated case. In fact, it was the young men and future leaders, like this boy, who were the most susceptible to disease.[22] Viral infections, such as smallpox, measles, mumps, and chicken pox occur more frequently among those in the prime of their life (15-30 years of age) because of their more active immune systems.[23] This demographic included men who were arguably some of the most physically and politically active individuals within Wendat society. Those who died, therefore, included not only potential leaders but current leaders as well.

Wendat Civil Leaders

Civil headmen conducted the political and diplomatic affairs of the seventeenth-century Wendat. Although men traditionally occupied these positions, women controlled the selection of community leaders. The Wendat were a matricentric society, stressing female authority over kinship, food cultivation, and residency patterns, as well as the selection of male heirs and future headmen.[24] This process usually involved the oldest or most senior woman of a clan nominating a male member of her clan for the position after consultation with other women. When the clan mother voiced her selection, the existing headmen approved or rejected the choice.[25] Following the men's vote, women still exercised their influence over the power of appointed male leaders. Typically, the clan or village held a feast in honour of the newly chosen headman, and if at this feast "two women came and [pitched] the tone of the feast, they expected to see only broken heads under the [headman]."[26] In other words, if the women did not accept the new headman, his leadership would be doomed to failure. Women may not have been eligible to hold political office, but they were nonetheless important decision makers throughout the selection process and the subsequent careers of Wendat civil leaders.

Civil headmen directed affairs of state and foreign relations, and also organized feasts, dances, games, and the councils of peace. Their duties included a variety of jobs, but excluded leading war councils and campaigns. The headmen were representatives of community villages, clan segments, and at times the Confederacy at large. A headman had to prove himself worthy of the position: individuals had to demonstrate intellectual superiority, diplomatic skill, and bravery, and they had to enjoy widespread support from their community.[27] Wendat villages often had more than one civil leader, although each headman was no more powerful than the next. They did not receive presents or gifts for their appointments, but they did command respect and obedience from their people. Significantly, while these men held great power, they were not dictators of political decisions and they could not act alone. French explorer Samuel de Champlain took note of the Wendat system of civil leadership, observing that "the older and leading men assemble in a council, in which they settle upon and propose all that is necessary for the affairs of the village. This is done by a plurality of voices ... They have no particular chiefs with absolute command."[28] Civil leaders had to facilitate productive communication and formidable consensus in order for them to execute foreign as well as domestic policy.[29] These skills, always in demand, become even more critical during times of social insecurity. The series of epidemics in Wendake throughout the 1630s made the headman's role all the more crucial: as the Wendat sought solutions to a dwindling population and unstable political network, the innovative leadership and diplomacy of certain headmen became critical.

Taretande

The influential headman Taretande serves as a case study demonstrating the effects of loss of leadership experienced by the Wendat during the 1630s. Taretande was a civil headman of the Southern Bear nation, a Bear clan member, and he belonged to the village of Ihonatiria.[30] Since the arrival of Christian missionaries, but more specifically the Jesuits, Taretande had maintained an anti-European policy of resistance and rejection. At first, Taretande's resistance took the form of public mockery. The Jesuits took up residence in Ihonatiria, and often held religious ceremonies and invited the Wendat to attend; missionaries enticed the Natives by offering tobacco. Taking advantage of this situation, Taretande accepted the invitations only to make jokes about Christian rituals and beliefs. He took tobacco and declared for all those present that this sacred medicinal plant was the only reason he was there.[31] By chastising the Jesuits in a public forum, Taretande demonstrated a number of important policies in regards to his leadership. He was not afraid of the French and was comfortable confronting them publicly, and he expressed his skepticism about the superiority of the Christian faith and remained loyal to Wendat traditional beliefs. Finally, his public displays suggest he spoke for other members in his society, which encouraged him to continue this type of mockery on more than one occasion.

As the epidemics became more severe and the death rates increased, so did Taretande's resistance to the Jesuits. In addition to the informal displays of hostility at Christian ceremonies, the civil leader took action during official councils throughout the mid-1630s. At a meeting on 4 January 1636, for example, Taretande lashed out at the Jesuits in attendance, throwing burning coals from the council fire at them and making verbal threats. Headmen gathered at this general meeting to discuss the popular belief that the Jesuits were responsible for the diseases afflicting the Confederacy. Taretande went to great lengths in his address to the council to blame the Jesuits for making their communities ill. He concluded his oration by declaring that if anyone in his family should die, he would "split the head" of the first Frenchman he saw.[32]

After the January council, Taretande made certain to put his words into action by suggesting a policy of Jesuit eradication. His request gained support from at least six other Bear nation headmen, resulting in a subsequent meeting between Taretande, his younger brother Sononkhiaconc, and the Jesuit missionaries. This private meeting took place at the Jesuits' cabin on the evening of 4 January, the same day as the general council. Once again, Taretande hounded the Jesuits to admit their guilt in their involvement in the epidemics. He accused them of sorcery, which could be punishable by death. Taretande eventually confessed the council would not agree unanimously on a death sentence; however, he warned that a number of headmen had resolved to expel the Jesuits from Wendat country and send them back to Quebec in the spring.[33] Thus, Taretande made the Jesuits aware that he represented a growing faction within the Bear nation that desired the complete removal of the missionaries from Wendat society. The missionaries in turn acknowledged Taretande as a formidable opponent, passionate in his convictions as well as motivated to implement his policy.

Taretande's family supported his position. Jesuit records indicate with extreme annoyance that Sononkhiaconc made fun of the catechisms in the same manner as his brother. Equally annoying was the refusal by the children in Taretande's house to listen to the Jesuits' teachings. On several occasions the Jesuits had visited the home, trying desperately to share their Christian education. They met with so much opposition that they eventually gave up and stopped their visits entirely.[34] Significantly, the most opposition from a single member of Taretande's family was by his mother, the so-called renegade Christian.[35] This woman had accepted baptism in 1635, which made her one of the first converts by the Jesuits. This seems to have been a superficial conversion, however, in that she often abandoned her ties to Christianity, choosing to support Wendat traditional practices instead.[36] It is likely she shaped her family's anti-Jesuit advocacy, given the power of women as Wendat advisors.

The Jesuits' intense dislike of Taretande and his family and the family's persistent rejection of the missionaries are further highlighted in the Jesuit documentation of the Wendat family's collapse in the wake of disease. Only a few days after Taretande's private meeting with the Jesuits, three members of his family fell ill, followed by his mother, his brother, and finally the headman himself. The entire household was cut off from society so that they would not infect others. Quickly, the illness took its first victim, a sixteen-year-old sibling of Taretande. Unfortunately, there was little time to grieve this loss, as the family realized that their mother, the "renegade," had also died. Like a game of dominos, one after another, brothers and sisters all succumbed. Left alone, Taretande spent his last hours in meditation, trying to escape the insufferable physical pain that engulfed his body, and the sorrow of his many losses. On 12 January 1637, Taretande joined the rest of his family in the Land of the Dead.[37]

Despite their weakened condition and the notion put forth by missionaries that Christian baptism might cure their disease, no one in Taretande's family converted during their illness. Taretande's mother, for instance, used the last of her energy to insist that she regretted her earlier baptism and that she did not believe in the Christian faith.[38] The persistence of anti-Jesuit sentiment, led by Taretande and supported by his family, must have made a strong impression on those within the wider community. There was a clear rejection of the Jesuits during a time when not only the fate of the missionaries was uncertain but the fate of the Wendat as well. Taretande's skill and determination provided a response and strategy to deal with the turmoil faced by the Wendat. By purging the community he hoped to eliminate a potential cause of illness and conflict. He had persuaded a number of civil headmen to support his endeavours, and had executed his plan by meeting with the Jesuits and communicating the coalition's desire to have them removed by the following spring. In spite of these seemingly successful negotiations, however, there is no reference to Taretande's removal policy after his death. In fact, the Jesuits did not leave Wendake the next spring, which indicates a lack of engagement by the surviving Wendat leaders to implement the plan. It would seem that Taretande's death represented the loss of not only a leader but also his policies.

Aenon

Taretande was not the only headman responding to the intense atmosphere of unrest in the 1630s. Many other leaders took up the call for guidance and strategy. Of particular significance was the influence of another Bear clan headman, from the Northern Bear nation, named Aenon.[39] In contrast to Taretande, Aenon spent the 1630s campaigning in support of the Jesuits and the French. This headman was involved in all aspects of Wendat diplomacy, and an active participant in the developing fur trade economy.[40] He had the talent to persuade and the confidence to put his plans into action. In fact, it was the Jesuits' belief that no other headman could prevail if he were in competition with Aenon.[41]

Much like his contemporary Taretande, Aenon was a prolific orator. Most frequently, he voiced his perception of the French and his relationship with them. In a speech made in 1635 to Father Brébeuf, Aenon explained:

> The French have always been attached to me, and have loved me; I have always assisted them in every way I could, and they have not found in all this land a better friend than I. This has not been without incurring the envy of others throughout the Country ... whatever may be said, I shall, all my life, love and serve the French, in every way I can.[42]

It was Aenon's utmost desire that the French and Wendat maintain an alliance, facilitated through Wendat diplomats and French missionaries. In his view, the nature of this alliance required mutual respect and support. He acknowledged differences in religion and culture, but asserted that both parties should accept these distinctions and that they should not be stumbling blocks to diplomatic relations.[43] Aenon also placed great importance on a military alliance between the French and Wendat. He equally emphasized the Wendat need for firearms and the French need for able-bodied men to protect them. According to the headman, this type of reciprocal exchange would allow for both parties to effectively combat the Iroquois and continue to live in Wendake.[44]

Aenon did much more than talk about his aspirations for an alliance. In 1635, finding Father Brébeuf alone in his cabin, the headman took the opportunity to have a private conversation with the missionary. Aenon asked Brébeuf what the Wendat could do to get additional aid from the French. The question carried urgency, as the Wendat were in the midst of dealing with a series of Iroquois attacks. Brébeuf responded only that it was important for the Wendat to pray during these difficult times. Aenon agreed to do so to gain favour with the French.[45]

On 21 July 1635, Aenon once again tried to draw the French to the Wendat. This time he met with several French missionaries at the French village of Trois-Rivières, and agreed to escort Fathers Chastelain and Garnier into Wendat territory. Initially, the Jesuits' destination was undecided, but Aenon seized this opportunity to make a case for his own village and suggested that he would take Father Chastelain to reside with him. Despite the fact that there were six other Wendat headmen present at this meeting, all expressing a desire to keep the two missionaries together at a village other than that of Aenon, it was Aenon who departed from Trois-Rivières with Chastelain in his canoe.[46] In this case, Aenon's wish to have a Jesuit reside within his village and the successful negotiations of his request demonstrate the leader's ability to act on his own while still working towards an overall alliance between the greater Wendat community and the French. By having Chastelain close by and living among his people, Aenon secured his ultimate goal of maintaining a direct connection to the French.

Aenon also initiated the idea of a "Centre Lieu."[47] This plan involved the amalgamation of five villages into a massive fortified community. The main impetus for the fort was to defend the Wendat against pending Iroquois attacks. For six months Aenon lobbied the French to join the Wendat in this endeavour. He delivered numerous speeches, held meetings, and continuously argued the need for full commitment from the French to join the Centre Lieu. Finally, in the spring of 1636, Aenon sent a message to Father Brébeuf requesting a meeting. Brébeuf agreed and the two met soon after. Brébeuf was so impressed with the headman's speech that he felt he could not do it justice by writing it down; nonetheless, he recorded the speech because of its importance.[48] Aenon's ideas, although perhaps not as eloquent in written form, demonstrate his role as an effective liaison during the negotiations over this Centre Lieu:

> I have sent for you [Father Brébeuf] to learn your final decision. I would not have given you the trouble to come here, had I not been afraid that I should not find at your house the opportunity of speaking to you. Your Cabin is always full of so many people visiting you, that it is almost impossible to say anything to you in private; and then, now that we are on the point of assembling to deliberate regarding the establishment of a new Village, this interview might have aroused the suspicions of those who wish to keep you.[49]

Even within this first paragraph (there are eight in total), one can see Aenon deserved his reputation as an effective diplomat. He assessed the situation and took into consideration all factors that might influence the missionary's decision, and he tried to respond to Brébeuf's concerns.

Aenon understood that to win his case he needed to eliminate outside interference. Furthermore, he was able to balance the urgency of his request and need for a final commitment by the French through an appeal to the missionary's desire to feel wanted. He knew that Brébeuf would be pleased and more inclined to listen if he addressed the fact that there were other villages interested in having the French priests live with them.[50] Brébeuf was so delighted that he made a note explicitly stating his satisfaction: "We have to praise God, that he gives us the favour to be loved and sought after throughout the Country ... but, if we have regard to importunities, assuredly [Aenon] will prevail."[51]

Because of Aenon's apparent affection for the French and his role as a leading correspondent between the Wendat and French, he often mediated between those who resisted the Jesuits' presence and those who supported them. Through speeches made at various times during his leadership, Aenon made significant calls for the Wendat to maintain and confirm their alliance with the French. On one occasion, for instance, the men of Aenon's village called an assembly, inviting both Father Brébeuf and Aenon to attend. They charged Aenon to represent the council at this meeting and apologize for any past messages of animosity, such as Taretande's threats. In so doing, Aenon asked the French to "think no more of what had passed ... [and to forget] the evil designs that [the Wendat] had had upon [the Jesuits'] lives."[52] Brébeuf responded by saying that he forgave them. Through Aenon, the Wendat were able to make amends with the French, thus sustaining the possibility of an official alliance for the future.

Similarly, Aenon's diplomacy ameliorated another crisis that transpired when Taretande threatened to "split the head" of a Frenchman. In response to Taretande's overt hostility towards the Jesuits, Aenon attempted to smooth over the situation by defending the missionaries and stressing the importance of the French alliance. He informed Taretande that threats towards the Jesuits would only lead to the "destruction and ruin of the country."[53] Aenon then turned to the Jesuits and added that "[the missionaries] should have no fear; and that if they were to settle down in his village, [they] should always be very welcome there."[54] The outcome of this mediation is unclear, but the attempt by Aenon to mend the divisions between the Bear nation and the French missionaries is obvious. Rather than fighting the arguments put forth by Taretande, Aenon focused tactfully on the overall future of the community. He attempted to calm the fears of the Jesuits by demonstrating that Taretande and his supporters did not represent all the headmen, and offering the welcoming atmosphere of his own village as proof.

Aenon's role as a mediator took on even greater significance when he saved several missionaries' lives. Although the public threats towards the missionaries at the 4 January meeting were serious, the extent to which the Wendat expected to follow through remained ambiguous. There was, however, at least one occasion when an entire council endorsed a series of threats, and the headmen agreed to kill the Jesuits. Aenon attended this meeting and listened carefully as decisions were passed. After the other men had said their part, Aenon had the last word, and he attacked the council's decision. According to Father Le Jeune, Aenon continued to reprimand his fellow council members "in such a way that they came and begged the Fathers not to write any of these evil thoughts to [the superiors], lest they should be badly treated in the places where [the] French are."[55] Aenon's speech had a significant impact on the council's decision and the immediate plan to slay the priests was put on hold.

Aenon's actions throughout the 1630s were persistent and consistent with his unwavering belief in the utility of a French–Wendat alliance. This policy inspired numerous speeches, military strategies, and diplomatic ventures, all of which were in stark contrast with the equally passionate Taretande. Yet, despite how much these two headmen differed, their lives were cut short in the same way, in the same year. As with Taretande, the dynamics surrounding Aenon's death are symbolic of his perspectives and policy in life.

In early August 1637, Aenon made a trip to Trois-Rivières to meet with Charles Jacques de Huault de Montmagny, the governor of New France, in order to discuss the likelihood of confirming an alliance. Upon arrival, Aenon was infected with the disease he had evaded for almost a decade. Despite his weakened state, the headman called for interpreters and asked to see the governor. A meeting took place, at which Aenon presented Montmagny with a gift and proceeded to beg the French man to favour the Wendat.[56] He then turned his attention to his Wendat kin and pressed them "not to do any harm to the French in his country."[57] The poor condition of Aenon's health only worsened, making his call for the governor and his people to unite the final act in his influential life. Understanding that death was near, Aenon's last recorded words were addressed to those who surrounded him. Known as an eloquent speaker and a man who knew how to select his words wisely, his last remarks not only attested to his feelings but also encapsulated his dedication to solidify an alliance once again. His statement was as follows: "Well ... I have been requested to come to the French, I am here; it is well that, since I must die, I die near them."[58] His belief in the importance of the French never wavered, even upon death.

On 6 August 1637, Aenon was laid to rest. Significantly, the headman's bones were not buried in Wendat country, but alongside the French in their cemetery at Trois-Rivières. Considering the Wendat concept that one must live life the same way their bodies rest after death, Aenon's burial symbolized one last attempt at solidifying a Wendat–French alliance.[59]

Despite his hard work and creative diplomacy throughout the 1630s, Aenon's vision never became a reality. Just as Taretande's anti-French policies died with him, Aenon's Centre Lieu was never established and the French alliance remained ambiguous.[60] In light of the considerable losses sustained through the deaths of headmen such as Taretande and Aenon in 1637, one may begin to understand the particular ways in which the epidemics impacted the Wendat Confederacy.

Women and Disease

Epidemics affected Wendat women in important ways. The loss of so many civil leaders made the choice for future headmen marginal. Women were forced to limit their selections, which in turn limited their ability to project influence on community politics. Lack of remedies for European diseases also complicated women's roles and status, as many Wendat sought baptism as a solution. Conversion, regardless of individual intentions, constituted a direct attack on Wendat matricentric structures, bringing with it patriarchal regimes and male-dominated social systems.[61] Many Wendat women outwardly rejected the entire notion of Christian baptism, despite the chance that it might save a life. The Jesuits deemed Arakhie's mother a "wretch" because of her adamant objection to Christian practices.[62] On several occasions, the missionaries tried to convince this woman to allow her sick son to be baptized, but she unequivocally denied them their request. She maintained that baptism was not the solution to her son's illness and forced Arakhie's mouth shut any time he began to speak otherwise. She was so strong in her conviction that when the Jesuits persisted to campaign for a Christian conversion she threatened the priests with a burning brand if they did not leave her house immediately.[63]

Taretande's mother showed similar disdain for Christianity. As noted earlier, she recanted her youthful baptism. In light of her outward support for traditional spiritual practices, the Jesuits deemed her a "renegade." On several occasions she made public displays of her dislike of Christian beliefs. If Jesuits requested that she teach her fellow Wendat the missionaries' lessons, she refused; when asked to make the sign of the cross she screamed at the priests for not respecting Wendat traditions.[64] Her stance did not diminish when she became sick. Despite numerous visits by the local missionaries during her illness, when asked if she was not in the least bit appreciative of her baptism, she yelled with full force, "No!"[65]

Wendat women had very few options to prevent their loss of power by the 1640s. Either they could openly declare their anti-Christian sentiment and hope that the legacy of a matriarchal heritage would serve to maintain its influence on community members and leaders or they could convert with the belief that the new religion would bring strength and rejuvenation to a dwindling population. This would give them a new spiritual role to replace their diminished political influence, but the choice was not to be taken lightly. By the late 1630s and well into the 1640s, any woman choosing to convert was simultaneously taking a gamble on not only her own life but those of her kin as well. If her village and/or kinship network was not predominantly Christian, she faced a life of isolation and lack of aid in times of distress.[66]

The Wendat convert Anne is a prime example of the devastating repercussions that could result from a decision to attain baptism. In 1640, Anne was seventy years old and a woman of high rank within her community. She had two daughters and a niece, all of whom had been baptized. Anne was also baptized during the epidemics. The women's conversion meant that Anne's family faced ostracism by the rest of the villagers, who were traditionalists.[67] This isolation would have been difficult in its own right; worse, the loss of Anne's daughters and niece due to disease left the household paralyzed. The aged clan mother was left alone to care for three orphaned grandchildren. She was sickly, weak, and blind.[68] In normal circumstances, women from the rest of the village would have come to Anne's aid, but in light of the tensions between Christians and traditionalists, no one helped. Anne was unable to collect firewood and her weak eyesight made it nearly impossible to make food or clothing. Of course, her breasts lacked the milk necessary to feed the children. Starvation set in, and at least two of the three infants did not survive.[69]

Considering the devastating results of Anne's circumstances, the adamant rejection of the Jesuit faith by Taretande's and Arakhie's mothers seems all the more understandable. These women (Anne included) were faced with insurmountable odds. Death surrounded them, and choices needed to be made. Yet all of the options carried serious risks. The French alliance and the decline of civil headmen meant a loss of matricentric political power, while the alternatives of conversion also required departures from customary sources of female power. Options were limited, to say the least.

Conclusion

The 1630s represented a time of great loss, but it was simultaneously a period of creative strategizing and active diplomacy made all the more urgent because of the many threats to Wendake. The impact of disease on Wendat society directly affected leaders and their policies. Wendat headmen were not merely passive bystanders to disease but active agents attempting to find solutions in order to save their community. Unwilling to sit back and allow the catastrophe facing them to take hold, headmen resisted the demise of the Confederacy by drawing lines and defining tactics in relation to the epidemics. Solutions were limited, however, and often these tactics became overt campaigns to support or reject the Jesuits and religious conversion.

The victim trope, too often applied in discussions of disease and Native society, distorts the type of decision making and activism attributed to Taretande and Aenon. One scholar addressed this issue by asserting that the historian's constant depiction of Natives as victims

> [fails] to acknowledge the tenacity with which native peoples, in the face of increasingly unequal odds, continued to defend their lands, customs, and personal dignity ... This behavior constitutes a record of continuing resourcefulness and adaptability under conditions of stress that had never been paralleled in North America in prehistoric times or at any time in the history of most other peoples.[70]

Taretande and Aenon were more than victims; they were active agents who swayed others and pursued policies to help their people. Their loss, then, had reverberations for Wendat resistance. Moreover, the Wendat lost not only these proven leaders but also people like the young Arakhie, whose potential we will never know, and the "renegade" mother who watched helplessly as her children collapsed around her. They serve as reminders that the numbers representing the extent of loss felt by North America's Native population are not just statistics; they are human beings. They are the medium by which individuals living in the present can approach the anxiety, sadness, and despair engulfing the Wendat Confederacy throughout the 1630s.

2

A Culture of War

Wendat War Chiefs and Nadowek Conflicts before 1649

By the 1640s, the socio-political and even physical environment in which the Wendat lived changed forever. Key civil leaders and a substantial portion of the population had died. With the loss of so many current and future male leaders, women's power became uprooted and rearranged, essentially narrowing their ability to assert authority over political leadership. Since choices of eligible candidates were few to nonexistent, clan mothers were forced to make do with the men who had survived the epidemics. The process for selection became superficial.

Still, these obstacles served as inspiration for new strategies of resistance. One of the most significant developments of this period was a shift in leadership, as war chiefs began to take on the civil responsibilities of trade, politics, and security that had previously been the preserve of the civil headmen. A war headman commented on this phenomenon in a 1638 peace council. He explained:

> My Brothers, you know well that I hardly ever speak except in our war councils, and that I concern myself only with the affairs of arms; but I am obliged to speak here, since all the other Captains are dead. Now before I follow them to the grave I must free my mind; and perhaps it will be for the good of the country, which is going to ruin.[1]

This speech gives some insight into who replaced headmen like Taretande and Aenon. Although it seems likely that both war headmen and civil leaders died throughout the epidemics, war leaders had had less contact with the French during the 1630s and were therefore less likely than their civil counterparts to contract European diseases. Since choices were so limited after the epidemic, women turned to war chiefs as an alternative option to civil headmen.[2]

Although both the civil headman and war chief positions involved similar responsibilities in terms of guiding their respective communities, there were clear differences between the two. War chiefs usually attained their position through demonstrations of bravery and military might. They were responsible for training and leading a unique faction of Wendat society – the warriors. But they did not have the power to reward or penalize anyone, not even the warriors.[3] Women called upon war chiefs of their community to lead and organize war councils and to deliberate on military campaigns during times of conflict. They did not engage in civil affairs.[4]

This all changed in the wake of the epidemics. As early as the summer of 1637, one of the most influential war leaders of the Confederacy engaged in civil diplomacy, signalling a more general shift in roles. Ondesson was a prominent member of the village Angoutenc and the Hawk clan.[5] This community was one of the hardest hit by the epidemics, which left survivors agitated and in search of answers. The Jesuits visited this village twice during the summer of 1637 and found that the majority of the community blamed their desperate situation on the presence of the French in Wendake.[6] In reaction to this hostility, Ondesson acted as an emissary of goodwill to the Jesuits.

On 8 July 1637, the war chief personally invited French missionaries to an upcoming civil council. Ondesson explained that many, including himself, felt afraid of the Jesuits. He believed this fear might be dissipated if the Jesuits clarified their purpose at the council. The Jesuits approved Ondesson's request and the two groups agreed to hold a civil council later that week – the war headman's diplomacy was a success.[7] Similar progress took place at the council itself. After the traditional rituals of speeches, smoking, and introductions, the Jesuits addressed the Wendat, explaining their good intentions towards them. Deliberations by Angoutenc leaders followed; in the end, Wendat delegates decided to welcome the Jesuits into their community and encouraged future visits by the French.[8] Although the Jesuits' record of the council proceedings do not explicitly mention Ondesson's participation, it was nonetheless critical to its success. Ondesson's diplomatic overtures towards the French initiated the council in the first place. His appointment as ambassador for the village's civil matters highlights the ways in which war leaders became more familiar with civic duties, especially concerning international relations, and shows how the Wendat managed to use existing institutions to respond to the twin challenges of epidemics and war.

The Jesuits made specific reference to Wendat war headmen becoming more involved in French–Wendat affairs in their 1642 report. Specifically, the missionaries remarked on the increased baptisms of war leaders, linking the "marked degree" of Wendat Christian converts to the number of Christian war chiefs.[9] Reflecting on this apparent shift in conversions, Father Paul Le Jeune noted that during the 1630s "hardly could one find, hitherto, among our Christians two or three warriors" but now "we have counted in a single band as many as twenty-two Believers, – all men of courage, and mostly Captains or people of importance."[10] Of particular interest to the Jesuits were the leaders Thomas Sondakwa from the Wenro nation, and Mathurin Astiskwa, and Martin Tehoachiakwan, both from the Cord nation.[11] According to the missionaries, it was the baptisms of "persons of such importance that brought about many others" and Wendat actions confirmed these notions.[12] War chief Martin Tehoachiakwan expressed a clear desire for his people to follow him in the Christian faith. In a public plea to his community he asserted:

> The enemies are at our doors ... I withdraw from misfortune; let who will, follow me; our affairs are in a desperate state ... I do not fear the Iroquois; I dread the more inhuman cruelties of the devils in hell, in a fire that is never extinguished. I abandon you, without abandoning you, or rather I abandon your follies; I abandon our evil customs; from this moment, I renounce all kinds of sin, and know ye that tomorrow I shall be a Christian.[13]

Although Tehoachiakwan's desire to encourage conversion may well have had a spiritual element, the fact that the French began to give European weapons to converts might also have played a critical role in his newfound Christian zeal.[14] Unlike the Iroquois, the Wendat were not able to acquire guns in significant numbers.[15] The French, who were the primary European trading partners of the Wendat, refused to trade guns for furs.[16] This was not always the case in Euro-Native relations: the Iroquois formed a trading partnership with the Dutch, who freely exchanged guns for pelts.[17] Nonetheless, French missionaries gave guns to actual or potential male converts, thus leaving some room for hope that the French might change their policy and begin to trade weapons.

The Wendat perceived French firearms to be crucial to military and diplomatic success. One headman declared, "On this account the whole Country [Wendake] turns its eyes upon you; we shall esteem ourselves quite beyond fear, if we have you [the French] with us; you have firearms, the mere report of which is capable of inspiring dread in the enemy, and putting him to flight."[18] Father Le Jeune remarked, "The use of arquebuses, refused to the Infidels by Monsieur the Governor, and granted to the Christian Neophytes, [was] a powerful attraction to win them."[19] Jesuit Simon Le Moyne confirmed the link between conversion and access to guns when he expressed his frustration in 1639 that the majority of converts were men; women took little interest in the process.[20] The need for French military support had not diminished since Aenon's quest for a Centre Lieu. Thus, conversion represented an alternative attempt at attaining weapons from the French. War headmen sought to strengthen their connection to the French with an acceptance of the Christian faith.

The participation of former war headmen in civil initiatives and foreign affairs represented an important shift in Wendat diplomacy and leadership. In 1638, a war leader defined his traditional role within the community as restricted to war councils, concerning himself only to the "affairs of arms."[21] Yet, in the aftermath of the epidemics and the death of many civil headmen, this same war leader regretfully noted that he was now forced to partake in civil matters for which he had little background. The war chief expressed particular concern about his lack of familiarity in international diplomacy, and specifically negotiations with the French. In an attempt to explain his situation, as well as justify his involvement in a civil council, this war headman asserted, "I neither hate nor love the French; I have never had anything to do with them, and we see each other for the first time to-day."[22] It seems that the interaction of Ondesson and other Christian war chiefs' interactions with the French not only broke with common practice but even transgressed their traditional role, yet the war leaders proceeded with these efforts. As a result, war chiefs not only came into contact with the French on a more frequent basis but also became key negotiators in terms of Wendat–French relations. With the loss of civil leaders due to the epidemics, the Confederacy was forced to restructure its polity, creating replacements, new strategies, and forms of leadership.

Although scholars argue over the causes for an increase in warfare in the 1640s, attributing it to the economic aspirations of the Iroquois and a desire to replenish diminishing populations, the connection between an increase in war headmen in civil matters offers another possible explanation.[23] Less familiar with negotiations of peace, war leaders began to shape Wendat society and policy towards situations that they had more experience in orchestrating. The Confederacy was anxious to respond to their circumstances, yet unlike Taretande and Aenon, who sought solutions through diplomacy, these new headmen resorted to strategies more in line with their role as war chiefs. Conflict and warfare became a feasible means for the Confederacy to retaliate against the devastation experienced in the 1630s. As a result, Iroquois–Wendat conflicts would overwhelm and dominate Wendat society for the next ten years.[24]

The Wendat drew on both old traditions and new innovations in shaping this culture of war before dispersal. As with the spread of disease, there were few Wendat who were not directly affected by the wars with the Iroquois. Some historians have argued that warfare "was at the heart of Native culture" during this period, calling it a "chronic" aspect shaping the Wendat world,[25] while others note that it was an intrinsic and important part of daily life, regarded as a "normal and inevitable social phenomenon."[26] Often the Wendat are depicted as weak and passive in their battles with the Iroquois during the 1640s, especially when their defeat in 1649 is framed as the culmination or resolution to these conflicts.[27] Despite this interpretation, the Wendat were far from submissive victims succumbing to Iroquois military might. The defeat of 1649 overshadows Wendat traditions of military success. In reality, 1649 was the culmination of decades of warring, interspersed with intricate customs of captive exchange and decisive Wendat victories.

Nadowek Warfare

The Wendat engaged in numerous battles throughout the history of the Confederacy. In most cases these conflicts were with other Nadowek groups. Motives for war were neither religious nor territorial in Nadowek society.[28] The most common reason to go to war was to avenge a death. This particular type of war often began as a blood feud, when one group refused to give appropriate gifts in compensation for killing a member of another group. This denial was understood as an act of aggression and relatives of the deceased felt it necessary to wage a so-called mourning war.[29] These wars were waged to restore lost population, ensure social continuity, and confront emotional pain.

Nadowek battles took place between spring and summer, which allowed the warriors better coverage behind the full trees.[30] These expeditions ranged in length from four to six months.[31] They involved surprise attacks and included hundreds to thousands of warriors.[32] This type of warfare was so intense at times that women had to be accompanied by men when venturing out to the fields.[33] Scholars have summarized warfare among the Nadowek as an activity "aimed at subduing an enemy, taking prisoners, and returning them for adoption. The underlying motivations included the acquisition of personal prestige by young warriors, [and] revenge."[34] War offered a means for young Nadowek men to gain status among their people.[35] They hoped for recognition for personal skill and bravery that could lead to prominent roles within the community. Accordingly, young men were generally supportive of war.[36]

The Nadowek identified other Natives as enemies and appropriate rivals if they were affiliated with a foreign tribe that did not have a recognized bond through trade and reciprocity.[37] Perhaps one of the most enduring conflicts was the traditional and seemingly continuous battle between the Wendat and Iroquois. In his detailed accounts concerning the Nadowek, Samuel de Champlain described a bloody encounter between the Wendat and one hundred Iroquois. This battle, known as "the Battle of the Richelieu River" took place on 19 June 1610. Champlain's involvement in the affair arose when a Wendat messenger came to ask for the Frenchman's help; he described the conflict and its aftermath:

> Both sides began firing swarms of arrows, one of which pierced my ear and entered my neck ... The French covered the Indians with musket fire ... Then, ... the French stormed the fort, swords in hand, and killed all but fifteen of its occupants. The rest were taken prisoner ... The only booty found inside the camp were some beaver skin robes and the bloodstained fur clothing worn by the dead. The Indians did not bother to plunder the latter and derided the French who did so ... The Indians scalped the dead or cut off their heads as trophies, and returned to St. Ignace Island, taking their prisoners with them.[38]

This example illustrates several key points concerning the nature of Nadowek warfare, including the fact that combatants could number in the hundreds, battles were fought around fortified camps, and the attainment of booty was not an objective of warfare. Once the battle came to a close, victors scalped the dead, and in some instances they took live captives back with them.

The production of military equipment and supplies was an important aspect of the preparation process. Arrows were some of the most common weapons produced. Using a sharp knife or sharp-edged stone, they would carve a straight and long arrow. Subsequently, the arrow was fledged with eagle feathers. Sharp-pointed stones or bones were then attached to the strongest point of the tip of the arrow using fish-glue. Although the arrows had a dual purpose – they were also used for hunting – there were several military implements made specifically for warfare. Missionary Gabriel Sagard's observations of warfare preparation stressed the production of wooden clubs made and used for warfare.[39] Warriors carried shields that covered nearly the entire body; the shields were decorated with a round piece of bark with the "armorial bearings of [the warrior's] town or province painted upon it, and fastened to the end of a long stick, like a cavalry pennant."[40] An aquientor covered the warrior's arms and legs, serving as protection against the onslaught of arrows. Aquientors, or cuirasses, were made with white rods, all about the same length, sewn together and tightly interlaced with cords.[41]

Food was an element of great importance to a successful campaign. The Wendat expected warriors to perform at great distances from home. If the warriors did not have proper nutrition they could not fight effectively and would be forced to retreat in search of food supplies. Such was a case described by a Wendat when they were at war with the Seneca. The Wendat expedition had to call off their war party and retreat to the nearest village to replenish their weak bodies because they had run out of food. The four-day delay cost the Wendat the battle.[42] The food for Nadowek war parties required careful preparation; bags of cornmeal were scorched and then roasted in ashes. This food supply was easy to transport, could keep for a very long time, and was easy to prepare. When the warriors wanted to eat, all they had to do was soak the cornmeal in water.[43]

Nadowek warfare also included a unique pre-battle ritual.[44] The French lawyer and New France traveller Marc Lescarbot described the "Fort Fight" ritual in his observations of the Nadowek:

> They make a fort, within which all the young men of the army place themselves; then the women come to compass them about, and to keep them as it were besieged. Seeing themselves so environed they make sallies, to slip away and deliver themselves out of prison. The women on the watch drive them back, arrest them, do their best to capture them; and if they are taken the women rush on them, beat them, strip them, and from such a success draw a favourable presage of the impending war, while if they escape it is an evil sign.[45]

Jesuit Pierre François Xavier de Charlevoix offered a similar description. He summarized this somewhat puzzling episode by stating, "Warriors, before taking the war-path, fought with their wives, and if they got the worst, had no doubt of the success of their expedition; but if, on the contrary, their wives were the weaker, they augured ill."[46] The Jesuits described the lessons learned through this custom and how the Wendat applied them in the context of actual battles. The following is a Jesuit missionary's account of a battle between the Iroquois and the Wendat:

> About two hundred Iroquois ... encountered some advanced-guards of that Huron troop. The latter straightway took flight after some skirmishing, and were eagerly pursued until within sight of our fort – many having been killed while they were in disorder in the midst of snows. But the more courageous of the Hurons, having stood firm against those who joined combat with them, had some advantage on their side, and constrained the Iroquois ... These Iroquois were forced into that palisade, and about thirty of them were taken captives.[47]

The success of the Wendat who stayed and faced the Iroquois and the death of those Wendat who fled demonstrate the importance of standing one's ground in times of battle. Participation in the Fort Fight was ritualized, symbolizing adversity that acted as a means to measure the capability of their warriors before entering battle. In essence, this is what the Fort Fight ritual sought to engender by confirming the strength of the warriors; if they were not strong enough to face their wives and be beaten and humiliated by them, then how could they possibly face their enemies?

Women and War

Despite the usual emphasis on men in discussions of war and battle, women shaped Nadowek warfare in significant ways.[48] Women, generally clan mothers, initiated the call to war, usually because there had been a death in the family and they desired to be compensated for that death through a mourning war.[49] A woman did this by approaching a war chief within the community whom she deemed to be influential and requested that he call a war council to try to persuade other members of the village to agree to go to war.[50] The following is a description of how this process took place:

> When, then, this matron judges it time to raise up the tree again, or to lay again on the mat, someone in her family whom death has taken from her, she addresses herself to some one of those who have their *Athonni* [sire] at her home and who she believes is most capable of executing her commission.

> She speaks to him by wampum belt, explaining her intention of engaging him to form a war party. This is done.[51]

The "matron's" choice concerning which "sire" would represent her at the council was an important one. This individual brought the clan mother's desire and justification for war to the table for discussion. If he was a poor orator, or if he lacked influence and respect within the community, her message might be lost and her call for war refused.[52]

Power to confirm or deny participation in warfare constituted one of the most significant contributions by women to Nadowek military conflict. According to missionary Joseph-François Lafitau, "the matron, who has the principal authority ... can force these children to go to war if it seems best to her, or keep them at home if they have undertaken a war displeasing to her."[53] If the war council agreed to go to war but the reasons for battle proved weak, or arguments were not convincing, the women had the power to veto the decisions of male council members.[54] Thus, the culture of warfare in Nadowek societies was one shaped by both men and women. Europeans placed more emphasis on the men because men received tangible benefits for fighting: personal and political prestige, as well as respect. To an outsider, it would seem likely that men maintained the key roles of influence within warfare because on a superficial level they were the ones that stood to gain or lose the most from successful military campaigns. Since women acquired little in these personal areas of accomplishment, European observers assumed that women did not contribute significantly to the interests and outcomes of warfare – also, that was the case in their own societies.

Another reason why women's involvement has been eclipsed by male roles in warfare is the lack of a physical presence of women at the war council. According to Brother Gabriel Sagard, women and young men took no part in the council.[55] Sagard did not consider the extremely influential presence of women behind the scenes; he might not have understood this aspect of war culture. Women not only participated on a pragmatic and symbolic level by starting the fire that was the heart and centrepiece of the council but also demonstrated their significant authority by instigating the call for an assembly in the first place.[56] Therefore, although women were not physically present during the war councils, their aspirations and political points of view gained expression through their male deputies. The Jesuits acknowledged the extent of female power within Nadowek war councils through an observation of one highly respected

Wendat woman. "This woman held a high rank and [was] much respected; ... the Elders would decide no important affair without [the woman's] advice."[57] Therefore, the Jesuits acknowledged, "the women ha[d] the chief authority amongst all the nations."[58]

Nadowek warfare involved a series of perpetual complex rituals. Beginning with the production of equipment, food, and the execution of the Fort Fight, young warriors were prepared to go to battle against the enemy. The call to war was not a simple process, however, and only took place after a multi-layered consultation between war chiefs, clan mothers and the community.

Captives

The most important objective of Nadowek warfare was the acquisition of captives.[59] Both the Wendat and their enemies placed great emphasis on the conduct and treatment of prisoners of war. Captives usually faced three possible outcomes: death, torture, or adoption into the captor society. Because most wars were waged in the hopes of renewing populations, and replacing a member that had been killed in a previous battle, prisoners were frequently subject to the last of the three options.[60] As with the decision to go to war, women had the final say in matters concerning the fate of captives. Lafitau asserted that

> the matrons to whom the captives are given are so entirely mistresses of the latter that the wish of the entire village could not save them if the former are desirous of throwing them into the fire nor could they be put to death if these women wish to grant them life.[61]

All scenarios involved highly ritualized events. The adoption process, for instance, featured a series of symbolized public gestures introducing the individual captive to the community. During these initial stages of the so-called probation period, potential adoptees could choose to conform to their captor's society and assimilate, or resist, risking maltreatment, slavery, or death.[62] On 2 September 1637, a Wendat contingent defeated an Iroquois war party and brought back seven captives.[63] The Wendat held a council and decided that the prisoners would be split up among the Wendat nations who had helped in the battle, namely, the Cord, the Rock, and the Bear. When the captives arrived in each respective village, another council was taken to decide the fate of the captives.

Out of these seven Iroquois, one man, named Joseph by the Jesuits, was deemed fit for adoption by the headman Saouandaouascouay of the village Arontaen. At this time, however, the condition of this Iroquois warrior was questionable. Joseph had a badly bruised hand and one finger that was not entirely cut off but wrenched away; the blow of a hatchet had nearly severed the thumb and forefinger of the other hand, the joints of his arms were badly burned and one of them was deeply cut. The injuries to his hands became so severe over the next few days that when they removed the bandaging the hands were half putrefied, with worms gnawing at his marrow, and there was an overwhelming smell of decay. The community made the decision for adoption in the absence of Saouandaouascouay, who had gone hunting, in consideration of the fact that this Wendat headman had recently lost his nephew to the Iroquois. The parade to Arontaen was elaborate. The captive wore fine beaver robes with strings of porcelain around his neck and on the crown of his head. Thirty to forty individuals escorted him, and a large group greeted the party on arrival. Joseph feasted on squash, sagamité (a Wendat delicacy), and fruits. In crossing certain houses he received items in order to make a feast, and another household invited him for a banquet of stewed dog. At the banquet Joseph was approached by a headman from the village who remarked, "My nephew, thou hast good reason to sing, for no one is doing thee any harm; behold thyself now among thy kindred and friends."[64] This signalled the amicable nature of the events and the relationship desired by the Wendat with the Iroquois Joseph.

It was on 4 September that Saouandaouascouay returned from his hunting trip and was finally introduced to his adopted nephew. He could not hide his disappointment at the captive's condition: fifty years of age and badly injured from his battles. Taking this into consideration, the Wendat headman had to decide whether it was better to honour the adoption or put the ailing Joseph out of his misery. He approached Joseph with the following appeal:

> My nephew, thou must know that when I first received news that thou wert at my disposal, I was wonderfully pleased, fancying that he whom I lost in war had been, as it were, brought back to life, and was returning to his country. At the same time I resolved to give thee thy life; I was already thinking of preparing thee a place in my cabin, and thought that thou wouldst pass the rest of thy days pleasantly with me. But now that I see thee in this condition,

> thy fingers gone and thy hands half rotten, I change my mind, and I am sure that thou thyself wouldst now regret to live longer.[65]

Had Saouandaouascouay not changed his mind and decided to have Joseph killed, the captive would have become part of Saouandaouascouay's family and Wendat society – a nephew to Saouandaouascouay, living among them. The circumstances of Joseph's fate reflect the extent to which these adoptions were taken seriously. Enemies became brothers, nephews, and sons.

Although adoption was a prevalent cause for warfare, some scholars assert that torture and death were far more common. Through this line of argument Wendat rituals are judged as a "sadistic game," revealing a "sinister aspect of the psychological finesse that was a very important part of their culture."[66] Others contend that "the process should be seen less as an exercise in ingenious varieties of cruelty than as a ritual humiliation of enemies and controlled release of mourners' emotions."[67] From the victim's perspective, torture represented three things: a reminder of the captors' dominance, a test of perseverance, and an altered state of mind (similar to a vision quest) that would lead the captive to a new life.[68] Therefore, torture was not an arbitrary demonstration of egotistic dominance or a display of conquest; rather, it was a calculated representation of strict Nadowek cultural codes that were accepted by both the captive and the captors. The case study of Eustace Ahatsistari demonstrates these circumstances and suggests the latter portrait comes closer to the truth for the Wendat.

Perhaps one of the most well-known Wendat war chiefs of his time, Ahatsistari was an accomplished warrior and leader within his community. Writing on Ahatsistari's military exploits, one scholar has aptly deemed him "the bravest of the braves," "a man who excelled and exalted in feats of war."[69] In the summer of 1642, Ahatsistari led a Wendat expedition, escorting forty Frenchmen from Trois-Rivières to Ste. Marie. During this voyage a number of human footprints thought to be Iroquois came to the attention of Ahatsistari. There was a momentary discussion of whether or not to proceed, but Ahatsistari had the last word: "It matters not; I noticed by their tracks that they are not in greater number than we; let us advance, and fear nothing."[70] This decision had tragic ramifications for the group; a nearly equal force of Iroquois warriors concealed in the bushes attacked the Wendat and took Ahatsistari as a captive, along with roughly twenty-two other prisoners, including Jesuit Isaac Jogues.[71]

Eight days after the initial capture, the ceremonial torment began.[72] First, the captors gave thanks to the Creator for having caused these captives to come to them. This was followed by a salute of arquebus shots into the air to symbolize the victory. Then they set up a stage on a hill, where, armed with sticks and thorns, they formed two lines, hundreds on each side. The captives were forced to run the gauntlet naked and endure each individual slash to the skin. Many did not make the length of the line and collapsed on the ground halfway. Out of the Wendat captives, Ahatsistari received by far the worst of these measures. After the gauntlet, the Iroquois cut off both thumbs from his hands, and thrust a pointed stick through the incisions to the elbow. On the tenth day after the capture, the party arrived in Iroquois country, continuing their journey for another four days, eating only a few wild fruits along the way.[73]

Upon arriving at the first Iroquois village, the community's youth lined up outside the gated entrance to greet the prisoners. They were armed with sticks and iron rods. The slower the procession walked, the harder the blows to the captives became. That night, the captives were taken to separate homes where they were tied down. Children were encouraged to throw pieces of coal and burning cinders at their stomachs. Following this first day and night, the captives were brought to a scaffold where they endured similar torture for three days. The process was continued in two additional villages over several subsequent days. The encounters only grew in intensity. By the third village, captives had thorns or pointed sticks thrust into their open sores, to the point of renewed bleeding.[74] At last, Ahatsistari's life was brought to an end by fire. As he burned, a missionary recorded his last words. He pleaded with his fellow Wendat that "the thought of his death should never prejudice the peace with the Iroquois."[75] Thus, it would seem that Ahatsistari, despite his horrible experience, respected the ritual as a natural result of warfare. Captive torture was not personal, but rather essential to the larger Nadowek cultural system.

Not all captive experiences fit the categories of adoption, torture, and death. There are cases in which captives escaped, either by their own volition or by that of their captors. In 1647, for instance, the Wendat had captured the prominent Onondaga headman Annenraes. After holding several councils to deliberate the fate of prisoners, the Wendat decided to let him return to his country as a kind of peace offering. The Wendat and Onondaga had been at war during this period and the headmen were hoping to create a truce through this manoeuvre. Consequently, Annenraes was equipped with presents and returned to his country.

On his travels, the Onondaga headman encountered three hundred Onondaga warriors who were on their way to avenge his assumed death. Upon seeing their beloved leader alive, the group decided to retreat and cede for peace instead.[76]

Other captives escaped on their own. The fourteen-year-old daughter of the Wendat man Antoine Otiatonnety was captured by the Iroquois, and while being held overnight, she heard her captors discussing her potential death. Not wanting to see her end, she gathered her courage and ran from the Iroquois village out into the bush a fair distance away. An Iroquois search party scanned the perimeters for three days and nights, coming very close to the girl on several occasions. In order to not give up her location, the girl remained still, eating and drinking nothing throughout this time. Deciding on the third day that she could not remain without food any longer, she took the risk of exposing herself and fled towards the Neutral nation, where she hoped to find sanctuary. The girl walked for three straight days, crossing a river and many kilometres of land. On the third day, she encountered a group of Iroquois and Neutrals. The Iroquois recognized her as the escaped captive and threatened to return her, but the Neutrals declared her safe, because she was within their territory. Finally, the Iroquois conceded to the Neutrals and allowed the girl to continue to the next Neutral village, where she broke her fast and then made the final trip home to Wendake.[77]

Captives had to adapt to survive, and the experience can be seen as a necessary "flexibility" or "duality" for Nadowek captives.[78] In some cases, captivity provided a means to benefit the Wendat, as escapees could provide valuable intelligence about the Iroquois war machine, as well as serve as diplomats on the Confederacy's behalf. On 14 July 1648, the Wendat man Armond, who had just escaped from a hundred Iroquois who were camped near the French settlement of Trois-Rivières, went to warn the French that the Iroquois were planning an attack on the settlement in the near future, but that he had tried his best to dissuade them. The Iroquois had made it known that their attack was in response to the Frenchmen's poor treatment of Iroquois captives. This Armond denied; he argued that the French, like the Wendat, treated prisoners very well and in the customary fashion. This seemed to pacify the Iroquois to some degree, according to Armond, and they agreed to put off the attack for the time being, but only as long as they received notice that the French had kept their brethren alive.[79] In this case, Armond acted as both informant and diplomat. He penetrated the Iroquois inner councils and obtained valuable information concerning their war strategy while quelling the potential for conflict.

On the Homefront

The effects of the loss of loved ones, whether they were adopted or killed, had serious ramifications for those back home. In the case of Eustace Ahatsistari, the results fed into the already changing dynamics of the Confederacy. Ahatsistari was a Christian, baptized just before he ventured out on his last expedition in 1642.[80] With the news of his death, many of his comrades, out of respect and a desire to see the fallen warrior in the afterlife, converted to the Christian faith.[81] These men defended their decision in relation to a speech delivered by Ahatsistari just before he left. The surviving war chiefs used this message as a guide to their actions. Ahatsistari said:

> Let us inform our Relatives who are not of the same Faith as we, even if they may be our fathers and our children, that we do not wish our bones to be mingled together after our death since our Souls will be eternally separated, and our affection will not continue beyond this life.[82]

Ahatsistari was asking that his remains be buried separately from non-Christians. If his comrades did not convert, they would not be able to rejoin their beloved leader. Ahatsistari's death also fed the growing contingent of Wendat chiefs converting to Christianity for guns. In these cases, conversion was used initially out of a respect for Ahatsistari but nonetheless fostered closer interaction between war leaders and French missionaries.

On some occasions the loss of a close family member or friend could have devastating effects back home. The news of such a loss could send relatives into a spiral of depression, unable to cope with the reality. Amantacha (baptized as Louis de Sainte-Foy) from the Wendat village of Teanaostaiae fell captive to the Iroquois and was put to death in October 1637. For some time, the family refused to accept that he was gone. In January, one of Amantacha's uncles received news from a "reliable source" that his nephew was still alive. This only fed Amantacha's parents' hopes and they continued the denial for another two months. In March, however, nearly five months after the initial news, Amantacha's mother declared her son dead. The Jesuits visited the grieving family that same month, following the customs of the country by giving four hundred porcelain beads and two small hatchets as condolence gifts.[83] It was during this visit that the missionaries learned of the depths to which this family had fallen.

With the acceptance of his son's death, Amantacha's father, a hard-headed traditionalist, took his own life, unable to cope with the loss of his son. Apparently, having suffered from severe bouts of depression for many months, the father asked his daughter to gather the root *ondachienroa.* This root was known for its medicinal value, but it could also be used as a quick poison if prepared properly. The daughter, believing the root would be used to cure her father's ailments, went out twice to collect enough root to satisfy her father's request. After some preparation, Amantacha's father ate the root, which resulted in a high fever and his death shortly thereafter.[84]

Repercussions of war and the practice of taking prisoners were not only personal experiences but also ones felt by the entire Wendat community. Although warriors and war chiefs were most certainly taken as captives, so too were young girls and old men. The loss of these individuals had major impacts on Wendat society in terms of Christian conversion and personal stability of the community.

Wendat Victories

Despite an emphasis on Wendat military losses (perpetuated with the constant focus on 1649), the Wendat represented a strong adversary to the Iroquois. Regardless of their weakened state, the Wendat secured numerous victories leading up to 1649. Two cases in particular demonstrate the ferocity and ability of Wendat warriors during these years. In the summer of 1642, Ahatsistari led a successful expedition against the Iroquois that would contribute to his already prestigious reputation. His party, having perceived a number of Iroquois canoes with much greater numbers than their own, began to panic; they petitioned Ahatsistari to retreat. He refused to give in and pushed his warriors to face their enemy head on. He enticed them, saying, "No, no, my Comrades. Let us attack them ourselves."[85] Taking it upon himself to lead the Wendat contingent, Ahatsistari was the first to strike at the Iroquois. As the canoes approached, the war chief leapt from the shore into a canoe full of Iroquois warriors. He proceeded to crack the head of the first person he came in contact with and throw two others overboard before he himself jumped into the water, upsetting the entire canoe. He swam with one hand while managing to kill others. The shocked Iroquois retreated. Ahatsistari and his men pursued them, picking up those who remained in the water and bringing them back as captives and symbols of this extraordinary victory.[86]

Similar circumstances took place in July 1648. An Anishinaabe scout discovered Iroquois tracks close to a French settlement, and sent word of a pending attack. The inhabitants fired the cannon (which was the usual way of signalling a potential attack). There were five Wendat in close proximity to the town, and upon hearing the cannon they hurried to see if they could be of assistance. However, they were confronted by a large Iroquois group of approximately eighty warriors before reaching the French, and were forced to begin combat with only two French farmers as allies. Still, the battle ended with an Iroquois retreat.[87]

The victories of 1642 and '48 were not the only military successes for the Wendat during the 1640s, yet they are representative of the ability of Wendat warriors to defend themselves against the Iroquois in a formidable way. These accounts also present instances when the odds were against the Wendat. Outnumbered and caught by surprise, Wendat warriors were victorious despite the fear of defeat.

Conclusion

The 1640s was a decade engulfed in Nadowek warfare and conflicts. Disease pushed the Wendat and their rivals to compete on a more frequent basis. The increase in warfare affected not just war chiefs and warriors but the community as a whole. Nadowek war culture took priority as the production of military supplies and the defence of villages became paramount to the security of the Confederacy. Women contributed significantly to this practice. Although out of the public eye and often overlooked by European observers, Nadowek women did not lack in influence. They not only produced food and weaponry and participated in the Fort Fight ritual but also made critical decisions concerning calls for war and the fate of captives. Community members respected the process, facilitating a continuation in customary warfare techniques and conventions.

The Nadowek tradition of captive adoption and torture remained an integral component to warfare throughout this period. Adoption replenished Nadowek numbers, encouraging diplomatic manoeuvres, and allowed for intelligence exchange. This interchange of people represented community growth and development, as citizens were both lost and gained. Through this process, kinship networks expanded and cultural customs evolved. Strangers could become nephews, replacing lost loved ones.

Given a second chance, adoptees bolstered their new family in numbers as well as skill. However, not everyone was deemed acceptable: injured and aged candidates risked rejection. Torture and death served as a normative feature to these events. The system of torture was complex and highly ritualized, rooted in long-standing traditions. Despite these outwardly grotesque and brutal physical performances, the Nadowek endorsed the beating and mutilation of captives as part of a natural life cycle. Pain served as a gateway to a new beginning, whether as an adoptee or in the Land of the Dead. It tested the strength and endurance of captives, while fear of further persecutions could dissuade support for future attacks.

A combination of economic aspirations and repopulation strategies motivated these conflicts, while the emergence of Wendat war chiefs in civil affairs also shaped circumstances. In the end, the Wendat acted as instigators and defenders within these struggles. There is no evidence to suggest that the Iroquois were any more militarily capable than the Wendat in the years leading up to their dispersal. But with the close interaction between the Wendat and the French by mid-century, Wendat communities became weakened with disease and by political divisions between pro- and anti-Jesuit factions. Nonetheless, examples of Wendat victories are a testament to the fact that although ultimately defeated by the Iroquois, the Wendat continued to represent a potential threat to their Nadowek enemies, resisting Iroquois attacks at least until 1649.

PART 2

Evacuation and Relocation

BEGINNING IN 1648, AND despite noted Wendat victories, the Iroquois managed to displace and overtake several Confederate villages. These defeats led the Wendat to reconsider their policies. Creative diplomacy and strategic military strikes on the Iroquois proved inadequate as their Wendat enemies burned villages, took captives, and killed large portions of the population. This section explores the resulting shift in Wendat tactics after the Iroquois conquest of Wendake. The decision to evacuate the mainland and eventually the homeland entirely was not an easy one, nor was it made in haste. The Wendat consistently followed customary protocol – organizing councils, consulting clan mothers, and creating consensus. The initial exodus did not lead to immediate dispersal and division within the Confederacy. Instead, after over a year of uncertain settlement, starvation, and isolation within Wendat country, the Wendat considered various long-term options. In the end, the Wendat directed their own removal: rather than simply reacting to European or Iroquois decisions and events, they engaged in a series of Native-orchestrated initiatives, influenced by traditional coalitions and kinship networks. The Wendat used their unique cultural capital to call French and Anishinaabe allies to their aid.

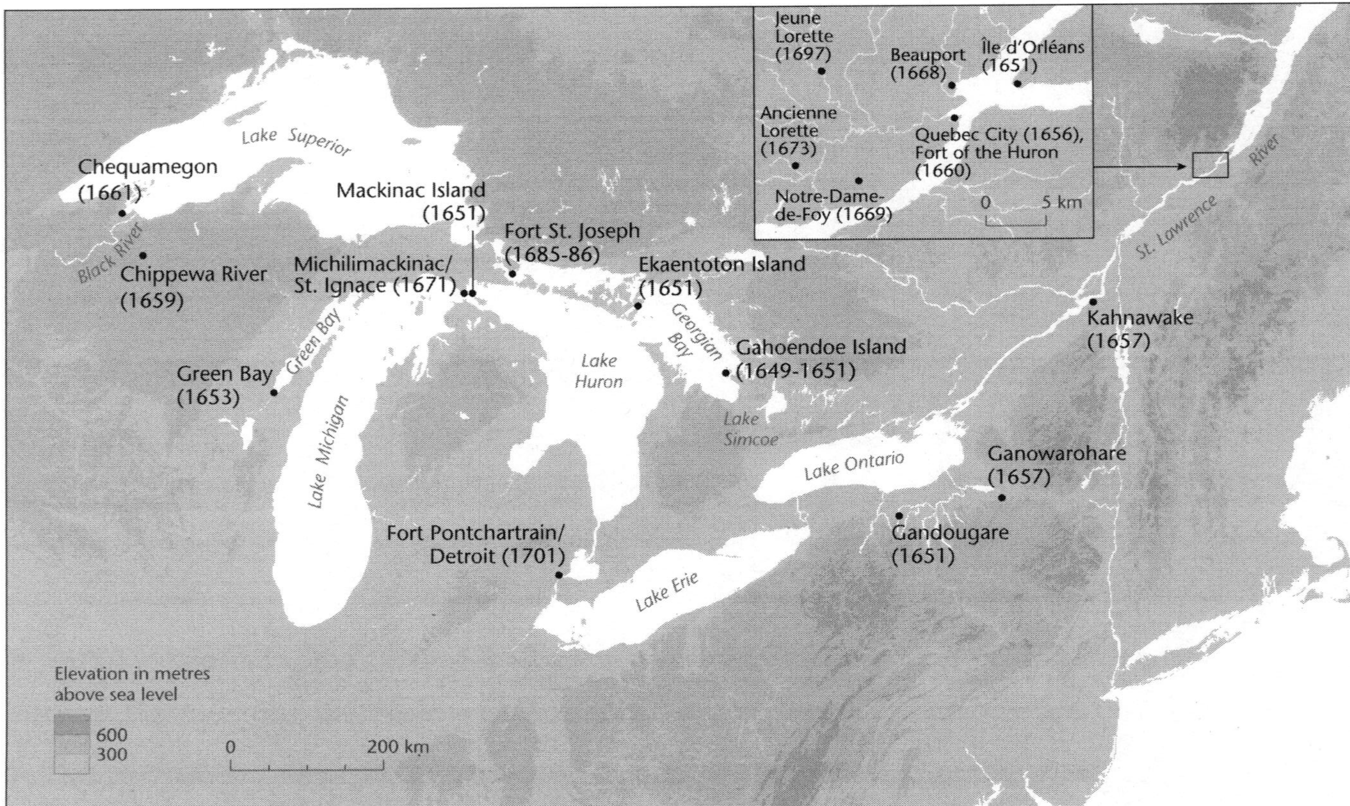

Post-dispersal relocations, 1650-1701

3
Wendat Country
Gahoendoe Island and the Cost of Remaining Close

DURING THE SUMMER OF 1648, the Iroquois executed a successful military invasion of the northern Wendat village of St. Joseph. Over four hundred families lived within this settlement, and the Iroquois victors took seven hundred captives.[1] Seven months later, the notable Wendat war chief Étienne Annaotaha from the village of St. Louis expressed a premonition that St. Joseph was only the first of many future Iroquois victories. The headman's worries became reality on 16 March 1649, when a thousand Iroquois warriors marched on the village of St. Ignace, resulting in four hundred casualties. In less than twenty-four hours, Annaotaha's St. Louis also fell, although most of the villagers had already fled as a result of his earlier premonition.[2] Convinced that an inevitable Iroquois victory would lead to total extermination, the remaining Wendat urged Annaotaha to leave. The headman replied in despair, "There is no longer time for them to flee across the snow. Let us die."[3] The Iroquois, who proved victorious in a brief amount of time (the battle took place between dawn and 9:00 a.m.), proceeded to burn the entire village to the ground. Many Wendat were killed. Jesuits made a record of the events, observing a terrifying scene where "children were broiling beside their mothers; where husbands saw [their wives] roasting near [them]."[4]

After a brief pause, the Iroquois returned to St. Ignace to regroup for an attack on the village of Ste. Marie the next day. This time, however, over three hundred Wendat warriors travelled to Ste. Marie to help in the defence. They managed to repel the Iroquois, who began a long and destructive retreat, taking with them hundreds of Wendat captives and provisions while burning whatever they could not carry.[5]

Scholars have attributed the Iroquois victories during the spring offensive of 1649 to several factors. The Iroquois acquisition of firearms and the Wendat lack of comparable weaponry most certainly played a role. In addition, the timing of the attack on St. Ignace (in mid-March) surprised the Wendat, who were used to the conventional Nadowek seasonal warfare that took place in the summer after the fields were planted. The spring attack happened when almost all the winter provisions were used and food resources were at their lowest. This tactic also made escape difficult, as the snow, ice, and freezing temperatures restricted movement and the lack of brush made hiding nearly impossible. The number of Iroquois warriors also presented a formidable advantage. Nadowek battles usually included small bands of warriors; the fact that the Iroquois attack comprised over one thousand able-bodied men allowed them to take hold of one village while sending more men to continue the military campaign on other unsuspecting communities. Iroquois might held extra longevity as their population had not been affected by European disease to the same extent as that of the Wendat. Finally, the Iroquois strategy of fighting at night violated customary practices of Nadowek warfare and caught the village by surprise. These departures from traditional tactics made the attacks all the more devastating for the Wendat.[6]

The decisive Iroquois offensives had both immediate and far-reaching repercussions. In addition to the many men, women, and children taken as captives, the Wendat lost approximately 630-880 warriors.[7] The loss of so many young men weakened the Wendat ability to fend off future invasions, and destabilized the psychological state of victims' families and loved ones. The destructive nature of the Iroquois retreat further debilitated Wendat survivors; the Wendat faced the horrific realization that they would not be able to plant or harvest crops for the coming year because the Iroquois had managed to take their corn seed supply. There was also the possibility that the enemy took their remaining provisions for the winter months.[8] The Iroquois attacks created a crisis situation for the survivors: if the Wendat remained within the borders of Wendake mainland, they faced starvation.

Understanding the severity of these circumstances, over six thousand Wendat convened at the village of Ste. Marie to evaluate their options.[9] After much deliberating, the majority resolved to move to the island of Gahoendoe, located roughly five kilometres from the most northern part of Wendake and the southern tip of Georgian Bay.[10] Gahoendoe became a Wendat refuge for more than a year. This period, deemed by one scholar as "the hungry winter" (although spanning from spring 1649 to spring 1650), represented the first major attempt at relocation by the Wendat, yet its importance in the process of Wendat dispersals has received little attention.[11] For the most part, historians treat Gahoendoe as a brief stopover in the much longer and geographically distant Wendat dispersal. It is framed as a complete failure and the impetus for the final evacuation of the Wendat from their homeland. Quick descriptions such as these fail to explain the circumstances that led to the Wendat evacuation of Gahoendoe.

This chapter explores the decision-making process that preceded the move to Gahoendoe in 1649, and the factors that pushed the Wendat to reassess their choice a year later. It considers how the Wendat negotiated their removal, and what aspects informed their decisions. Wendat political and commercial networks relied heavily on geographic location, with specific emphasis on waterways. Gahoendoe represented an attempt by the Wendat to maintain their role as diplomats and fur traders through spatial power.[12] In this light, the island relocation became an integral part of a calculated plan to overcome the military defeat by the Iroquois and keep a foothold in the geopolitical world of the northeast. The failure of this experiment, and the Wendat final resolution to abandon the Gahoendoe strategy in 1650, signalled a major turning point in Wendat survival, but still a calculated one, embedded in traditional networks and identities. While disease and the Iroquois attacks significantly weakened the Wendat and drove them to leave Wendake, the food crisis on Gahoendoe in 1649-50 was the most important factor shaping the future of the Wendat and their subsequent exodus from Wendat country.

The Decision

The Wendat reacted to the news of the defeat at St. Ignace and St. Louis with a combination of grief and panic. In the village of Ossossane, people heard about the overall Iroquois victory two days after the confrontation at Ste. Marie. Shocked and frustrated, wives cried out for their husbands and mothers for their sons. According to Father Pierre-Joseph-Marie Chaumonot, not a single cabin remained untouched by these events; the wails of mourning family members and friends could be heard throughout the village.[13] Sorrow soon gave way to an overwhelming sense of anxiety about the future. How would they overcome these losses? Would the Iroquois return? How would they defend themselves? For many, these questions pointed to the ultimate demise of the Wendat, and the people expressed this fear both privately and publicly. In Ossossane, an aged man became so agitated that he began to run from one end of the village to the other yelling that the Iroquois were sure to return and with the loss of so many warriors, the village's ability to defend itself was hopeless.[14] His disillusionment pushed him to shout, "Run away! Run away! Save us! Behold the enemy army who has arrived to take us!"[15] In reality, the Iroquois were not attacking the village, but paranoia surely affected many in the already anxious community.

Luckily, this type of reaction did not consume the majority, and before long Wendat from all the villages began to congregate to constructively address their situation. Ste. Marie became the nucleus of this activity. Staying in the established villages within Wendake was not an option because of the lack of food supplies and the likelihood that the Iroquois would return. A plan of evacuation and relocation was the next logical solution.

Dividing up into small bands and families seemed a reasonable strategy that would allow for easier mobility and the potential to evade detection from the Iroquois.[16] Others thought that keeping villages together would create greater security.[17] One group put this plan into action and created a new village, later named St. Charles by the Jesuits. They built cabins and fortified their surroundings. They relied on fishing for subsistence, although they also managed to retain a small amount of corn.[18] Although some advocated these small-scale relocations throughout the Wendake mainland, others believed the tactic too precarious, since villages such as St. Charles seemed too distant and isolated from the larger Wendat community.[19] Indeed, many of these groups would find themselves exposed to Iroquois attacks and a lack of supplies and provisions.[20] The alternative to remaining on the mainland was to venture across the water to one of the numerous islands located near by. Although some groups decided to move out on their own to various small islands, the majority agreed to remain together and relocate the entire population to one island.[21] At first, Ekaentoton Island, located north of Lake Huron, approximately two hundred kilometres (108 nautical miles) from Ste. Marie, and already inhabited by the Anishinaabeg and a Jesuit mission, seemed attractive.[22] During the deliberations at Ste. Marie, the Jesuits informed the Wendat that they thought Ekaentoton was their best option.[23] The land was said to be good and the fishing excellent; the island was approximately 1,718 square kilometres with 108 freshwater lakes.[24] The presence of other missionaries on the island enticed the Jesuits to support a move there. For the Wendat, however, the move was more complicated. Current interpretations point to the long frost season at Ekaentoton as the main reason for Wendat reservations towards the relocation, but the Wendat may have also been considering the geopolitical ramifications of such a move.[25] By joining the Anishinaabeg who already lived on the island, the Wendat would relinquish their position as middlemen within the French–Wendat–Anishinaabe fur trade. Traditionally, the Anishinaabeg traded furs to the Wendat in exchange for corn and the Wendat in turn traded the furs to the French for European goods.[26] If the Wendat relocated to an Anishinaabe settlement, the French would have no need to go through the Wendat to receive furs – they would have direct access to the Anishinaabeg.

The Wendat rejected the Jesuit proposal of Ekaentoton in 1649 and sought land closer to home. Located approximately forty-two kilometres northwest of Ste. Marie, the island of Gahoendoe was one of the largest islands within Wendake.[27] The 13,413 acres of land comprising Gahoendoe could provide ample space for the cultivation of fields, and the fishing was known to be plentiful.[28] In addition, there was already a Wendat village on the island, and it was common knowledge that they had planted their corn for the year.[29] The island's five-kilometre distance from the mainland made it a secure location; close enough to access the mainland, but far enough away that any pending attack could be foreseen from the island's eastern shore (the western shore had no significant land mass in proximity). Its northern location was also an advantage because it was one of the islands farthest from Iroquois country.

While these were important factors, the relationship between the occupied space of Gahoendoe and the resulting maintenance of power within the geopolitical and economic Wendat world was taken into consideration. Wendake was the heart of commercial activity for the St. Lawrence fur trade, and Gahoendoe was not only within the influence of the Wendat territorial authority but was also already an established stopover for the Anishinaabe and Wendat fur trade.[30] The Wendat had used it as a meeting ground in the past, a position that would only be augmented further if the Wendat community took the island as their primary place of residence. Despite the frequency of warfare and the latest Iroquois attacks, trade between the Anishinaabeg, Wendat, and French continued throughout 1648 and 1649, with an accumulation of over five thousand livres in beaver furs.[31] Thus, Gahoendoe provided a decent subsistence culture and physical defence, as well as a good location to secure Wendat hegemony in the fur trade and their traditional role as middlemen.

The majority of Wendat resolved to move to Gahoendoe, having reached consensus within each village. As a final step in solidifying the pending removal, twelve of the most prominent headmen invited the Jesuits to join them. This request could have been made for several reasons. Although there were already Christian converts within the group, the headmen inferred there would be the potential for future conversions if the Jesuits agreed to move with them. This was most likely done to appease the Jesuits, with the hope that the Wendat would also gain military defence and provisions; the Jesuits had guns and other goods the Wendat needed.[32] Because the Wendat fended off the Iroquois at Ste. Marie, the Jesuits of that mission had maintained decent amounts of livestock and agricultural provisions. In their storage, the missionaries had at least ten fowls, two pigs, two bulls, four cows, and a substantial amount of corn (that had been provided by the Wendat in the last harvest).[33] The prospects of keeping the Jesuits within the Wendat sphere of influence also remained crucial to trade networks with the French. By maintaining a close relationship with the Jesuits, the Wendat simultaneously secured future relations with the French.

The official invitation to the Jesuits followed customary Wendat diplomatic protocol. The headmen called a council in which they spoke about the Wendat decision and the reasons they wished the French to accompany them. They pointed to the weakened state of their people and their inability to properly defend themselves without French help. They urged the missionaries to have compassion on their widows and children. The headmen concluded their three-hour oration with the proposition that many of the Wendat would consider Christian conversion after relocation. Subsequently, the headmen gave the Jesuits ten wampum belts that represented "the voice of the women and children."[34] The Jesuits resolved to "follow [their] flock, and flee with the fleeing."[35]

The Wendat engaged in calculated planning and strategic decision making to facilitate their move to Gahoendoe. Despite the limited options, Gahoendoe represented the best opportunity for survival. Much of the scholarship discussing this point in Wendat history tends to overemphasize the role of the Jesuits in these deliberations. The public history site of Sainte-Marie among the Hurons, for instance, presents a sign depicting those who moved to Gahoendoe as a group of Jesuits and "some Wendat followers."[36] Similarly, Mackinac State Park describes the Wendat as being "lured" by the French.[37] Even prominent scholars assert that the Wendat looked to the Jesuits for leadership in these matters.[38] However, the actual circumstances depict a different situation. The move to Gahoendoe was clearly a Wendat decision. Jesuits wanted to go to Ekaentoton; an idea rejected by the Wendat. Further, the Jesuit decision to accompany the Wendat to Gahoendoe was made in response to invitations instigated by the Wendat.

The Journey

It took less than two weeks to pack up and strip the village and mission at Ste. Marie.[39] They burned the village to the ground in less than an hour.[40] Similar operations took place in at least fifteen other Wendat villages. These settlements were burned in the hope of preventing the Iroquois from using them for refuge in future campaigns.[41] While most Wendat left near the end of March, several small groups remained on the mainland throughout the summer to try and gather sufficient provisions for the fall and winter months.[42] This strategy was crucial to ensure that upon arrival the Wendat community would have enough food to last them until the next harvest.

The exact path to Gahoendoe is unknown, although the most likely route was by canoe out the Wye Marsh adjacent to Ste. Marie. They could follow the shores of Matchedash Bay, beyond present-day Beausoleil Island and Giant's Tomb, round the northern tip of land that points to the greater Georgian Bay. The journey ordinarily took a day, but was made longer by the large number of people travelling, and hesitancy from fear of Iroquois attacks.[43] Some members of the fleet made the mistake of taking refuge at night for sleep and were attacked by Iroquois war parties that continued to keep watch on the Wendat from the shore.[44]

The Jesuits and their European contingent, as well as the remaining Wendat, followed this first wave of migrants on the evening of 14 June 1649. In addition to canoes, this group built a raft out of fifty- to sixty-foot logs. They maintained a strategy of only paddling at night, and thus it took them several days to make their final destination, despite the fact that they had calm winds and no rain.[45]

Population

Historians have never fully explored the demographic information concerning those who relocated to Gahoendoe.[46] The Jesuits recorded that approximately three hundred Wendat families occupied the island before June. Another report indicates over a hundred "cabins" by 1650.[47] If one Wendat family comprised approximately five to eight people, then a minimum of fifteen hundred people lived on Gahoendoe before the major migration in the spring of 1649.[48] In addition, one cabin, or longhouse, housed roughly sixty to eighty people.[49] Thus, one hundred cabins translate into a minimum population of six thousand. Combined, these numbers indicate that the entire Wendat population of Gahoendoe was most likely close to eight thousand.

Current archeological data supports these estimates. In the early 1990s, Northeastern Archeological Associates excavated the Charity Site, originally one of the largest Wendat settlements on Gahoendoe in the seventeenth century.[50] The data collected at this site and several others from the surrounding area revealed over a thousand people living within one settlement and confirmed that there was at least one site with over one hundred longhouses. Further evidence of material culture, such as a hundred decorated pots, a hundred ceramic pipe sections, sixty glass beads, and a considerable amount of European metal, point to the fact that the Wendat had not only settled the area but also transported their culture and rituals to the island.[51] Taking these numbers into consideration, as well as the loss of over seven hundred warriors in the spring campaign against the Iroquois, the Wendat community on Gahoendoe represented at least 86 percent of the entire Wendat population.[52]

This group mirrored the various factions within the Confederacy. Those who moved to Gahoendoe represented all the villages and nations of the Wendat.[53] Scholars have argued that the majority of those relocating to the island were from Christian villages and nations, but there is little evidence to support this beyond a 1649 letter from the Ursuline nun Marie de l'Incarnation, who believed the entire island was made up of Christians.[54] In addition, the Christian hypothesis is based on Jesuit reports of many converts and their baptismal records.[55] The use of baptismal records presents two problems. One, the fact that there were Wendat asking for baptism in 1649 suggests that many were not Christian when they first sought to relocate. Similarly, the headman's oration at Ste. Marie just before the move implied that many Wendat would consider baptism if the Jesuits also moved to Gahoendoe. Moreover, the Jesuit practice of baptizing the dying and the Wendat custom of seeking conversion in an attempt to overcome death had not ceased during this period. So although it is true that the Jesuits recorded three thousand baptisms, this indicates the number of Christian *souls* among the Wendat, not necessarily the number of Christian *people.*

The loss of so many warriors in the spring of 1649 has led scholars to suggest that the majority of the population was made up of women.[56]

The Iroquois wars had taken hundreds of able-bodied men from this community, and the Jesuits contend that there were "hundreds and hundreds of widows who had lost entire households."[57] Although the Jesuits' constant reference to Wendat "families" when discussing population size seems to complicate the validity of this argument, there is no doubt that hundreds of men were lost in the recent war. If the overall population before 1649 was around ten thousand and 86 percent moved to Gahoendoe after the dispersal, it is unlikely that the Wendat population had such an extreme gender ratio unbalance. This is not to make light of the loss of hundreds, perhaps over a thousand warriors, but in the context of the entire population, it is hard to believe that nearly 90 percent of the survivors were women. One faction was most certainly comprised of men – the sixty Europeans who came to live among the Gahoendoe Wendat. This group consisted of thirteen Jesuit fathers, including Fathers Pierre-Joseph-Marie Chaumonot and Paul Ragueneau, four assistants, twenty-two donnés (a secular employee of the Society of Jesus), eleven domestics, six soldiers, and four "boys."[58] In sum, the refugee population on Gahoendoe was comprised of all Wendat nations, including Christians and traditionalists. Moreover, women constituted a significant portion of the community, but family units still existed.

Settlement

The ways in which the Wendat organized their settlement on the island illustrates a continuation of past practices of agriculture and village composition while also highlighting innovations for a more secure community. The structuring of this space and thus the physical ordering of Wendat daily lives were direct reflections of underlying cultural principles and belief systems.[59]

They built two large Wendat villages, and several longhouses that were located in more remote areas.[60] The village now called the Charity Site was located roughly one and a half kilometres northwest into the interior on the shore of present-day Douglas Lake. Houses within this community were for the most part customary longhouses, although they were shorter and narrower than those found on the Wendake mainland. They were also built closer together than Wendat settlements of the past. This new structuring had very little to do with any alterations to the population; archeologists agree that the houses were still able to hold the customary sixty to eighty people.[61] Rather, the new design was most likely an attempt to optimize the amount of space on Gahoendoe. Back on the mainland, villages usually relocated every eight to ten years in order to rotate the soil of their fields. The limited amount of land on an island would have restricted this strategy and so preserving space was important to ensure the availability of land for the future. The close proximity of the houses to one another may have also been a defensive strategy. Closer, tight-knit villages were easier to defend in the case of an Iroquois attack.

The Wendat managed to clear and plant at least one field by June 1649 at the Charity Site.[62] Cornfields were an integral part of Wendat subsistence culture and it was paramount that all the villages cultivated the land for food to sustain the isolated island population. Prospects for agriculture were good; in general a Nadowekian population of twenty thousand people can subsist off of seven thousand acres.[63] Taking into consideration the size of Gahoendoe (13,413.1 acres) and the population of the Wendat (eight thousand), there would have been ample space for the cultivation of crops. Gahoendoe presented some difficulties, however, as it had dense forest; trees had to be cleared and the ground tilled before any crops could be sown. Although this undertaking took priority in terms of community building, only one out of ten families contributed in any significant way.[64] Some scholars suggest that the preparation of fields was men's work, and have connected the inability of the Wendat to plant crops to their dwindling male population.[65] Given the new data on Wendat gender ratios at Gahoendoe, however, the inability of most families to contribute to the fields might have been a result of the many other tasks required by the Wendat during this period. A combination of building houses, finding food, and protecting the community from potential Iroquois attacks occupied the majority.

The Wendat located their second large settlement, named Ste. Marie II by the French, a few hundred metres from the southern shore of Gahoendoe, within plain sight of mainland Wendake, and close to the Jesuit mission.[66] In addition to at least a hundred longhouses built in the same fashion as those on the Charity Site, Ste. Marie II included fortifications. It appears that the Wendat decision to have the Jesuits accompany them paid dividends; under the guidance of several skilled soldiers, the Europeans immediately built two forts, one around the mission and the other circling the Wendat village.[67] This project was made easier with the help of the Wendat, and the realization that the ground naturally provided stone and mortar without any digging. The structure encompassing the mission followed seventeenth-century military guidelines and was approximately 120 square feet with bastions at each corner.[68] French soldiers were later posted at the bastions for twenty-four-hour protection.[69] This arrangement was completed by the end of the summer.[70]

According to Father Ragueneau, the fortification was an improvement in comparison to the wooden palisade that had been constructed at Ste. Marie I on the mainland. For the most part, the Jesuits felt confident that the stone was impenetrable by the Iroquois. In addition, they believed the stone walls surrounding the settlements were high enough to repel the enemy and strong enough to withstand a battering ram.[71] Most Wendat also felt secure on the island, asserting that the location and buildings allowed for optimal defence against an Iroquois attack from the mainland.[72]

In their longhouses, design, and fortifications, the construction of Wendat villages on Gahoendoe reflected both customary practices and alternative innovations. They required a large amount of labour and dedication from every member; each contributed to the building of residences, palisades, and fields. The French furthered Wendat aspirations of security by applying their experience with mortar and stone fortifications to these communities. Up until this point, the decision to relocate to Gahoendoe must have seemed a success, providing potential to maintain the Wendat Confederacy and its people, but food shortages soon created a new crisis.

Food Crisis

Despite the fact that the Wendat had planted their crops by spring, it became evident after a few months at Gahoendoe that food was going to be an issue. Some Wendat expressed anxiety over the lack of rain as early as June 1649.[73] Indeed, these worries were well founded, as the droughts of 1649-50 and the pending crop failure would culminate in a food crisis that proved to be the most disastrous force affecting the future of the Confederacy. The causes of the famine on Gahoendoe have been the subject of debate by scholars. Some argue the famine was the result of a pre-1649 Wendat focus on trade and a neglect of their fields, as they obtained corn from other Nadowek societies such as the Neutral and Petun. Others discount this theory and assert that the food crisis was correlated with the depopulation of the Wendat during the Iroquois attacks in 1648-49 and the inability of the survivors to cultivate their fields out of fear of the Iroquois. This, they contend, along with the Iroquois destruction of so many Wendat fields and provisions, would have made it difficult for the Wendat to create any kind of substantial surplus to be transported to Gahoendoe. Further, the immediate crisis occurred because of the small yield of fish on Gahoendoe and the limited amount of food reserves of the Jesuits.[74]

Even though there is little to support the first theory, the second explanation serves to only partially describe the circumstances leading to the famine. A lack of provisions would have created significant problems for an isolated population, and the inability to obtain alternative food supplies, such as fish, would have certainly exacerbated the situation.[75] It is also correct to assume the amount of food in the Jesuits' storage was lacking. The Jesuits had about five hundred bushels of corn and the equivalent in acorns.[76] Still, further examination is necessary to understand the severity of the situation.

First, acorns and corn do not have the same nutritional value. While one cup of dried Indian corn represents about 108 calories and provides 78 percent of the carbohydrates, 12 percent of fats, and 10 percent of proteins of a human's daily requirements, the same amount of acorns represents 142 calories, 42 percent of the carbohydrates, 52 percent of fats, and 6 percent of proteins.[77] More importantly, the amount of work to attain the nutritional value from these products differ greatly. The Wendat preferred corn because it could be easily prepared for consumption. Once dried, it could be ground, boiled, or roasted in abundance because the kernels were ready to be eaten.[78] Conversely, acorns were a time-consuming product; the edible portion is found within the hard shell of the nut, accessed only by cracking the exterior or boiling the acorn as a whole to break the softer shell. Access to the insides is only half the battle, however, as the bitter tannins within the nut need to be leached in order to make it edible. This process of boiling or soaking could take anywhere from a few hours to a number of days, and required several changes of water.[79] Thus, the reality of the situation was that acorns and corn were not equal in terms of nutritional value, preparation, or desirability by the Wendat. Still, emphasis on the lack of Jesuit supplies holds true. If corn *was* the most preferred provision, five hundred bushels could feed fifty people over the winter months – a number that made little to no difference to eight thousand starving Wendat.

These factors could have been overcome if the crops planted in the spring of 1649 had matured. In this case, both theories overlook a second important detail – the effects of a drought that took place during the summer of 1649. Tree-ring data for the entire Mississippi area suggests that the mid-seventeenth century was not an era typified by regional droughts, compared to the conditions of the late sixteenth century, or the century-long megadroughts of the twelfth and thirteenth centuries. Nonetheless, Jesuits were seriously concerned about the lack of rain; and it seems likely that a local drought contributed to the Wendat crisis. The Jesuits took note of it and the constant need for rain even before the extent of the drought was fully realized.[80]

The Wendat addressed the crop failure and pending famine in a number of ways. Alternative foods were the first line of defence. Despite their distaste for labour-intensive acorns, these nuts became the number one source of nutrition. Groups were sent out to collect acorns in the late months of summer and autumn to acquire provisions for the winter. In addition, a bitter root called *otsa* was often collected. Those who did not have the luxury of these items relied on wild garlic that they baked under ashes or boiled in water.[81] Other Wendat stripped trees of their bark and boiled it. This created a bitter broth they drank to give their bodies the impression of being full.[82]

Eventually, the hunger became a pandemic and famine plagued the entire population. For those who had not, or could not, obtain other wild foods, bartering for supplies became an alternative. Some sold their material possessions to other Wendat in exchange for meals of acorns or broth. Many of these items were clothing and it became common practice for desperate Wendat to take the clothes from deceased bodies and trade them for food. This happened so frequently that one dying man pleaded with his companions to "bury me now, at once; for my life is over, and thou seest plainly that I am numbered among the dead. Now, what I fear is this, that, if I should die before being buried, other poor people, as destitute as I am, may rob me of these rags that cover my nakedness, to put upon themselves."[83]

Another option was to seek out the reserves of the Jesuits. Although in small amounts, the readily accessible supplies stored at the mission enticed many Wendat to meet the priests and request aid. Not surprisingly, the Jesuits favoured Christian converts with rations. To implement distributions in a controlled fashion, the Jesuits introduced a coin that was a small piece of copper stamped with a sign designed for the acquisition of food. They instructed coin holders to line up at midday. Jesuit favourites received Indian meal boiled in water, while others could obtain acorns or smoked fish.[84]

As spring drew near, those who had survived the winter ventured off the island in search of a wider supply of food, particularly acorns that could be more easily collected on the melting mountain tops of the mainland. They also checked fishing grounds exposed to the southern sun. These risky endeavours occasionally led to death. In early March 1650, a large group of men, women, and children attempted to cross to the mainland for this purpose. They split up into small bands to make an attack from the Iroquois more difficult. Barely out of sight of the island, the ice cracked and several drowned. Others remained paralyzed on the surface, unable to move out of a fear of falling through, while equally aware that the amount of noise created by the catastrophe would alert the Iroquois on the mainland. Survivors remained exposed out on the ice overnight, until a Wendat rescue party deemed it safe to make a crossing the next day.[85]

As the famine peaked in the winter of 1649, the Wendat were pushed to the brink of survival. People transgressed social norms, implementing survival tactics that would never have been condoned in a healthy Wendat society. Some ate the excrement of animals and humans, while others dug up the corpses of animals to eat the boiled fur and bones. This was followed by cannibalism, which, for the purposes of physical nourishment, was strictly forbidden in Wendat society. Yet, brothers ate brothers, mothers their children, and children their parents. The Jesuits observed, "Everywhere, corpses have been dug out of the graves; and, now carried away by hunger, the people have repeatedly offered, as food, those who were lately the dear pledges of love."[86]

In the end, the combined effort to attain food through alternative supplies, bartering, Jesuit provisions, escape to the mainland, and cannibalism were not enough to save the majority of the population. Echoing the epidemics of the 1630s, families and loved ones watched each other die with very little opportunity to save them. One young mother, for instance, was found dead, while her two infant children continued to suck at her breasts; shortly after, the children also died. Many parents did not have the strength or resources to help their children, let alone themselves. In another case, a mother visited the Jesuits with her four children. Despite the children's repeated attempts to press their mother for milk, her body could no longer provide nourishment. The mother caressed the weeping children at her feet, one by one until they each died; she did not have the energy to bury her family and left the children in the hands of the Jesuits, who promised to take care of the bodies before she herself expired.[87]

The lack of normal refuse such as animal bones and the minimal remains of corn and acorns in archeological surveys are a testament to the extremely dire situation.[88] Jesuit baptismal records serve as an additional source. Nearly three thousand baptisms took place between March 1649 and March 1650.[89] This number indicates the number of deaths or at least those expecting to die and who were accepting baptism.[90] This does not count the traditionalists who were not included in these records, but were nonetheless afflicted by the famine. The Jesuits asserted that "hundreds and hundreds died" on Gahoendoe; the reality was that it was most likely thousands.[91] Bad luck and drought, not poor Wendat preparation or decision making, had undermined the resettlement. Regardless of causes, the catastrophe required immediate action.

Exodus

The food crisis pushed the Wendat to reconsider their move to Gahoendoe and shaped their entire experience on the island. Instead of a place of refuge, it became a death trap. With the coming of spring, Iroquois war parties became more active on the mainland, creating increased anxiety within an already weakened population. On 25 March 1650, a group of Wendat were attacked while they attempted to harvest fish from the mainland coast. The Wendat dispersed in all directions, leaving distances of twenty-four kilometres between each group. This strategy did not dissuade the Iroquois, however, and the entire company was lost except for one man who managed to escape and return to the island to share the details of the attack.[92] In early April, two other bands, headed by the Wendat leaders Andotitak and Thawenda, lost a brief battle that took place about forty-eight kilometres in the interior.[93] Roughly eight days later, the island Wendat received news that two large Iroquois war parties were on their way to Gahoendoe with the intention of attacking the Wendat and destroying their fields.[94]

The culmination of the winter famine and the present and pending Iroquois attacks resulted in a quest for new strategies. If the Iroquois were to land on the island, the surviving Wendat were too weak to orchestrate any kind of formidable opposition. Moreover, the depopulation of the island community and the weakened state of the remaining Wendat made it difficult to plant the crops needed to survive further occupation of Gahoendoe. These factors persuaded the Wendat to plan an evacuation.

In deliberations at a night council, headmen discussed the different destinations for relocation. The majority felt it wise to split up entirely, grouping into small bands and hiding in the forests of Wendake unfamiliar to the Iroquois. Others suggested that some move south to the Susquehannock and their allies of New Sweden, or to the west with the Anishinaabeg, while some entertained the thought of joining the Iroquois. Still, some suggested that they might move closer to French settlements for protection. In the end, the group agreed upon a strategy of calculated dispersal.[95] The majority of migrants would leave immediately, taking various routes to a number of different locations. A small contingent would stay behind, however, to salvage the limited amount of crops that had already been sown. This group would leave the island after the harvest.[96] Women, children, and older individuals that could not make the journey would also remain behind.[97] Two headmen delivered the news to the Jesuits; they explained their desperate situation in the following way:

> My brother ... thine eyes deceive thee when thou lookest on us: thou believest that thou seest living men, while we are but specters, the souls of the departed. The ground thou treadest on is about to open under us, to swallow us up, together with thyself, that we may be in the place where we ought to be, among the dead.[98]

Shortly thereafter, the Wendat evacuated Gahoendoe, taking nothing but themselves and the unwavering hope that they might survive.[99]

Étienne Annaotaha and the Last Stand

The situation was precarious for those Wendat who stayed. Towards the end of autumn, the Iroquois set up a fortification on the mainland, intending to capture any Wendat who strayed from the island.[100] After completing the fort, a group of Iroquois ventured to the island and executed what seemed to be an ambush. The Wendat manned the defences and prepared themselves for a violent conflict when, to their surprise, the approaching enemy sent word that they did not wish to fight but make peace. The Iroquois enticed the Wendat with promises of presents attesting to their goodwill. Étienne Annaotaha, a Wendat with a well-known adventurous reputation, stepped forward to discuss these assertions. The Iroquois brought him to their camp and presented him with gifts. Annaotaha replied, "It is not to me ... that these presents should be given"; he felt they should go to the Wendat headmen and council on Gahoendoe.[101] He requested they keep him as a hostage until the return of their emissaries. The Iroquois considered the situation and resolved that it would be Annaotaha himself who would accompany three ambassadors to the island; a number of Wendat would be kept at the Iroquois camp to ensure the return of their envoys. Annaotaha called for the people to come together once he returned to Gahoendoe:

> My Brothers ... Heaven is propitious to us to-day, because to day I have found life in death, not only for myself, but for all those who will not refuse the happiness that comes to our doors from the side whence we feared our greatest misfortune. The Iroquois have changed countenance, for their hearts have altered; their thoughts are no longer of blood or of fires, except to change them into bonfires.[102]

The Wendat reacted positively to these overtures; headmen expressed their satisfaction and the women gave equal assurances that they believed this was truly a salvation.[103] They welcomed the three Iroquois ambassadors into their homes and gave them the best food the famished community could provide.

But the true circumstances of the situation, much more complicated and potentially disastrous than a customary truce, emerged. As the Iroquois enjoyed their feast, Annaotaha took aside the most important Wendat headmen and informed them that he was convinced the Iroquois were laying a trap. The headmen organized a secret council to discuss the matter further. They believed Annaotaha's suspicions had merit, considering the most recent attacks and deceptions by the Iroquois over the last year. Consequently, they decided that they could not trust the Iroquois and would implement their own plan of deception. The headmen dispersed throughout the village asking the women to begin pounding corn and collecting provisions in preparation for their move to Iroquois country in three days. The women remained uninformed of Annaotaha's suspicions of the Iroquois; he told them only that they should prepare food for the journey to Iroquois territory. They accepted the instructions and kept busy with preparations for the next few days, which led the Iroquois to believe in the willingness of the Wendat to join them. On the day of departure, Annaotaha approached the large group of Iroquois who had ventured to the island to help in the relocation. He invited over thirty of the most prominent war chiefs and young men into the confines of the Wendat village. This was the last act of deception, for as the thirty warriors entered the fort, they fell into a Wendat ambush. Before being put to death, one of the warriors admitted that the Iroquois truce was a lie and that their plan had been to capture and defeat the Wendat. The majority of the Iroquois were killed; only three escaped.[104]

Historians have largely overlooked the legacy of this expedition. One scholar, for instance, summarizes the Wendat experience at Gahoendoe and their final evacuation this way: "After a terrible famine during the course of the winter, the Iroquois broke through in 1650 and massacred the survivors."[105] This interpretation replaces the Wendat victory with an Iroquois massacre and implies there were no Wendat survivors. Yet it was a Wendat victory, not an Iroquois one. The results of the Iroquois loss were twofold; first, upon hearing of the Wendat victory, the Iroquois fled the island and returned to the mainland, abandoning any design for immediate retaliation; and second, the Wendat became convinced that the Iroquois would return in order to avenge the deaths of their comrades and implement their goal of Wendat eradication.[106] To avoid this fate, the remaining Wendat evacuated Wendake to join their dispersed Wendat kinsmen.

Conclusion

The Wendat chose Gahoendoe Island because of its combined opportunities for defence, preservation of trade, and its potential for fishing and agriculture. The geographic location of the island satisfied all of these elements, including their desire to maintain spatial power within their geographic sphere of influence. Iroquois raids, always a threat, largely failed during the year at Gahoendoe. Stone walls and cement fortifications, as well as French soldiers and firearms, easily protected the compact island villages and their strategic sites. Approaching enemies could be seen long before they landed on Gahoendoe. In regards to trade, there is nothing to suggest that Gahoendoe would not have served its purpose as a meeting ground for exchange between the Anishinaabeg, Wendat, and the French. Before word of the evacuation reached the French settlements east of Wendake, for instance, a fur brigade had already departed with Gahoendoe as their final destination for trade.[107] These factors remained fundamental to the Wendat project of resettlement; if it had not been for the drought and subsequent food crisis, the plan might have worked.

The drought of 1649-50 was the most decisive issue shaping these circumstances. It changed everything. The climatic situation damaged the prospects of any substantial food supply for the Wendat population, and compromised their security. People were weak and dying and the community began to collapse both physically and socially, transgressing cultural norms to the point of cannibalism. The defensive advantages of the island location differentiated the Wendat from other people within the region. Unlike their mainland counterparts, such as the Iroquois and Anishinaabeg, the Wendat were trapped within the confines of the island's perimeter. If agriculture was not a feasible option on the mainland, for instance, communities could resort to hunting and gathering, venturing out farther and farther from their villages in order to meet the needs of their people. This was not an option for the Wendat, and the human population quickly depleted what little game, roots, and acorns they might have found on the island itself.

The decision to leave Wendat country was most certainly made out of desperation and in reaction to a seemingly hopeless situation, but even in this emergency the Wendat held councils and considered various strategies of relocation. In the end, the communal resolution to evacuate Gahoendoe was a calculated attempt to reorganize Wendat society for continued collective survival, not inevitable defeat, even if this meant dividing the community. The exodus from Wendake initiated a new phase of Wendat life, focused on dispersal and migration. Thus, although the epidemics of the 1630s and the Iroquois attacks of the 1640s were crucial in the final decision to leave Wendat country, it was the food crisis and the often overlooked Gahoendoe experience that pushed them, as one Jesuit described, "like wolves from the woods," to reshape their community into a diaspora entity and a reconfigured Wendat world.[108]

4
Anishinaabe Neighbours
The Coalition

Making and maintaining relationships within a system of North American networks was fundamental to the Wendat dispersal of the seventeenth century. This became even more evident with the decision to move beyond the borders of Wendake. Wendat decisions were not made in isolation, but called upon the input and influence of their allies. Central to this process was their preoccupation with the Wendat–Anishinaabe Coalition. This alliance was over two and a half centuries old at the time of the dispersal, yet it remains overshadowed by accounts that privilege the Wendat and Iroquois Confederacies in terms of seventeenth-century Great Lakes geopolitics. While historians consistently acknowledge that the relationship was close and that the Wendat and Anishinaabeg joined together to conduct trade and military campaigns, they differ on the specific details of the alliance and continue to consider it relatively "ambivalent."[1] Wendat descendants offer another perspective; they have preserved a standing knowledge of the Coalition's importance. The nineteenth-century Wendat Grand Chief from Lorette Michel Sioui described the legacy of the relationship by stating, "We, the Hurons of Lorette, have always had great affection for our brothers the Algonquins ... and we still do."[2] The chief then presented a wampum belt he said attested to this alliance and explained, "This is the belt that is proof of what I say. We have, or our ancestors for us, fixed this contract with the Algonquins so that we may always be able to hunt together."[3] More recently, scholar Georges Sioui, also a Wendat from Lorette, attempted to clarify the nature of the alliance for the general public. For Sioui, the historical relationship between these two groups was "symbiotic," flourishing because of a "sensitive and sympathetic awareness of each party's situation by the other." He asserts, "These two families, each with essentially distinctive qualities, had a long relationship ... that was harmonious."[4] Thus, Sioui contends the relationship was in fact rooted in difference, from which each group benefitted.

Evidence from the Wendat dispersal bears out this interpretation of the Wendat–Anishinaabe relationship, and offers a new way to view Native American alliance-making within the context of North American systems of power. Rather than an "ambivalent" organization of autonomous nations, the Coalition functioned as an established alliance that fundamentally shaped the nature of the Wendat dispersal. It is because of the resilience of the Coalition that the Wendat privileged Anishinaabe communities for relocation in the early stages of their dispersal, demonstrating an unwavering allegiance well beyond 1650 and into the second half of the seventeenth century.

The Wendat–Anishinaabe Coalition, 1300-1650

The cultural encounter between the Wendat and Anishinaabeg began as early as A.D. 1000. Around that time the Wendat migrated north into present-day Ontario and the Great Lakes region. Evidence suggests that this movement into Anishinaabe territory continued as far east as present-day Quebec City, although by 1550 many of these Wendat ancestors (known as the St. Lawrence Iroquois) had evacuated their eastern settlements (Stadacona and Hochelaga). The foundations for an established relationship between the newly arrived Wendat and their Anishinaabe neighbours did not fully take shape until the thirteenth century, when the Wendat settled permanently within the Georgian Bay area. At the time of contact with Europeans, the Anishinaabeg controlled most of the Ottawa Valley, as well as the surrounding area both north and west.[5]

Significant differences separated the Anishinaabeg and Wendat. Whereas Wendake included a concentrated number of settled villages with an emphasis on agriculture, Anishinaabe territory was vast and comprised of smaller, spread-out villages of a hundred to five hundred relatively nomadic people who centred their lives around the cyclical movements of wild game rather than the planting of corn.[6] Similarly, whereas the Wendat preferred to live in large longhouses, the Anishinaabeg constructed smaller wigwams that could house a family or two. Anishinaabe society was patrilineal (they traced their family lineage through male ancestry), rather than the Wendat custom of matrilineality.[7] Language variance was comparable to the contrast between Indo-European languages and the Altaic linguistic group, making the linguistic differences between the Anishinaabeg and Wendat as stark as that between Germans and Turks.[8] In regards to religion, the Anishinaabeg produced few Christian converts in comparison to the Wendat, as the former continued to privilege the uniquely Anishinaabe notion of the Great Spirit, or "Manitou."[9]

Despite these seemingly diametrically opposed characteristics, the Anishinaabeg and Wendat cultivated a "brotherhood" and coalition based on a shared partnership between territory, kinsmen, spiritual beliefs, trade, military defence, and diplomacy. The coming together of Anishinaabeg and Wendat likely occurred due to their close geographic proximity. Not only did the boundaries of their communities overlap, but in many cases both lived within the villages of the others. It was customary, for instance, for Anishinaabe groups to winter among the Wendat, establishing their wigwams within the confines of a village's palisade walls.[10] These wintering groups could average up to seventy people.[11] Likewise, the Wendat travelling through Anishinaabe territory and in need of shelter and food found welcome from Anishinaabeg who provided them with materials to ensure the success of their expeditions.[12] Shared residency also offered benefits in the form of security and protection when military attacks by the Iroquois drove both the Anishinaabeg and Wendat to seek refuge within the others' communities.[13]

Intermarriage further linked these two groups. Although the Wendat custom of matrilocality probably resulted in an overrepresentation of Anishinaabe men in Wendat villages, the union of men and women and their resulting offspring fostered a system of kinship integral to Native alliances.[14] The incorporation of new members into each respective society was also facilitated by adoption. Jesuit records indicate at least one case in which the Wendat raised an Anishinaabe orphan from early childhood.[15]

In view of the extended and sometimes lifelong shared residence of the Anishinaabeg and Wendat, it is not surprising certain aspects of each community were acculturated by the other. Spiritual charms were one of these elements. The Anishinaabeg had many powerful charms within their belief system. The Wendat bought the *onniont,* or serpent charm, for instance, so they could benefit from its power. This charm, with its snake-like features, was an armoured spirit that roamed the forest and if caught would render the captor good luck.[16] Through the Wendat acquisition of the *onniont,* they incorporated an Anishinaabe spiritual practice. Aside from the potential to attain personal "luck," Wendat motivations to acquire the charm may have reflected a Wendat belief that their neighbours to the north possessed "superior powers of achieving harmony with the spiritual world."[17] The Anishinaabeg had a different relationship with the earth due to their emphasis on hunting rather than agriculture. The Wendat, therefore, saw their alliance with the Anishinaabeg as a way of finding "spiritual regeneration and equilibrium," to balance their own alternative emphasis on agriculture.[18]

The Wendat and Anishinaabeg also shared in the same trade network. Predating the European fur trade, these groups engaged in a reciprocal exchange with one another. This trade was based on the premise that the Wendat would provide a surplus of corn and agriculture produce, and sometimes additional items such as fishing nets and wampum, to their hunting neighbours of the north. This led the Jesuits to qualify Wendake as the "granary of most of the Algonquins."[19] In return, the Anishinaabeg delivered a surplus of meat, fish, and furs, usually through exchange when the Anishinaabeg made their journey to Wendat country for their winter sojourn.[20] This system of reciprocity was only strengthened with the introduction of a European market for fur. As a result, the Anishinaabe and Wendat Coalition entered into an alliance with the French – the Anishinaabeg provided furs and the Wendat secured diplomatic initiatives.[21]

Joint military expeditions and defence strategies were also part of the Coalition. On numerous occasions, Anishinaabeg and Wendat engaged in military combat with a common enemy.[22] Although many assume the Wendat pulled the Anishinaabeg into Iroquois conflicts, the Anishinaabeg had a similar, yet autonomous, history of warfare with the Iroquois dating to the sixteenth century.[23]

The Coalition served as a customary vehicle for unified representation in diplomatic endeavours. In most cases, equal numbers of Anishinaabeg and Wendat delegates conducted treaty and council negotiations on behalf of the Coalition. Samuel de Champlain described his meeting with two war chiefs (one from each group) to discuss a truce and future resolutions towards peace.[24] On other occasions, however, one ambassador might represent both groups, suggesting a high degree of unity and shared purpose. At the French village of Trois-Rivières, the Anishinaabe headman Simon Pieskaret represented the entire Coalition in 1647. Under this guise, Pieskaret held responsibility for maintaining peace with the French and punishing any Wendat or Anishinaabeg who tried to hinder this goal.[25] The Coalition acted cohesively, in a similar way to the Wendat Confederacy.

The degree to which this close relationship existed culminated in a shared participation in the most important Wendat ceremony – the Feast of Souls. This burial ritual offered a familiar stage for cultural exchange and understanding, as well as a forum to renew and solidify the Coalition in a formal setting. Participants gathered together to mourn the loss of life while also rejoicing in the affirmation of current relationships. The Wendat and Anishinaabeg approached their interaction with other nations by acknowledging that strangers could either become enemies or be turned into symbolic kin people.[26] The Feast of Souls reflected those ideals and called upon both groups to make invitations to each other to participate in the ritual and unite.[27]

Evidence suggests this ceremony was specific to the Coalition, as it was only the Wendat and those Anishinaabe nations who came in close contact with the Wendat who made it a customary practice.[28] Although the Anishinaabeg customs differed slightly from that of their Wendat neighbours, the Wendat probably communicated the tradition to the Nipissing, who then shared it with other Anishinaabeg in league with the Wendat.[29] In order to demonstrate the profound connection between the two groups, the Anishinaabeg modified their tradition by including a special meal prepared in honour of the Wendat. This was delivered separately to the Wendat in order to demonstrate their unique status within the ritual. While it was customary during the Wendat feast to hold a council that incorporated all the nations (both Wendat and Anishinaabeg), the Anishinaabeg organized two separate assemblies, one for each respective group. At the Wendat council, gifts were delivered to the visiting headmen and the Anishinaabe hosts expressed the important role the Wendat played within the Coalition and the great respect the Anishinaabeg had for them.[30]

The Feast of Souls demonstrates the deep bond between these two groups. By burying their dead together, they confirmed their dedication to each other. The feast's spiritual and diplomatic overtures reiterated the nature of the alliance. While they operated as separate and distinct nations, the Wendat and Anishinaabeg chose to maintain ties to their greater confederations, which in turn dedicated them to an even larger coalition between the larger Wendat and Anishinaabe communities.

Post-Dispersal Coalition, 1650-1701

According to scholar Harold Hickerson, the Coalition began to disintegrate after 1650 and the dispersal of the Wendat Confederacy. He attributes this to the declining practice of the Feast of Souls throughout the rest of the seventeenth century, although he acknowledges that there were at least two different feasts hosted by the Anishinaabeg in 1660 and 1670 with Wendat guests.[31] It is assumed that the Coalition intentionally abandoned the ceremonies, when in reality neither group may have had time to conduct the feast given the pressures of Iroquois warfare and relocation. Both groups customarily held the feast during periods when the community had time to prepare the elaborate elements of the ceremony, which could take over a year, and the Wendat feast usually coincided with the movement of a village. The dispersal disrupted this pattern, as Natives built and abandoned villages in haste during the first few decades, while later they constructed permanent residences, making the practice of relocation obsolete. The fact that other Coalition customs of joint diplomacy, trade negotiations, and military expeditions continued well beyond 1650 testifies to the Coalition's persistence.

In November 1652, for instance, a council was held at Trois-Rivières between the Wendat–Anishinaabe Coalition, the French and the Iroquois. During the proceedings the Coalition delivered a gift to the Iroquois delegates on behalf of both the Wendat and Anishinaabeg.[32] A similar council followed in September 1655. Much like in the pre-dispersal period, the group elected an Anishinaabe headman to speak on behalf of the Coalition, while other Wendat and Anishinaabe leaders attended as witnesses. In this case, the Anishinaabe ambassador, Kahoka, expressed the Coalition's desire for the safe conduct of the visiting Iroquois and likewise an Iroquois respect for the rules of the host village.[33] These proceedings illustrate a consistency concerning the Coalition's diplomatic function. In essence, they continued to engage in foreign relations as one cohesive unit. They gave gifts on the Coalition's behalf and elected representatives to lead negotiations for the entire group.

Shared trade practices also flourished during this period. A fur brigade, including four Coalition headmen, conducted trade at Montreal in 1689. At the negotiations, a Wendat leader presented the French with a wampum belt and explained that it was to ensure the French gave special privileges to the Anishinaabeg, with decent prices on trade items.[34] This request offered a clear attempt by the Wendat to ensure the prosperity of their Anishinaabe allies. The Wendat used their close and familiar relationship with the French in order to help members of the Coalition gain a similar status with their European trade partners. This would have strengthened the efficiency of the Coalition as a whole.

Trade between Anishinaabeg and Wendat remained consistent with pre-dispersal practices. Although the Anishinaabe communities became more sedentary and the Wendat incorporated more hunting into their subsistence strategy, the exchange of corn and hides remained integral to the nature of the relationship.[35] If anything, the Anishinaabeg's role as providers became more significant during this time as the Wendat crops failed and refugees sought to offset the famine with game and fish from the Anishinaabeg. The legacy of success from the previous reciprocal exchange before the dispersal encouraged the Wendat to depend more on their Anishinaabe suppliers during their struggle.

Despite the exodus from Wendake and intermittent peace negotiations with the Iroquois, the Coalition maintained its agreement to provide mutual protection and act as a collective military unit. For the most part, the Coalition continued to focus on their joint dislike for the Iroquois. In 1652, the Anishinaabeg and Wendat organized and directed an expedition of over one thousand allies against their common enemy. The main architects of this endeavour were a mix of both groups and included seven principal men: Aennons (Bear nation), Mangouch (Nipissing), Onda,enronk (Bear nation), Eentawai and Totraenchiarak (Rock nation), Teochiawente (Ottawa), and Otontagonen (Ottawa).[36] This group arrived together at Trois-Rivières and informed the French governor of their plan to attack the Iroquois in the autumn; they made a collective invitation for the French to join the Coalition in this campaign.[37] A similar expedition took place in 1660 that included four Anishinaabeg, sixty Wendat, and seventeen Frenchmen. They planned to confront the Iroquois as they returned from a hunting expedition, with the hope the enemy would be weakened by their long journey and lack of provisions near the end of their exploits. The ensuing battle took place over two days. Despite a concerted effort, the Coalition and French lost because the Iroquois had prior warning.[38] Thus, the military contract of the Coalition continued to function as it had before. Delegates from various member nations joined together in pursuit of military expeditions, alliances, and defence. They approached outside groups, such as the French, to join in their exploits and expressed their military policies through representatives of the entire Coalition.

In addition to diplomatic, trade, and military missions, the observations of contemporaries who engaged with the Coalition in the post-dispersal period point to the persistence of the alliance after 1650. The French certainly saw them as a solid unit. Claude-Charles Bacqueville de la Potherie, a historian living in New France, explained that French colonists viewed the Anishinaabeg and Wendat as "part of the same body."[39] Similarly, in 1676 French businessman Charles Aubert de La Chesnaye noted that the Wendat and Anishinaabeg possessed equal amounts of influence throughout the Great Lakes region, with the Coalition representing the majority of the people and territory.[40] Speaking explicitly about the nature of the relationship after a sermon delivered to both groups, Father Louis Hennepin concluded that the Wendat and Anishinaabeg were "in a Confederacy together against the Iroquois their common enemy."[41] Father Pierre François Xavier de Charlevoix expressed his lasting impression of the alliance over seventy years after the dispersal. He remarked on the longevity and persistence of the alliance in a letter to his superiors written in 1721. Charlevoix explained that the Anishinaabeg were the "inseparable companions of the Hurons from the time both were driven from their country by the Iroquois."[42]

The French perceived the Coalition as a legitimate and official alliance. They understood it as a solid partnership in which the Wendat and Anishinaabeg were in essence one "body." This perspective shaped the ability of the Coalition to operate in its full capacity. Since the French represented one of its main allies outside the Coalition, it was important that Europeans understood and accepted the Wendat–Anishinaabe alliance in order for the Coalition to function properly.

Iroquois perceptions of the Coalition depict a similar acknowledgement of the union between the Anishinaabeg and Wendat. On 19 November 1653, the French governor announced the Mohawk were making preparations to send a wampum belt with the intention of presenting it to the Coalition in the near future. The Mohawk message assured the Coalition that "whatever the Hurons and Algonquins may do, [the Mohawk] shall remain at peace with them."[43] This act acknowledged the partnership between the Anishinaabeg and Wendat and respected the contours of the Coalition, including the fact that all representatives of the alliance had to be present for any formal negotiations to take place. On 3 September 1655, for instance, the Iroquois approached the Wendat to conduct a formal discussion of peace. This meeting ameliorated an earlier oversight, when the Iroquois neglected to address both members of the Coalition the year before when the Iroquois had tried to confirm a treaty with a group of Anishinaabeg at Trois-Rivières. The Iroquois gave the Wendat three wampum belts to entice them to engage in talks once again and tried to assuage any doubt concerning Anishinaabe support of these negotiations by pointing to the fact that the Anishinaabe ambassador Kahoka had already agreed to accompany them back to Iroquois country.[44] In this case, the Iroquois had transgressed the policies of the Coalition. Their disregard for the solidarity of the alliance led to their inability to push forward peace negotiations with both the Anishinaabeg and Wendat. Thus, they had to accept the dynamics of the Wendat–Anishinaabe alliance and shape their own foreign policy so that they met the requirements of the Coalition.

Despite the relatively firm alliance cultivated within the framework of a multi-dimensional association, the post-dispersal Coalition was not without its moments of weakness. Insecurity from both parties could foster conflict with potentially devastating repercussions. In one case, the Wendat leader known as Le Baron was accused by several Anishinaabe headmen of making secret peace negotiations with the Iroquois and agreeing to accompany this traditional enemy on a campaign against the Miami.[45] This meant that Le Baron had acted outside the Coalition, disregarding its function as a collective military unit. Diplomacy defused the conflict, however, when Le Baron denied the accusations and the Wendat agreed to engage in a subsequent expedition with the Anishinaabeg against the Iroquois to prove their loyalty and dedication to the Coalition.[46]

Demonstrations of allegiance were also expressed through penalties for disloyal behaviour. During a Coalition military expedition against the Iroquois, one Wendat and one Anishinaabe scout were sent out to detect the enemy and report back to the main group that was comprised mostly of Anishinaabeg. The Iroquois captured the Wendat scout, who divulged the location of the Coalition's men. The Iroquois took the information and conducted a successful attack on the scout's unsuspecting allies.[47]

Soon after, the Anishinaabeg approached their Wendat kinsmen and demanded redress for this treachery. The Wendat held a council and decided that the transgression was so severe that the only punishment suitable was death. They sentenced the scout to be mounted on a pole and killed by a hatchet: "Thou deservest death, for having betrayed our friends and our allies." The culprit responded, "It is true ... kill me."[48]

First Wave Migrations, 1650-51

Much like the pre-dispersal period, the Wendat and Anishinaabeg continued to share residency with one another after 1650. Relocation strategies stemmed from old customs of sharing space, whether it was an Anishinaabe band wintering within a Wendat village, a Wendat war party replenishing their provisions in Anishinaabe territory, or simply the incorporation of a new husband or wife after marriage. This habit fostered shared knowledge about convenient locations for protection in times of insecurity.

Although the majority of Wendat moved to Gahoendoe to stay within Wendake's borders, their historical relationship with the Anishinaabeg persuaded a number of smaller groups to seek out Anishinaabe communities for shelter and safety in the hopes of evading the Iroquois. The first wave of Wendat migrations from Wendake began haphazardly before 1649, becoming more popular after the food crisis at Gahoendoe, and eventually formed a new dispersal strategy that led the Wendat to separate into smaller groups and spread across the Great Lakes as a diasporic community.

As early as 1645, a number of Wendat families chose to relocate to the Anishinaabe village of Tangouen. The community was located in a fairly remote region, unfamiliar to the Iroquois. These Wendat refugees hoped the village would protect them, and the village accepted them without hesitation.[49] In other circumstances both the Wendat and Anishinaabeg established new villages that included members of both groups. St. Charles, organized in the wake of the Iroquois attacks in 1649, was one such village. It was located approximately six days' journey from Gahoendoe, chosen for its potential for agriculture, fishing, and isolated setting. The inhabitants built longhouses, wigwams, and fortifications. Eventually, the community invited two Jesuit priests to live with them and they built a Christian chapel out of tree bark. Despite the presence of the missionaries, St. Charles, much like Gahoendoe, included a mix of Christian converts and traditionalists. At times this dynamic led to conflicts, as some of the most outspoken traditionalists, who also happened to be the most affluent and influential members of the community, accused the Jesuits of ruining their country. Still, the chapel possessed both Wendat and Anishinaabe followers, and the conflicts resulting from the Christian/traditionalist factions seemed to have translated into confrontations only with the priests and not the rest of the village. Overall, the architects built the new village on the basis of the Coalition and a goal to make it a "new country." Unfortunately, the drought of 1649-50 also affected the crops at St. Charles and the fishing yielded little. The community resolved to move to Gahoendoe after one winter and join the majority of the Wendat in their relocation plan.[50]

Those who congregated on Gahoendoe remained open to an eventual relocation to Anishinaabe territory, whether northwest of Wendake or near Quebec. When the Wendat headmen presented their plan to the Jesuits in the spring of 1650, for instance, they expressed the desire of many to go to the Anishinaabeg, who would protect them. They explained:

> Their charity will alleviate, in part, our miseries; and, at the least, we shall sometimes find there a morsel of bread for our little ones, who, to sustain life, have for so long lived on acorns, and bitter roots. After all, if we must die with them, death there would be to us far easier than in the midst of forests, where no one would assist us to die well.[51]

They based their reasoning on past experiences that had included the generosity and charity of the Anishinaabeg to their Wendat kin.

The Anishinaabe island community of Ekaentoton remained another option, despite the initial refusal to move there. The idea resurfaced in the wake of the food crisis and the council negotiations at the final evacuation of Gahoendoe. Ekaentoton's distance from Iroquois country offered geographic protection, while its large space and friendly hosts offered familiar settings to rejuvenate the population. At the same time, a number of Jesuits had already relocated to the island in 1648. This would have encouraged both the Christians of Gahoendoe in terms of spiritual instruction and the traditionalists in terms of maintaining access to French guns and trade.[52] At least 240 Wendat resolved to relocate to this site.[53] Ojibwe oral traditions include an account of the arrival of the Wendat to Ekaentoton and Anishinaabe territory. Reverend T.C. Thomas transcribed the history in 1903:

> Dejected, disheartened, the Hurons presented themselves at the doors of the great council wigwams of the different nations whom they had made enemies by their former depredations; but rather than submit to be led by their own brethren, as a conquered race, throughout their possessions, those who came to the northwest called a council among themselves, in which it was determined upon what should be done. This council, according to tradition, must have been held somewhere on the northern shore of the Lake Huron ... The Hurons assembled themselves in council, and in the course of their deliberations, they desired several of their chiefs to visit the great Ojibwe family ... It was the policy of the Hurons to present themselves in a pitiable condition before their superiors, the Ojibwe family of the great lake, that they might the more easily obtain their favour and sympathy. Tradition informs us that they came and presented themselves before the council door of that nation and begged them to spare their own children's lives ... The Ojibwes saw them and yielded to pity and compassion. The Hurons were received as friends ... A situation was assigned them near by, where they and their children could reside and be near the villages of the Ojibwes.[54]

The relocation process in this case followed the customary traditions of cohabitations between Anishinaabeg and Wendat. Just as the Wendat had suspected, they found safety within the community, not as acculturated citizens, but as an autonomous faction with a separate space for residency, while retaining nourishment and protection. This scenario was only temporary, however, as the Wendat on Ekaentoton would relocate farther east in 1651.[55]

As dispersal became the main strategy within this period, and considering the vastness of Anishinaabe territory in the seventeenth century, the Wendat were not relegated to settlements within close proximity to Wendake. For many, the Anishinaabe communities farther east and west provided alternative options.

East of Wendat country a growing number of Anishinaabeg had begun to create a semi-permanent community in what the French would later call the town of Sillery. Located 941 kilometres from Wendake and roughly five kilometres from Quebec City, this community quickly became a mixed population of Coalition refugees. The Sillery Registry lists numerous Wendat baptisms during the 1640s; these included Wendat Christian names such as Charles Tgondatsa, Paul Atondo, Jean-Baptiste Okhuk8andoron, Thérèse Kinhrcha, Ignace Saoiiaretchi, Pierre Otarenti.[56] Totems on written contracts with the French also signal an Anishinaabe presence at Sillery.[57] After 1649 those Wendat seeking protection entered Sillery in even greater numbers; thirty families or roughly a hundred and fifty people in 1650 alone.[58] Intermarriage was prevalent at Sillery, producing children with ties to both Anishinaabe and Wendat ancestry.[59]

Much like St. Charles and Ekaentoton, Sillery housed both Christians and traditionalists. On 2 August 1646, the governor of New France, Charles Huault de Montmagny, signed over the land around Sillery (which the French considered their own) to the Jesuits to "better convert" the Natives.[60] Later in 1647, the Jesuits received 5,000 livres to aid them.[61] It would seem that the Native inhabitants of Sillery supported this move, as several Anishinaabe headmen signed the transfer of lands to the Jesuits in 1646.[62] The inclusion of priests in the community and the proximity to the French settlement of Quebec City fostered a close interaction between the Coalition and French settlers, demonstrated through cases in which French men and women became the godparents of Native converts. Paul Chomedey de Maisonneuve (future founder of Montreal) and Jeanne Mance (founder of the Hôtel-Dieu de Montréal), for example, served as the godparents of both Okhuk8andoron and Atondo. Similarly, the Wendat Tgondatsa had the governor [Charles Huault de Montmagny] as his godfather, who gave him his Christian name of Charles.[63] The Wendat presence within Sillery was substantial, but it served as a temporary haven for most. The 150 refugees, for instance, intended to move to a location farther east within a year or so. Still, the baptisms of Wendat children in 1659, 1660, 1662, and 1664 demonstrate that some Wendat remained.[64]

Located 402 kilometres from Wendake and 201 kilometres from Ekaentoton, the western settlements of Anishinaabeg near present-day Sault Ste. Marie, Ontario, presented another option for the Wendat. This group, whom the French called the "Inhabitants of the Sault" and the Wendat called the "Pauoitigoueieuhak," numbered roughly two thousand people in 1641. By the time Wendat refugees made their way out to this region, Jesuit priests already had a presence in the area, with a mission established about eighteen days' journey from the Anishinaabeg. The Pauoitigoueieuhak and the Wendat were familiar with each other due in large part to the networks provided by the Coalition. The Anishinaabeg of the Sault attended the Feast of Souls hosted by the Nipissing in 1641, where they invited the Jesuits and Wendat to visit them. They accepted the invitation and an expedition left near the end of September 1641; they arrived after seventeen days of water travel along Lake Huron. This trip allowed the visiting Wendat to not only engage with these Anishinaabeg but also become familiar with the land and route to this area. Discussions concerning Wendat relocation were probably not part of this visit, as it predates the major Iroquois attacks of the late 1640s; yet it may have served as a point of reference in 1650 when various locations were being discussed. The Pauoitigoueieuhak also had a reputation for accommodating refugees; they had welcomed the Potawatomi before 1640 into their community and provided protection for them against their enemies farther west.[65] Although far away, the familiarity, previous interaction, distance from Iroquois country, and reputation of Pauoitigoueieuhak would have been taken into consideration by those Wendat seeking to relocate. Eventually some Wendat did travel west, residing briefly among the Pauoitigoueieuhak before heading south and west within a year's time.[66]

Consequences

The Wendat–Anishinaabe Coalition shaped the first wave migration out of Wendake, and the Wendat decision to relocate within Anishinaabe societies influenced the future of the Coalition and the cultural frameworks of its members for the rest of the seventeenth century. Subsistence strategies and settlement patterns changed. Although the Anishinaabeg continued to return to their fisheries and trading centres, while living in villages during portions of the year, their former small-scale communities began to grow in population. One theory is that this swelling of the population was due in part to the fur trade and the desire of more people to seek out trade centres to acquire European goods.[67] The impact of Wendat refugees should also be considered, as they could have doubled the size of some villages.[68] A growth in population led to different forms of social interaction, based on more community-level activity. Whereas before, the Anishinaabeg usually privileged the needs of small bands and family units, in the post-dispersal period the larger networks of villages, nations, and the Coalition's aspirations took priority. This shift in focus led to an expansion of community-based activity and a larger sphere for decision making.[69] It reorganized the nature of Anishinaabe society and may have resulted in an increase in sedentary lifestyle as the century progressed.

The influence of Christianity on Anishinaabe communities increased with the relocation of the Wendat to their territory and the incorporation of Jesuits into these societies. For the Wendat, the prospect of conversion was not new. By including Jesuits in their dispersal and relocation plans (by either taking them with them such as on their journeys out to the Sault, or choosing locations that had recently acquired missions, such as Ekaentoton and Sillery), they were ensuring the potential for future baptisms. Their Anishinaabe neighbours were not as familiar with the Jesuits. Out of the eleven missions established in New France, only three were among the Anishinaabeg by 1648.[70] The new wave of Jesuits taking up residency among the Anishinaabeg after 1650, however, fostered increased interaction with the priests, extending the Jesuit missions among the Anishinaabeg as well.

Joseph Onahare is an example of the individuals affected by these circumstances. Joseph was an Anishinaabeg, raised within a community without a mission. He relocated to Sillery around 1650 and the time of the Iroquois attacks. There he was introduced to the Christian teachings of the priests; he attended their sermons and within a year's time was baptized. It is uncertain whether he arrived in the settlement alone and had a family elsewhere or whether he was orphaned like so many children during the epidemics, wars, and famine. Whatever the case, he did not have immediate family at Sillery. As a result, and on the occasion of his baptism, he was adopted by the Anishinaabe Christian Charles Kariskatisitch, who arranged for Joseph to be married to a local Christian

Native woman.[71] Joseph was later captured by the Iroquois and sentenced to death. Before his death, he delivered a message to his closest friend (who happened to be a Wendat from Sillery and who escaped soon after): "If ever, my dear friend, thou returnest to the country of the Anishinaabeg, assure them that the Iroquois, with all their tortures, have not succeeded in stifling the prayer on my lips, nor the faith in my heart. Tell them that I died gladly, in the hope of going very soon to Heaven."[72] Joseph represented a new generation of Anishinaabeg, who in the aftermath of the Wendat dispersal and relocations came in contact with Jesuit missionaries and consequently adopted the Christian faith.

In terms of the Coalition, the dispersal only served to strengthen it. The options made available to the Wendat during the early stages of relocation became more numerous through their established alliance with their Anishinaabe neighbours. This was the result of an official coalition of more than a hundred years. It was not "ambivalent" and did not disintegrate in the post-dispersal period. By taking up residency with Anishinaabe neighbours, the Wendat and Anishinaabeg interacted on a more frequent basis. They shared homes and villages, families and kinship ties that in turn maintained their connection. The Coalition continued to engage in diplomacy and military actions. Further, the acknowledgement of the Coalition by the French and Iroquois demonstrates that the Coalition was seen as a legitimate polity within this period.

Famine and warfare put the Coalition to the test in 1650. At this time more than ever the Wendat depended upon the alliance to ensure their survival; the Anishinaabeg were their first option for refuge, rejuvenation, and protection. Through this strategy and the willingness of the Anishinaabeg to support the Wendat and preserve the Coalition, the Wendat gained security and upheld their autonomy before moving on to future permanent settlements. In addition, the Wendat continued to have access to Anishinaabe furs, while the Anishinaabeg created closer connections with the French through Christian missionaries and gained access to firearms because of it. This collective residency resulted in a more thorough merging of territories and people, as the borders between Wendake and Anishinaabe country became blurred.

5
The West
The Country of the People of the Sea

LOOKING BEYOND 1650 AND the Anishinaabe enclaves and safe havens near Wendake, the Wendat sought refuge farther away from their homeland. As Jesuit François Le Mercier explained, because of the "devastation of the Huron country having made them apprehensive of a like misfortune, and the fury of the Iroquois having pursued them everywhere, they thought to find security only by retreating to the very end of the world, so to speak."[1] Anishinaabe communities such as Ekaentoton, Sillery, and the Sault remained temporary, transitional locations for the dispersed Wendat rather than endpoints of Wendat migrations during the seventeenth century. Much like the first wave, the Wendat made subsequent moves in response to the commercial and geopolitical contexts of the region. Within this second wave of migration, a Wendat diaspora truly began to take shape. Groups formerly allied in a settled political and geographic confederacy, in close proximity to one another, relocated to distant outposts hundreds of kilometres apart. The trajectories of these migrations focused for the most part east and west of Wendake.[2] Two groups of Wendat set out in 1651; the first headed west towards what the French called "the Country of the People of the Sea"[3] and later Michilimackinac, while a second group travelled east along the St. Lawrence towards Quebec City.

The establishment of permanent settlements was a long process in both cases, spanning nearly twenty years of temporary relocations until the 1670s. Ultimately, scholars have conflated both moves with a Wendat loss of cultural distinctiveness, arguing that in the west the Wendat adopted an Anishinaabe lifestyle, while in the east they assimilated to the French.[4] Although in some respects this might hold true, an analysis of community activity, social organization, and spiritual affiliation indicates that many Wendat customs endured the relocation process, giving these new communities uniquely Wendat ethnic characters.

This chapter is an investigation into the cultural dynamics of the Western Wendat community at Michilimackinac. It offers insight into the extent of assimilation and the persistence of Wendat culture in post-1650 Wendat society. A similar analysis will follow in Chapter 6, which focuses on the Eastern Wendat. The people of the west balanced cultural compromise and identity preservation as they endeavoured to both transform and maintain Wendat traditions within the community.

Early Migrations West: The Petun, 1649-51

For the most part, the first group of Wendat who moved west included representatives from the Bear, Cord, Rock, and Deer nations.[5] These same members sought refuge in 1649 with a community of Nadowek called the Petun by the French, and Etionnontateronnon, or "people of the hill," by the Wendat, who lived in villages located approximately fifty-six to sixty-four kilometres southwest of Wendake.[6] Both groups were ethnically Wendat; they spoke the same language and had similar cultural practices. They were so similar that the Petun may have even called themselves Wendat.[7]

Although the Jesuits established three missions among the Petun in the late 1640s (St. Jean, St. Mathieu, St. Matthias), evidence suggests that this community, much like its Wendat neighbours, was not entirely Christian. In 1649, after the Wendat relocation to the Petun, a council concluded that the French were traitors and caused the ruin of all Christian converted Native nations; eventually these allegations resulted in the murder of Jesuit Father Noël Chabanel.[8] The controversy highlighted the tensions between Christian and traditionalist factions within this community and more specifically among the Wendat refugees, a split that permeated social structures and governance. The anti-Jesuit council comprised both Wendat and Petun, suggesting at least a portion of the Wendat refugees were traditionalists. Further, a Wendat had allegedly committed the murder.[9] This type of internal conflict did not last long, however; Iroquois attacks became just as prevalent as those in Wendake and forced the Petun/Wendat community to focus their energy on military defence rather than infighting.

Much like the villages of the Wendat Confederacy, the Petun were overwhelmed by Iroquois attacks. Initial defeats prompted disbelief and shock; after the conquest of the town of Etharita on 7 December 1649, warriors remained in the village for half a day in silent meditation, cross-legged on the bloodied ground.[10] By this time, Wendat options were limited. Although some returned to the complicated despair of Gahoendoe, others looked beyond Wendake to the country of the People of the Sea.

The western Great Lakes represented a unique opportunity for these Wendat. It was predominantly Anishinaabe territory; thus there was potential to expand the Coalition's networks and kinship ties. Second, the Sault, as previously mentioned in Chapter 4, had a reputation as a refuge for other nations, exemplified by the movement of many dispersed Native groups to the area during this period.[11] The Wendat also desired to distance themselves from the Iroquois to ensure better protection, and they hoped that French missionaries and supplies might also move west.[12]

The shared cultural heritage between the Wendat confederates and the Petun offered yet another set of incentives. Both groups had prospered in the past by situating themselves within a predominantly Anishinaabe territory. Some scholars describe the Petun and Wendat relocations as mostly a Petun affair.[13] In this interpretation, the Wendat are merely followers due to their smaller numerical status within the group.[14] In fact, it was the Wendat, not the Petun, who had developed previous relations with the northwest, and who maintained a long history of successful trade negotiations through the Coalition. The Petun had no such reputation for diplomatic or trade networks, especially in the north, and were not skillful travellers.[15] Although numerically marginal, the Wendat would have influenced the community with their persuasive diplomacy, their established connections to the northwest, and their reputation as skilled canoeists and travellers. Either way, a group of approximately five hundred ethnic Wendat, whom the French would later term the "Huron of the Petun Nation"[16] and for the purposes of this study are referred to as Western Wendat, chose to abandon their villages for good in 1650. They stopped briefly at the Sault before moving on to Michilimackinac.

The Unsettled Period, 1651-71

From the Sault, as discussed in Chapter 4, the Wendat moved south towards Mackinac Island, or Michilimackinac, in 1651.[17] This site attracted the Wendat for a number of reasons. The island was about four kilometres in diameter, with stony peaks that allowed defenders to see potential attackers up to forty-eight kilometres away.[18] The location's climate was exceptional compared to other regions, as a typical winter did not start until January and spring arrived in early March, thus allowing for a long growing season.[19] The soil was also very good quality for corn. The Wendat, at the time of their relocation, would have heard about Michilimackinac's reputation for excellent fishing potential. Aside from the usual fish attained from other regions, such as herring, carp, pike, golden fish, whitefish, and sturgeon, there were three kinds of trout – one grew well over three feet in length. Jesuit records indicate that fish were so abundant that a man could catch up to fifty within the span of three hours. Finally, the geopolitical location of the island would have certainly influenced the Wendat decision to relocate there. It was situated in the strait connecting Lake Huron to Lake Michigan, inspiring contemporaries to call it the "key and door" to the lands and people beyond Lake Huron, and serving as one of the main passageways to gain access to the southern nations of the Great Lakes.[20] This spatial position would aid a successful relocation inspired by a need to expand commercial and kin networks while also maintaining a powerful role as fur trade mediators and political diplomats.

We know very little about the Wendat experience during their first few years at Michilimackinac; what does seem clear, however, is that despite the apparent distant location, the Iroquois followed them and within approximately two years forced the Wendat to change location. Their Ottawa (Anishinaabe) allies accompanied them on this journey to an island in Green Bay.[21] By 1653 they had established a camp at the entrance of the bay, but out of a desire for a more secure location they retreated to the Anishinaabe town of Teaontorai in the winter.[22] Once again, the Wendat–Anishinaabe Coalition proved essential, as Anishinaabe towns remained a safe haven for Wendat refugees well beyond the first wave of migration and served as a fundamental strategy for survival. The accompaniment of the Ottawa would have likely given the Western Wendat an extra advantage, as preexisting Anishinaabe ties may have facilitated the incorporation of the Wendat into Teaontorai.

After the winter, the Western Wendat and the Ottawa continued west to the banks of the Black River, which reminded them of the St. Lawrence. There, the Anishinaabe-speaking Potawatomi welcomed them and allowed the Wendat to reside among their sixty villages. According to the French trader Pierre-Esprit Radisson, the region comprised over one thousand people in 1659.[23] The welcoming atmosphere fostered by the Anishinaabe hosts was in part due to the Wendat–Anishinaabe kinship network. Radisson confirmed the persistence of the Coalition when he came across Wendat refugees in his travels, acknowledging that they were one association of both Wendat and Ottawa.[24]

By 1661, the Western Wendat had moved once again, this time to the very end of Lake Superior and the village of Chequamegon near the new

Jesuit mission of St. Esprit. According to Jesuit accounts, the majority of Wendat adults were either already baptized or had received baptism during their stay there. The missionaries asserted that these conversions occurred because of the Wendat exposure to Christianity through the missions in pre-1650 Wendake and their ability to retain their prior knowledge of Jesuit teachings throughout their relocation. Aside from interacting with French missionaries, the Wendat cleared and cultivated a number of fields for the purposes of raising Indian corn, which indicates that the Wendat had retained their traditional role as agriculturalists and perhaps suppliers to their Anishinaabe allies.[25] For the most part, the Wendat experience at Chequamegon remained peaceful – not an easy feat. Only 240 kilometres away were the Sioux, who were comparable to the Iroquois in terms of military reputation.[26] It is likely that the ability for Wendat to relocate to this area and maintain friendly relations with its inhabitants and the Sioux depended almost entirely on the continued alliance with the Ottawa and other Anishinaabeg.[27]

Unfortunately for the Wendat, peace did not last. Over the course of the winter of 1671, several murders took place involving the Wendat, Ottawa, and Sioux. Whatever the motivations behind the murders, the deaths complicated the previously amicable relationship among the different groups and threatened the security of the Wendat–Ottawa community at Chequamegon.[28] Fearing a retaliatory attack by the Sioux and upon having received word of a peace settlement with the Iroquois, the Wendat decided to abandon the shores of Lake Superior in the spring and return to their previous settlement at Michilimackinac where the French had recently established the mission of St. Ignace. They spent the winter making preparations and sent an expedition ahead to reconnect with those living at Michilimackinac.[29] At the same time, a number of the Ottawa decided to return to Ekaentoton on Lake Huron.[30]

The period of 1651 to 1671 proved significant for the Wendat for a number of reasons. Despite the physical and mental anguish of living in an unsettled and insecure community, the repeated removals provided opportunities for the Western Wendat. They forged intimate relationships with valuable allies through marriages, subsistence interdependency, and community projects. It is also likely that the Wendat were one of "various Nations" attending an Anishinaabe Feast of Souls in 1670, another indication of a persisting adherence to the Coalition.[31] Access to Anishinaabe people and fur stocks permitted a continuation of Wendat presence in the fur trade. In the spring of 1655, a Wendat–Ottawa contingent from the Green Bay area arrived in Montreal and Trois-Rivières with canoes laden with furs, which they exchanged in the customary fashion for French products.[32] Thus, commercial endeavours did not cease but in some ways flourished in terms of expanding trade and kin networks among the Anishinaabe nations of the area.

The route that the Wendat took over these decades also seems calculated. In essence, they traced a perfect geographic circle with strategic periods of settlement among some of the most powerful and numerous nations within the region. The connections fostered along this route, in combination with the circular trail, would have allowed the Wendat to shape the contours of their newly established influence in the area. This helped them to connect intimately with the landscape; they got to know the geography of the land on a personal level. Although the Wendat relocation to Michilimackinac was most likely the result of Sioux aggression, it may have always been their intent to return since their initial departure in 1651. Michilimackinac was ideal for many reasons, and now that the Wendat had established themselves among the People of the Sea they could conduct themselves as a people of the region.

The Michilimackinac Community, 1671-1701

Parhelion Premonitions

The Wendat knew of the advantages of Michilimackinac when they set out in the spring of 1671 to return. The appearance of parhelia on 16 March of that same year served to reinforce this decision: residents witnessed what appeared to be three suns in the sky.[33] They were separated by just over one kilometre and materialized first in the morning – about an hour after sunrise, and once again in the evening – an hour before sunset. Whereas the real sun was located towards the southwest, the second sun was located in the west and was surrounded by a scarlet band. The third sun had more of an oval-shaped iris, surrounded by a shimmering gold halo. A hazy mist filled the sky, filtering the light projected by the three suns. At one point, a dimmer fourth sun showed itself. When the false suns disappeared, they left behind two rainbows stretching across the sky.[34] The Wendat and Anishinaabeg viewed the parhelia as sky spirits, the false suns representing the real sun's wives. In contrast, the French missionaries saw the sundogs as God's symbolic reference to the Holy Trinity. Despite these differing views, both Natives and non-Natives acknowledged the suns as an indication of Michilimackinac's potential.[35] The parhelia promised a fruitful future for those living at Michilimackinac, and signalled that the Wendat had made the right choice in resettling there. This parhelia event symbolized the ways in which the shared experiences between the Western Wendat, Anishinaabeg, and French consistently fostered moments of difference, convergence, and persistence based on unique cultural perspectives. Ultimately, this inspired a community based on cultural compromise, a strategy that allowed the Wendat to create and maintain alliances and traditions.

The Population

By 1671, the country of the People of the Sea had become a crossroads for dispersed peoples from nations such as the Miami, Wea, Piankashaw, Kickapoo, and Mascouten. Some view the resettlement of these people in terms of "multiethnic villages" and "first republics," where tribal identity remained intact. They contend that the Wendat experience was an exception to this pattern, arguing the Wendat settled as a disjointed association of individuals who did not represent any dominant ethnic unity.[36] The basis of this assertion is unclear; it may be rooted in a misunderstanding of the ethnic similarities between the Petun and Wendat confederates, as well as in the developing diasporic nature of the contemporary Wendat living in the east at that time. Conversely, an analysis of the population at Michilimackinac reveals a community unified by distinctly Wendat cultural traditions while simultaneously interacting on an intimate and frequent basis with other groups.

When the Western Wendat left Lake Huron in 1651, they numbered no more than five hundred. By the early 1670s, and their return to Michilimackinac, Jesuits counted 380 people – with over sixty Ottawa also among them.[37] Less than ten years later, the population was estimated to have returned to approximately five hundred, while the Ottawa numbers had expanded considerably to fifteen hundred.[38]

The gender and age ratios of this Wendat community are hard to decipher. In terms of generational demographics, we know that there were Wendat at Chequamegon who had lived in Wendake pre-1650, which suggests that the western community included at least some elders. In addition, the records of a winter population census indicate that the community may have consisted of up to 60 percent women, children, and elders.[39] In contrast to the Wendat, the French population was entirely male. Fathers

Jacques Marquette and Phillippe Pierson headed the mission of St. Ignace, located nearby.[40] Roughly thirty "young" Frenchmen tried to make their way to the area in 1655, but postponed the trip to the following spring due to Iroquois raids.[41] The original expedition consisted of the Jesuit Fathers Léonard Garreau, Gabriel Dreuillettes, and their assistant, Brother Louis le Boesme, as well as at least three other "young" men who had resolved to carry the faith west.[42] Similar expeditions between 1656 and 1671 added at least thirty men to the French population.[43] In 1683, fifteen more French canoes made their way to Michilimackinac and established the military Fort de Buade.[44] This increased the population to such extremes that by the early 1690s the settlement hosted a population of approximately seven hundred French soldiers and traders.[45] Missionaries complained incessantly about the influx of French troops to the area and their "sinful" influence on the Native populations.[46]

By 1700, many of these men had formed close, even intimate ties with the Wendat. Intermarriage between the Wendat women and French soldiers was prevalent. A 1702 report listed French soldiers and traders who had married Wendat wives; at least one French commander had a Wendat child living within the Michilimackinac village.[47] Although Jesuits decried these relationships as sinful and extramarital affairs, the fact that many French men went to live in their partner's longhouse suggests that the Wendat viewed them as married couples according to their customs.[48]

Wendat spiritual beliefs at Michilimackinac were as diverse as in the past. Despite the influx of the French missionaries to the country and the Wendat ten-year sojourn near the mission at St. Esprit, the population at Michilimackinac was not entirely Christian.[49] Baptismal records indicate that the population was approximately 30 percent Christian. A 1676 report, for instance, noted the baptism of forty-five children and forty-seven adults.[50] Considering that the total number of Wendat was somewhere between three hundred and five hundred individuals at this time, the count indicates that at least one-third of the population became Christian. It is likely that this number increased as the Wendat and missionaries continued to engage with one another at Michilimackinac. Father Louis Hennepin alluded to an increase in baptisms, although he simultaneously mourned that many of the Wendat Christians were only superficially Christian, having converted out of curiosity rather than a dedication to the faith.[51] In sum, there were hundreds of Wendat settled at Michilimackinac. A disproportionate number were women, children, and elders. Many of the women married French men who had ventured west for work. In addition, the Western Wendat were both traditionalists and Christians, a characteristic consistent with Wendat communities of the past.

The Village

The Wendat village at Michilimackinac initially consisted of several longhouses and a chapel. Within a year's time, however, the Wendat began building a fort that was meant to enclose the village buildings. They created an activity area on the far end of the space, and included a number of fields used to grow corn for subsistence and surplus.[52] The Jesuits noted the abundance of the harvest and how the Wendat continued to use corn as a trade item with the Anishinaabeg to gain other valuable products.[53] The Jesuit mission of St. Ignace connected the Wendat village to a much larger Anishinaabe community approximately three kilometres away, composed of thirteen hundred people.[54] Overall, the Wendat village fit customary design in that it included longhouses and fields. The palisade or fort was also typical of a Wendat village; even the inclusion of a chapel was nothing new, as a chapel had been built in the community at St. Esprit, as well as in villages in Wendake.[55]

Cultural Matrix

The Christian influence on the Western Wendat grew stronger during their tenure within the community at Michilimackinac. Changes and new customs occurred and, as with many cultural encounters, some traditions gave way to the adoption of new practices. The situation at Michilimackinac in the latter half of the seventeenth century presents a case in which Native cultural practices did not disappear, nor were they forgotten. Instead, the community engaged in a series of cultural compromises rooted in respect and organized within a flexible framework of integration and accommodation. In this case, Christianity did not necessarily weaken the community, but rather secured it.

In 1674, Wendat medicine men met with Jesuits and promised that they would stop most of their curing practices and give preference to Christian teachings.[56] This was only partially realized in subsequent years, but the promise and willingness of the medicine men, probably under pressure from other members of the community, is an early illustration of Wendat appeasement towards French missionary initiatives in the area.

Around the same time as the medicine men's declaration, a prominent Wendat leader called an assembly with the intention of publicly expressing his views on French religion. This man invited all the local headmen as well as the Jesuits. To begin the assembly, the leader addressed each chief individually by name and then declared that he wished to tell them, and therefore the rest of the community, that he was Christian. He vowed he would not adhere to the power of dreams, or engage in traditional dances that were considered overtly sexual. Others in his house would follow him.[57] His message was passed throughout the village. This pattern of public expressions of loyalty to the French illustrates the changes taking place within the community; although there had been some Christians already within the group, now greater numbers adopted French customs. It is important to note that the leader who had declared himself a Christian did not necessarily reject Wendat tradition. His discussion of Wendat dances depicts compromise; he agreed to discontinue the practice of dances characterized by indecency while still honouring other dances.[58]

This type of cultural brokering fostered the need for new roles within Western Wendat society. In 1679, the Jesuits created the position "Officer of the Faith," who acted as a liaison between the French and Wendat. This permanent appointment encompassed a variety of responsibilities. Some of the minor tasks included announcing meeting times with the Jesuits, such as Sunday Mass and prayer times, by going to each house within the village several times a day. The most important task of the Officer of the Faith was his role as religious leader. After the sermon, the officer took over and reiterated what the Jesuits had said, elaborating on certain aspects of the sermon in order to clarify subject matter. The Jesuits endowed this person with the authority of a deacon or preacher. The officer received help from four Wendat "prayer officers" – usually two were in charge of organizing prayer meetings, while the other two were charged with leading the prayers and hymns during these meetings.[59] The new religious offices greatly enhanced understanding and communication between the French and Wendat. The Officer of the Faith, in particular, held a powerful role as mediator, translator, and leader within the community. Although there is no record of what the officer chose to preach about after the sermon, the power and influence of that choice would have significantly influenced Wendat perceptions of Christianity as well as their impressions of the French. There is no doubt that word choice, subject matter and interpretation shaped local relationships between these two groups.

In many instances, the Western Wendat Christians embraced Christian teachings by fusing European religious ceremonies with Wendat tradition. Sunday Mass was an example of this. In addition to the incorporation of the officer into the Mass, the Wendat and Jesuits prayed and sang in the Wendat language.[60] Although the priests made the translations, the Wendat act of singing hymns represented a performative symbolic expression that signified their accommodation and acceptance of this new practice and cosmology. Ceremonial offerings also became fusions of Wendat and Christian practices at Michilimackinac. After receiving the blessed bread, Jesuits distributed thirty-three porcelain wampum beads as a symbol of uniting the two cultures in devotion. The beads were placed on each person's bark plate, and the number of beads depended on the degree of devotion of the individual.[61] The mixing of Christian ceremony and Wendat diplomacy transformed the Sunday service at Michilimackinac. With Wendat translations and exchanges of wampum, the Christian Wendat and French were communicating within both cultural frameworks.

The Western Wendat celebrated Christmas in a similar syncretic fashion. In preparations for one Christmas, Wendat parents sent their children to gather materials to build a small nativity scene. The children gathered grass and wood and soon completed the structure. Subsequently, they confessed, took Communion, and attended midnight Mass.[62] To conclude these festivities, a few Wendat asked the Jesuits if it would be appropriate to process through the village to view the baby Jesus in the manger of the Wendat-made nativity scene. They explained that through this procession they wished to imitate the "three kings" whom the Jesuits had told them about. The Wendat prepared themselves for the Christmas parade by splitting the village into three groups. Each faction then designated a "king." The Wendat decorated their "kings" with wampum that was to be used as an offering to Jesus and each "king" wore a typical Wendat headdress instead of a European style crown.[63]

Once the procession concluded, the Wendat hosted a customary feast and dance in honour of the previous events. The women performed the dance, which was most likely the Wendat welcoming dance.[64] They arranged themselves into two lines on either side of the longhouse. Each woman took a turn singing and dancing, accompanied by their own personal refrain. In this case, some included refrains that addressed the baby Jesus; others honoured his mother Mary or gave thanks to the missionaries for organizing the event.[65] The Christmas festivities at Michilimackinac demonstrated a coming together of different belief systems. The procession and dance were simultaneously characterized by Euro-Christian customs and Wendat tradition.

Dances in general shifted in practice and meaning during this period. It was common Wendat practice that a number of dances include nudity and certain sexual acts – especially in the case of those performed as curing rituals.[66] The Jesuits remarked on these types of dances, which they called "the dance of the naked ones," and which had drawn attention from the Wendat Christian leader in the early 1670s.[67] Ultimately, as that leader suggested, the Wendat continued to practice their traditional dances with slight modifications at Michilimackinac. The Bear Dance offers an example.

In pre-dispersal times, several members of the Wendat community – mostly women, young girls, and three or four older women – performed the bear dance, so called because the dancers wore bearskins on their heads, in the hopes of curing women of a disease. The ritual included several rounds of songs and an initial dance performed in the nude. The sick woman was raised from her resting place and made to dance with the performers.[68] At Michilimackinac, the Wendat performed the dance in a similar manner. In one instance, a sick woman called together twenty women of the village to conduct the dance. The women wore bearskins and wampum around their necks. They proceeded to growl, hide, and act like bears, following the sick woman's instructions to throw certain items on the fire. The sick woman was then made to dance with the performers.[69]

For all intents and purposes, the nature of the dance remained the same. The songs, dances, regalia, and purpose had survived within the community's cultural memory. Yet, it purposefully did not include the initial dance that was performed in the nude, as a result of an earlier assembly held by the Wendat headmen, who had resolved to forbid the practice of nudity in community dances.[70] This decision was most certainly a response to Jesuit and Christian–Wendat pressure to engage in more "pious" activities.

Other ways that the Wendat incorporated Christian traditions into their customs included an offering to the priests that followed the first harvests of the field. The offerings of corn were placed at the altar and blessed by the Jesuit priest, followed by a brief sermon and a series of prayers where the Wendat gave thanks to God for giving them an abundant harvest.[71] This was one of the most popular forms of devotion, because the Wendat believed that a lack of devotion to the faith could lead to a failed harvest in the years to come. In addition, it motivated Wendat hosts of the traditional Feast of Squash to take special care to appease both Wendat spirits and the Christian God. They made the sign of the cross on several occasions throughout the feast, and especially during the meetings that convened afterward.[72]

Similar expressions of thanks and devotion were adopted into hunting rituals. This is likely the result of a combination of factors. At first, many Wendat chose to ignore the Jesuits' teachings that denounced the importance of dreams as guides to successful hunting expeditions. These dreams were used as premonitions, and if someone dreamed of a bear, for instance, the expedition would not kill bears in the hope that they would appease the spirits and that their choice would allow for other more profitable kills. According to the Jesuits, after several poor expeditions, a number of Wendat agreed to ignore their dreams and put their faith in Christian teachings. Subsequent hunting parties were very successful and brought home large numbers of bears, stags, beavers, and wildcats. This led many other Wendat to adopt similar practices.[73] In this case, the Wendat need for wild game drove them to incorporate Christian beliefs into their hunts, while the former importance of dreams was pushed aside.

Traditionalists and the Cultural Divide

The examples of Christmas celebrations, feasts, and dances as well as harvest and hunting rituals point to a fusion of Wendat and French values by the Wendat. This approach transformed Wendat society and activities, but in most cases it did not lead to an outright rejection of Wendat traditions in their entirety. Christianity influenced some Western Wendat more than others. Certainly, substantial portions of the population remained unconverted throughout their time at Michilimackinac. Despite the potential for factional conflict, however, it seems that the community continued to engage in joint activities, and that inclusion rather than exclusion was the dominant policy. Both Christians and traditionalists took part in the Christmas procession, for instance, and traditionalist women danced and sang at the celebrations that were held in honour of the infant Jesus, although it is unclear whether their refrains addressed the baby Jesus, Mary, and the missionaries in the same way as their Christian counterparts.[74] Moreover, during the Christian season of Lent, both Christians and traditionalists attended Friday morning meetings led by the Jesuits, where both groups engaged in conversations about spirituality, morality, and their perceptions of the French faith. Non-Christians were also invited to the community's evening prayer sessions and at times helped in their orchestration.[75]

A Wendat headman gave a public speech at the Feast of Squash in 1672 that expressed the traditionalist perspective at Michilimackinac. He called attention to the fact that non-converts respected the Christian faith and its followers. He then made the sign of the cross to publicly honour the Christians in attendance.[76] This display of respect for Christianity indicates underlying tensions within the community. Because of past conflicts between traditionalists and Jesuits as well as the Christian Wendat in pre-dispersal Wendake, it was important for Wendat leaders to make clear demonstrations of their amity towards their spiritual counterparts in order to appease any conflict that might arise. There seems to have been little overt opposition to Christianity from traditionalist Wendat at Michilimackinac. With the exception of the infrequent stealing of corn and wampum offerings and a few rumblings at the Feast of Squash when participants protested against the headman's making of the cross, overt actions of resistance were minimal.[77] The stealing of corn and wampum was most likely out of greed rather than a traditionalist protest to Christianity, especially since the culprits did not come forward. Most of the opposition towards the headman's symbolic sign of the cross gesture may have actually come from Christians themselves who viewed his act as degrading the purity of the cross. The community dynamic of Michilimackinac contrasted greatly with the days of Taretande and Aenon. Western Wendat leaders and the general public did not draw lines between community members based on religious affiliation – at least not in the public sense.

Foreign Relations and Cultural Connections

What effect did the acculturation of Christian practices and values have on Western Wendat alliance networks during this period? In regards to the Anishinaabeg, Christianity became an additional means for unification. Often, sermons were delivered simultaneously to both Anishinaabeg and Wendat at Michilimackinac.[78] More elaborate ceremonies also included both groups, such as the Christmas procession. In fact, the Wendat invitation to the Anishinaabeg to their Christmas feast and dance was one of the first Wendat–Anishinaabe declarations of their united devotion to Jesus.[79]

The Christian Wendat frequently visited Anishinaabe communities to pay respect to that village's Christians. During these meetings, the Wendat visited the Anishinaabe chapel, where the entire Wendat procession saluted the baby Jesus. This was followed by chants and prayers delivered in both Anishinaabe and Wendat. Subsequently, the Anishinaabeg provided a feast for their Wendat visitors, and an Anishinaabe headman addressed the group declaring that they were "all united as brothers to obey Jesus, and to entreat the divine Child to preserve their children."[80] This type of public fraternity emphasized the unity that still existed between the Wendat and Anishinaabeg, as well as their common desire to have strong relations with the French. It reconfirmed the Coalition as an important aspect of Wendat foreign relations and that the French were still integral allies to the Coalition.

Similar diplomatic gestures took place in response to an Anishinaabe transgression against the faith. Apparently, the Anishinaabeg had not paid due respect in 1679 to a cross that was erected within their community. After hearing about the circumstances, a group of Wendat decided to lead a procession to the Anishinaabe village so that the Anishinaabeg could make reparations for their actions. The Wendat arrived on a Sunday, carrying small crosses symbolizing respect for the cross. The Anishinaabeg welcomed them and both groups sang hymns in honour of Jesus and the cross.[81] In all likelihood, this meeting was less about transgressions and more about appeasement of the French: the incorporation of certain Christian practices into the Wendat community and the full conversion of many Wendat offered clear indications of a Wendat desire to have the French remain close to them. Cultural brokers such as the Officer of the Faith would have facilitated communication between these groups, while a tactic of respect and cultural flexibility created opportunities for future conversions, thereby enticing the Jesuits to stay. Thus, without fully committing themselves to Christianity, the community at Michilimackinac demonstrated a consistent devotion to the Jesuits and their mission within the area.

Leaving the Country of the People of the Sea, 1701

In 1701, the Western Wendat resolved to move south to Fort Pontchartrain (modern-day Detroit). It is believed that by this time the Western Wendat were role models throughout the region as traders and diplomats.[82] In essence, they had come full circle by the eighteenth century. In 1650, they had struggled to survive, but after fifty years they had recreated a community analogous with their previous geopolitical role. They situated themselves in a geographic location of central commercial activity, while maintaining their old alliances with the Anishinaabeg and French. They were able to do this through strategic diplomacy and cultural compromise, nullifying conflicts and seeking to expand trade and kinship networks.

The examples provided above give evidence that the Western Wendat did not transition into subsistence patterns more in line with their Anishinaabe kin, as some scholars suggest. Rather, they retained their Wendat identity in cultural and political as well as material terms. That said, the Anishinaabeg and the Coalition proved integral to the overall success of the relocation to Michilimackinac. The Ottawa that accompanied the Wendat during the "unsettled years" and who continued to live next to them at Michilimackinac convinced other Anishinaabeg to allow the Wendat to stay in the area.

In many respects, it seems that the parhelion premonitions of 1671 was correct: Michilimackinac's status expanded over the rest of the century; it became a major hub for the fur trade, military efforts, and politics of the seventeenth century. The establishment of a Wendat village in 1671 meant that the Western Wendat were at the heart of this activity. They had spent twenty years creating bonds with the people and land of the region, legitimizing their authority within the area.

6
The East
The Lorettans

WHILE CULTURAL COMPROMISE – a kind of acculturation between Wendat views and host nations – informed the survival strategy for the Western Wendat, settling in the east required a different approach based on cultural conformity. Surrounded by a primarily French population, the Wendat who ventured along the St. Lawrence towards Quebec and settled in Lorette enforced strict community guidelines that incorporated a public dedication to Christianity and allegiance to the French. Writing to his superior in 1710, the Jesuit Louis d'Avaugour summarized the unique character of the eastern Wendat community of Lorette. He argued:

> There are some who think, and therefore write, that the soil of Canada is thoroughly sterile and unfruitful; that the heralds of the Gospel reap therefrom hardly any fruit in return for long and painful labor. This single village of Lorette can teach them otherwise. In fact, I make bold to say that all the other missions of Canada are by no means as fruitful as this one.[1]

These Wendat were more than just the product of a hundred years of determined missionary zeal. Their "fruitfulness" and extraordinarily pious nature resulted from a conscious Wendat survival strategy dating to the 1650 dispersal. Some scholars view the Wendat migration east as a movement towards cultural and spiritual disintegration, assimilation, and dependency.[2] Yet, there are others who have demonstrated how Native people often chose Catholicism as a conduit for achieving power. In many cases conversion led to positions of mediation between cultural groups (Native and French), leadership in religious training, and the ability to influence commodity production and exchange.[3] This strategy was not new, as we have seen with the pre-dispersal conversions of headmen, war chiefs, and some female leaders, but became more pronounced during the eastern relocation. Acculturation offered socio-political and economic advantages, and proved essential to creating a successful and amicable relocation among the St. Lawrence French population. Thus, the so-called "Lorettans"[4] became exceptional Christians, much like d'Avaugour's commentary suggests. They developed a more conservative culture than their western counterparts, one that required major departures from customary behaviour mores and sociability from its members. This does not mean that the Eastern Wendat became French. Much like the Western Wendat, Lorettans retained an essential Wendat identity despite their unwavering dedication to the French and Christianity.

Negotiations: 1650

Several factors convinced the Wendat to move east to what Father Le Mercier called "the very ends of the world."[5] The disarray and mortality on Gahoendoe made it an unwelcome stop, and the Wendat viewed relocations to Anishinaabe villages as a temporary strategy. Eastern migration provided a familiar environment (both in terms of landscape and people). Historical connections through their ancestors' former habitation of Montreal (Hochelaga) and Quebec City (Stadacona) and frequent trade and travel to the area created an enduring bond between the seventeenth-century Wendat and the people of the St. Lawrence. Unlike their western counterparts, the Eastern Wendat did not have to introduce themselves or prove their usefulness to the local population, because their reputation was already well established throughout the region. In addition, a sizeable number of Wendat had already moved east to Sillery, Trois-Rivières, and Montreal, although many considered these locations too dangerous and vulnerable to Iroquois attacks.[6] This shaped a resolution to continue farther east to Quebec City. The Wendat believed that this predominantly French settlement would allow them to continue their ties with the French, and offer the possibility of creating a more intimate relationship than before; the Wendat could attain French military protection, as well as French material goods. Finally, the Wendat perceived Quebec City as the eastern end of the French world during this period. By positioning themselves at this point, the Wendat sketched their geographic and political stakes in North America. They had always had firm trade and diplomatic ties with the northeast. From Michilimackinac to Quebec City, the dispersed Wendat attempted to consolidate their authority from the concentrated centre of Wendake to the distant outposts of French, Anishinaabe, and Wendat spheres of influence.

The Wendat held a number of consultations to put this plan into action. First, they deliberated among themselves, and then dispatched a headman to Quebec City to propose an official Wendat relocation to the French. Two meetings took place over Easter weekend in 1650; both French civil authorities and missionaries attended, including Fathers Barthélemy Vimont, François Bressani, Jacques de la Place, and Daniel Richer.[7] The colony of New France built its policies on a "unique symbiosis" between the Church and civic administrators, making them "part and parcel" of all negotiations with Native nations, and these Easter discussions were no exception.[8] While the governor general technically controlled Native affairs, governor Samuel de Champlain had set the stage for a more complex set of relationships in 1632, declaring the French would trade with the Wendat only if Jesuits could establish themselves in Wendake.[9] Jesuits later took on full responsibility of Wendat trade from French merchants of the Compagnie des Cents-Associés (Company of One Hundred Associates).[10] In addition, the Compagnie itself created a policy encouraging Christian conversion. The Christian Wendat enjoyed lower prices for merchandise than their traditionalist counterparts; Christians also received guns and could enter French forts.[11] By 1642, the governor gave gifts only to converted Natives during trade and diplomatic negotiations.[12] In 1647, the colonial government established a new governing council. It included the governor of New France, the local governor of Montreal, elected representatives, *and* the superior of the Jesuits.[13] Missionaries and administrators, therefore, worked together in most cases to achieve colonial goals. This did not mean that they always saw eye to eye, but rather supported each other to achieve population growth, establish a trade network, and spread Christianity and French culture to Native Americans. Ideally, the latter process of "Frenchification" included the total assimilation of Native people into the French colonial population, which thus led to full French citizenry.[14]

In terms of Wendat affairs, governors often used Jesuits as mediators. The church controlled one-quarter of the colony's land holdings. Jesuits received twenty land concessions in New France, ranging from small building plots to large tracts of land outside of towns. Availability of Jesuit land holdings was a key component to the Wendat's strategic relocations east; equally important was access to missionary funds. The French population at Quebec suffered from the same poor crops because of the drought of 1650-51 and could not support hundreds of Wendat refugees.[15] Yet, French administrators saw the benefit of keeping their Native allies close to help fend off a series of Iroquois attacks throughout 1651-52.[16] The Jesuits' private resources offered a solution to this dilemma. Not only did the missionaries want to continue their work with the Wendat at Quebec, endorsing the relocation, but they also had the means to do it. After some discussion, the French agreed to welcome the Wendat and allocated 3,000 livres to help in the endeavour.[17] This negotiation of physical space had broad implications for the future; from the very beginning, relocation eastward depended on an amicable balance between the Wendat, colonial officials, and Jesuit priests.

Back on Gahoendoe, a council presented the details of the agreement to the community. Several headmen gathered to entice the missionaries to escort a portion of the Wendat to Quebec, and offered concessions concerning the relocation that they hoped would attract greater support. If the French agreed to supply land and provisions for the Wendat, the headmen intimated that the Jesuits could garner the conversion of the entire Eastern Wendat community. One headman articulated the Wendat perspective in the following way:

> Cast thine eyes toward Quebec, and transport thither the remnants of this ruined nation ... Thou bearest us in thy hands and thy heart ... If thou listen to our wishes, we will build a Church under shelter of the fort at Kebec [sic]. There, our faith will not die out ... Their charity will alleviate, in part, our miseries; and, at the least, we shall sometimes find there a morsel of bread for our little ones, who, to sustain life, have for so long lived on acorns, and bitter roots.[18]

According to Wendat tradition, this type of reciprocal relationship typified relocation. The Wendat had incorporated many refugee groups over the years and it was customary to welcome these groups by giving plots of land and provisions to establish themselves as part of the larger community.[19] Thus, the Wendat expected the French to accommodate their group, even though they understood that the situation was orchestrated under the pretext that the Eastern Wendat would become Christian.

The Wendat emphasis on Christianity may have been the result of previous French demands, by both missionaries and administrators, for Native conversions in relation to relocation. Earlier discussions concerning the settlement of the Wendat at the popular French trade centres of Trois-Rivières and Montreal would have set the standards for this particular relocation. In 1648, for instance, the Wendat gathered at Trois-Rivières to ratify the nature of settlement there. Four main articles of agreement were included in this discussion. First, the Wendat agreed to have an individual serve as a representative of the Church, much in the same way as the Officer of the Faith did in the West. This person would commit to being the most dedicated Christian and would take it upon himself to report the names of members of the Wendat community who resisted conversion to the Jesuits. Second, all Wendat who declared themselves Christians were subject to the Laws of Jesus Christ; if they transgressed these laws they would be punished in accordance with Christian rules. They promised to eschew drunkenness; any Wendat found guilty of this crime would be sent to jail and made to fast on water for several days. Finally, the Trois-Rivières council concluded that individuals who openly expressed resistance to Christianity would not receive defence or shelter from the French fort.[20]

Similar negotiations took place at Montreal with the governor. In this case, the headman Achindôanes spoke on behalf of the Wendat and asked the French governor to "take pity, be their father and protector."[21] He specifically requested that the sale of liquor be outlawed to reduce temptation; that the Natives be allowed to seek employment from the French in the making of canoes, snowshoes, and moccasins; that the French provide provisions when their community was in need (especially during the hunting season); that more land be provided if the community grew; and that the French supply a priest. Achindôanes concluded that in respect to community justice, the Wendat desired that if one of their dogs ate one of the Frenchmen's birds he would be subject to Wendat laws, not French ones. The governor agreed to the majority of the Wendat requests, although he argued about the acquisition of land and an inability to stop all sales of liquor.[22]

The experiences at Trois-Rivières and Montreal fit within a tradition of negotiation between the French and Wendat in cases of relocation; the Wendat agreed to endorse Christianity, while legal authority and rules of law continued to be a point of discussion. At Trois-Rivières, there was a strict code of Christian doctrine, while at Montreal there may have been instances in which Wendat justice trumped French law. In many cases, the two may have been compatible. Wendat desires to eradicate drunkenness because of its social toll meshed with Christian notions of piety; similarly, the request for charity in times of need echoed both Wendat and French customs. Thus, when the Gahoendoe council outlined their desire to relocate among the French, they were most likely aware that religious conversion would play a key role in the success of this endeavour.

Although the French in Quebec City accepted the terms presented to them by the headman, the missionaries on Gahoendoe were hesitant. A move from Gahoendoe meant a complete abandonment of Wendake, which seemed like admitting failure of the Wendat missions. The Jesuits took to prayer for forty hours and consulted each other on numerous occasions. Finally, Father Ragueneau concluded that "if we [the Jesuits] could conduct them [the Wendat] to the shelter of a French fort at Montreal, Trois-Rivières, or Quebec, it would be, we thought, their only place of refuge; that there, the assistance which we could render them would be more effectual, and their faith would be more assured."[23] In other words, the Jesuits accepted relocation as an opportunity to save their mission. The weakened Wendat needed the charity of the St. Lawrence French to survive. By establishing the Wendat in a region surrounded by French Catholics, the Jesuits might convert them more easily. In addition, they endorsed the policy that the Christian Wendat would take priority over non-converts and their families would benefit first from French shelters and charity.[24] The Jesuits agreed to move east, acting as escorts to the Wendat as they ventured towards Quebec.

The context of these discussions contradicts the common notion that the Wendat "followed" the French to Quebec. In reality, the Wendat, not the French, instigated the migration east and set many of the conditions for the relocation. In fact, it was the missionaries, if no one else, who were hesitant. Gaining French acceptance of the proposal was key, however, and a successful relocation could not have proceeded without the support of the missionaries. Thus, the Wendat engaged in negotiations, similar to previous discussions at Trois-Rivières and Montreal, in order to persuade the Jesuits. They used all their diplomatic skills both to create consensus in their own communities and to appeal to the divergent civil and religious communities of New France. A promise of Christian conversion proved essential to this process. Ultimately, by adopting this Christian strategy, the Wendat left a considerable amount of power in the hands of the Jesuits. Although the idea of relocation was a Wendat one, the situation permitted the terms of settlement and the future nature of the community to be dictated by the French.

The Journey: 1650-73

Approximately three hundred Wendat moved east in the spring of 1650.[25] The route was twelve hundred kilometres and took roughly fifty days.[26] The difficult journey took an enormous physical and psychological toll. Unlike the migration west, the Eastern Wendat had to cross the homeland of Wendake mainland, where they witnessed the abandoned villages, the decaying corpses of loved ones, and the ashes of houses torched in the evacuation process.[27] Constant fear of Iroquois attacks compounded the horror of the experience. The Wendat made note of recent paths created by the enemy and twice they came across abandoned Iroquois forts.[28] There was no time to bury the bones of the deceased or to stop and lament the loss of a territory.

Fear and paranoia dictated their movements to such an extent that any sign of human activity was assumed to be Iroquoian. Nearing the twenty-fifth day of travel, Eastern Wendat scouts noticed a trail of what they took to be the enemy. They reported their findings to the larger group, who immediately prepared for war. Children and women hid in the bushes while the men took to arms, retracing their steps towards the attackers. Just as quickly as they drew their weapons, however, they lowered them; to the war party's relief and surprise, the opposing group was not the Iroquois but a group of forty Frenchmen, as well as a few Wendat. Both groups took solace in the close call and used the opportunity to exchange information on Iroquois in the area. As it happened, the group moving west had just survived an Iroquois attack the previous night, in which they lost seven men. The encounter confirmed that their fear was warranted, and forced the Eastern Wendat to remain on constant alert for the rest of their journey.[29]

Despite the difficulties of the expedition east, the Wendat arrived at Quebec City in the spring of 1650. They were starving and weak; their journey had been long and dangerous, but they had finally made it.[30] Ursuline nuns who had established themselves at Quebec in 1639 were some of the first French people to greet the travellers. Writing in August 1650, Marie de l'Incarnation, who supervised the Order, expressed her view that the Wendat were indeed refugees, and promised that the Ursulines would try their best to help the Wendat through the initial stages of relocation until they could establish themselves independently from the French.[31] What the Ursuline mother neglected to add was that this charity was exclusionary and applied only to Wendat Christian families. Christians received clothing, food, and shelter within the seminary as well as among a number of French residents. The Ursulines' day-school also welcomed a small number of Wendat girls, where they received a European education in the Wendat language. This strategy, combined with a lack of supplies within the French community in general, left at least two hundred non-Christian Wendat without significant aid in the early stages of relocation.[32]

Eventually the Jesuits satisfied Wendat requests for settlement, however, and the community established itself at Île d'Orléans, three kilometres from the mainland and Quebec City. This took some negotiating on the part of the Wendat, Jesuits, and Éléonore de Grandmaison – the French woman who owned the land, which was divided into thirty portions, the largest tract being half an acre.[33] The Wendat agreed to an eight-year contract. They arranged to cultivate the land and establish residences separate from Grandmaison, as well as to help her with chores. Accordingly, the French landlady agreed to distribute food in times of need. In addition, the French governor agreed to build a fort to protect the Wendat from the Iroquois, and the Jesuits agreed to build a mission and chapel.[34]

The Wendat tenure at Île d'Orléans proved productive. Trade continued to be profitable during this period; the Wendat exchanged beaver robes with the French, trading up to two thousand skins a year.[35] Yet, they struggled with security as the Iroquois harassed them in various ways, alternating between incessant diplomatic meetings and violent attacks. The Iroquois hoped that they might convince the Wendat to abandon Île d'Orléans for Iroquois country.[36] Eventually the situation became so volatile that it culminated in what one scholar calls the "rape of the Quebec Huron" in 1656.[37]

Despite all the careful planning by the Wendat, the politics of the region grew increasingly tenuous for them. The French and Iroquois had just made peace and Jesuits established themselves in Iroquois communities. At the same time, several of the Iroquois nations competed to annex the Wendat, who engaged in diplomatic relations with several of them simultaneously in an effort to stave off attacks. This was not always successful; their dealings with the Onondaga incited a bitter reaction from the Mohawk.[38] To make matters worse, the French received word that the Mohawk planned to attack the Wendat at Île d'Orléans, and decided to remain neutral. The French gave the Mohawk presents in an attempt to discourage the pending attack, but offered no indication that they would provide military support for the Wendat in the event of an assault.[39] Subsequently, the Mohawk landed at Île d'Orléans on the morning of 18 May 1656 and laid siege to the unsuspecting Wendat as they worked their fields. Although some Wendat managed to seek refuge in the Jesuit mission, approximately seventy individuals were killed and a substantial number taken. The attackers left French residents untouched.[40]

The Mohawk victory engendered important repercussions for the Eastern Wendat. It proved that the island was not secure and that the

French, despite their continued protestations of friendship, were unable or unwilling to provide military protection for them. This realization led the community to abandon the island and relocate within the fortified walls of Quebec City on 4 June 1656.[41]

The Wendat at Quebec City established themselves in what the French termed "le Fort des Sauvages" or the "Native Fort," located in the centre of town.[42] Governor Louis d'Ailleboust de Coulonge ordered the construction of the fort, perhaps in reaction to the Mohawk assault; he issued a public decree that the French would support any Wendat or Anishinaabeg whom the Iroquois attacked in close proximity to a French settlement.[43] In addition to the fort, the Wendat received forty-four acres of land to cultivate on the south shore of the St. Lawrence.[44] Although the fort may have provided more protection, it did not safeguard the Wendat who ventured beyond it. During the following fourteen years, the Wendat within Quebec City faced continued French–Wendat–Iroquois hostilities, including the famous Battle of Long Sault and the escapades of Adam Dollard des Ormeaux in 1660. The French, Wendat, and Anishinaabeg lost this battle, but managed to protect the French settlements in the area.[45]

In 1667, the French and Iroquois entered into a peace agreement, and the following year the Wendat relinquished their Quebec City fort and moved briefly to Beauport, about five kilometres from the city's walls.[46] The details of this move are not clear but possibly resulted from the French–Iroquois peace. If the Iroquois had agreed to halt their attacks, the Wendat might have been more confident relocating outside the fort. The relocation to Beauport lasted only a year; by 1669, the Eastern Wendat had moved again, this time to Notre-Dame-de-Foy. The Wendat remained there for four years, enough time to cultivate their fields, build houses, and become attached to the land. A Wendat woman's reluctance to relocate in 1673 indicated the extent of this attachment. She told her friend in confidence about her personal struggle, and the friend reported the conversation to the Jesuits who helped in orchestrating the move. The conversation continued among them as the friend sympathized with the distraught woman: "I see very well that your regret at changing your village comes from the love that you bear to the Fields which you have here, and which you cannot transport so far."[47] For many Wendat, the relocation from Wendake took twenty years. They grew tired and frustrated about their inability to attach themselves to a land and village. It is perhaps for this reason, as well as the productivity of the fields at Notre-Dame-de-Foy, that the Wendat continued to return and cultivate their corn even after their leaving in 1673.[48] This said, the Jesuits associated the move with an increased population and a need for more land as the fields became exhausted.[49] The continued use of the fields implies that the Jesuits' explanation of the move may not describe the situation in its entirety.

What became known as "Ancienne Lorette" was the relocation site that served as the Eastern Wendat's home for the better part of the remaining century.[50] Many search parties and consultations on the destination took place until the group finally selected the location, eleven kilometres from Quebec City.[51] Modern Wendat traditions support this account, as Eastern Wendat descendant Alexandra Martel explained to a reporter in 1965. According to Martel, the main reason behind the selection of Lorette was its location beside the falls of the St. Charles River.[52] The Jesuits highlighted the importance of the river and remarked on how it was "a brook of excellent water."[53] In December 1673, the Lorettans began construction and over several months erected their village in relation to the water on a high tract of land just beyond the brook.

During this time a village plan was drawn up. The physical setup offers perspective into the Wendat diaspora culture that the villagers created. At the centre stood the chapel, surrounded by twelve to thirteen bark longhouses, each connected by a twenty-foot road that led directly to the church. All of this was set high on a tract of land that had a direct view of Quebec City.[54] The church remained central to the Wendat relocation process and settlement strategy. It was literally the force that connected the community through roads, rituals, and relationships. Moreover, the view of Quebec City was a constant reminder of the French presence in the area and the Wendat connection to them. The Jesuits described the location as "one of the most pleasing in all this country."[55] The Lorettans grew satisfied enough to remain in the vicinity indefinitely.

The two decades of relocation for the Eastern Wendat differed from that of their contemporaries out west in several key respects. Whereas the Western Wendat spent the 1650s and '60s expanding their networks throughout the upper Great Lakes, the Eastern Wendat remained confined to restricted spaces allocated by the French. This led to isolationism, as the French began to dictate Wendat interactions with other nations. All the while, Iroquois intrusions, both diplomatic overtures and violent assaults, remained a constant concern. Thus, the long journey of relocation to the East resulted in a settled community that had survived continual Iroquois attacks and French neglect. The negotiations of spatial occupation created a community dependent on Jesuit support, which in turn required that the Wendat prove themselves worthy Christian allies. Some scholars argue that during this period the Eastern Wendat "joined the growing ranks of Indians who ceased to be treated with respect by Europeans once they ceased to be an economic asset."[56] As we shall see, however, these Wendat retained respect through Christian zeal rather than beaver pelts.

The Lorettans, 1673-97

Population

The Wendat population at Lorette had experienced years of demographic shifts.[57] After the settlement at Île d'Orléans, many more Wendat ventured east to join them. In 1651, forty additional canoes joined the original three hundred Wendat who left Wendake. This group came from Ekaentoton and included roughly 240 people.[58] During the same year, the Wendat residing at Sillery moved to Quebec in a forced removal dictated by the French sale of the Jesuit lands at Sillery.[59] This group numbered close to 120.[60] It was also in 1651 that the additional group of Wendat who had remained on Gahoendoe to harvest crops made their way to Quebec.[61] This number increased again on 26 April 1654 with the arrival of the Wendat from Trois-Rivières.[62] Thus, by the end of their tenure at Île d'Orléans, the Wendat population could have been over seven hundred people; this is corroborated by Father Léonard Garreau's assertion in 1652 that there were at least two hundred Wendat men hunting and four hundred to six hundred women in the fields at any given time.[63] This far exceeds previous estimates of thirty families, or roughly 240 individuals.[64]

But these high numbers did not last. Due to Iroquois raids and Wendat agreements to relocate to Iroquois country, the population dwindled to approximately 150 members by 1670.[65] Although the number of Wendat adopted into Iroquoian society is unknown, we can roughly calculate the number of dead and captured Wendat. From 1650 to 1656 there were approximately six battles between the Eastern Wendat and Iroquois; the most extreme was the Mohawk attack in 1656.[66] Ninety-three Wendat became captive or "lost"; out of these, seventy-one to eighty-five people were captured in the 1656 battle.[67] Taking into consideration the hundreds of Wendat residing at Île d'Orléans during that time, and the Jesuits' account that only seventy people were saved, there must have been *hundreds* of casualties.[68] Combined with the numbers of Iroquois adoptees, this gives at least a partial explanation to the eventual decline in population and the low number of 150 by 1670.

The ethnic composition of the original Eastern Wendat group included the Bear, Cord, and Rock nations.[69] By 1656, however, most of the Bear and Cord had joined the Iroquois. The Lorettans primarily consisted of members of the Cord who chose to remain in the Quebec region despite Iroquois pressure to leave.[70] The Cord nation was not known to be any more inclined towards the French than the other nations, nor did they have a reputation as more Christian. The Jesuits asserted that by the time the Wendat removed to Lorette they were a "church fully formed," no longer counting "therein the number of the baptized, except by that of the children who come into the world."[71] Taking this at face value, it seems the Lorettans had kept their promise and were mostly Christians. The Christian character of the Eastern Wendat attracted other Native people to Lorette. Large portions of these visitors were Iroquois and would eventually be incorporated by the Wendat. By 1675, the population of the community rose to roughly three hundred individuals, including both Wendat and Iroquois. In that same year, twenty-two Iroquois adults were baptized.[72]

Although the late seventeenth-century historian Claude-Charles Bacqueville de la Potherie deemed the Native society at Lorette "one of the largest villages in New France," it was an ethnic minority among the growing French population of the St. Lawrence.[73] By 1660 the French numbered approximately ten thousand, making the Lorettans roughly 3 percent of the entire population.[74] This had far-reaching implications, not least of which was intermarriage. The Wendat entertained marriages with the French for several reasons. First, marriage represented a symbolic union for the Wendat, one that created customary kinship ties. Christian marriages also signalled a public display of Christian piety among the Wendat. Second, European women were still underrepresented among the French: Christian Wendat women provided an alternative for French men. Finally, it was during the 1660s that the French began to enforce their policy of "Frenchification."[75] Thus, French administrators pressured the Wendat to marry the French with the hopes they would assimilate into French society. On 19 September 1662, for instance, Marie Félix Arontio married Frenchman Laurent du Bocq. She received 500 livres from the property of her deceased mother as a dowry.[76] Eight days later, thirteen-year-old Catherine Annennontak married Jean Durand. Her dowry was 260 livres.[77] This tradition continued throughout the century. On 9 September 1698, the notary Guillaume Roger recorded the marriage of the Wendat woman Elizabeth-Agnès Michel to Louis Durand (the son of Jean Durand and Catherine Annennontak), which included a dowry of 500 livres.[78]

Children resulted from these unions. Marie Félix had seven children with du Bocq and Catherine had three children with Durand, as well as an additional five children from her second marriage to Jacques Couturier after Durand's death.[79] It is not clear whether the couples remained in the Wendat village or returned to a French community, though it was Wendat custom to invite the Frenchman into his wife's home. The Jesuits indicate that the population in Lorette continued to grow.[80] Taking this into consideration, it is likely these mixed families continued to reside in Lorette, creating generations of Lorettan children that were biologically both French and Wendat.

Compliance

The Eastern Wendat living at Île d'Orléans, Quebec City, Beauport, Notre-Dame-de-Foy, and Lorette needed to make overt gestures to convince the French they would honour their promise of conversion. It was no longer enough to express interest in Catholicism, attend Mass, and speak about Christianity, because other Native people were doing that by this time. The Wendat needed to be exemplary Christians to stand out. This was not an easy task, as Christian doctrine demanded changes in Wendat cultural traditions. Previous practices of premarital sex, nudity, alcohol consumption, and gambling were forbidden. Nevertheless, the advantages that came with religious conversion, such as French support and Wendat survival, were too important to ignore. It was for this reason that community members imposed strict guidelines on their citizens, with heavy repercussions in the case of disobedience.

Embracing Christianity required major cultural shifts for the Wendat. Extramarital relations and public nudity became virtually non-existent. Christian marriages became the norm, along with a Christian sense of purity that forbade public kissing and flirting. This represented a marked departure from earlier Wendat resistance towards Catholic marriage contracts and from habits of sexual liberty that existed in Wendake. Even the missionaries were surprised at the Wendat decision to encourage changes that departed so drastically from previous times.[81]

Similarly, theft had been a common activity among the Wendat before the shift to Christianity. In the pre-dispersal period, Jesuits called this an "addiction." It is unclear, however, the extent to which these activities were seen as "stealing" from the Wendat perspective, since Wendat concepts of personal ownership and property rights differed from the French. Regardless, theft and "borrowing" of property became less frequent after 1650. The Eastern Wendat made a concerted effort to demonstrate their restraint by seeking out the Jesuits if they found any item whose ownership was in question. This could involve things as small as pins and nails found in the street. When found, the Wendat brought them to the Jesuits in the hopes that they would restore them to their rightful owners.[82]

Alcohol consumption among both French and Native populations had always been a major concern for the Jesuits. Although the Wendat and Jesuits repeatedly tried to limit the trade of this commodity, they could not stop it. French traders often tried to entice the Natives by saying, "What crime is there if by the way, or when weary from one's journey, or for a guest's or friend's sake, one quaff a cup of wine?" The Lorettan Wendat reply is indicative of their unwavering perspective on the matter: "It is just as thou sayest, brother," they would respond, "but we have promised Mary that we would never drink even a single cup."[83] The Wendat placed special emphasis on teaching the immorality of drunkenness and the ways in which it opposed the Christian faith.[84] Together, the missionaries and community pressure succeeded in technically abolishing drunkenness in Eastern Wendat society during this period. Father d'Avaugour asserted that he saw not a single instance of public drunkenness in his five years at Lorette, a remarkable change from earlier Jesuit observations.[85] A French merchant also took note of the sobriety of the Wendat. He could not help "admiring the temperance and constancy of the Lorette Hurons" whom he had encountered on a recent trip: "They never could be induced by us to taste a drop of wine, even to touch it with their lips, being satisfied with bread and a little tobacco."[86]

The Wendat pressured visitors to adhere to the community's culture of conformity. Large numbers of Iroquois came to the Wendat village for Christian instruction from missionaries and Wendat converts. By 1675, approximately 17 percent of the Lorettan population was Iroquois.[87] The Iroquois received rigorous religious training.[88] At first, newcomers found it very difficult to transcend the differences between Iroquoia and Christianized Eastern Wendat society. One young Iroquois struggled with how to explain his new life among the Wendat to his fellow Iroquois. He believed "the manner in which the hurons lived Was so surprising and so different from that of other savages that he expected that The account he would give of it would be looked upon as a fable."[89] Nonetheless, many Iroquois adhered to the transition and became exemplary Christians.[90]

The Wendat enforced these guidelines throughout the community in a number of ways including public humiliation, reprimands, and by burning houses. In extreme cases, individuals could be subject to a multitude of punishments culminating in permanent exile. The entire community participated in these strict measures. In one case, the Wendat accused a wife and husband of alcoholism in the early 1670s. Upon finding them guilty, the couple was exiled from the community and forbidden to return under any circumstances. To prove this point, the villagers burned the couple's house so they would have nothing to return to.[91] Exile was a devastating sentence, as it almost certainly meant death. Without food or shelter and left vulnerable to enemy attacks, those without community had little hope for survival, so fear of punishments pressured Lorettans to conform.

Punishment for children differed from that of their parents, but was nonetheless critical to the success of the Christian strategy. Wendat youth represented the future and their character formation required careful consideration. The Wendat always had a special affinity for the younger generations and encouraged them to use their childhood to explore and experiment. The French made particular note of the nature of Wendat children and child-rearing in the pre-dispersal period. Samuel de Champlain, for instance, believed "the children of these nations [were] extremely free."[92] Recollet Brother Gabriel Sagard made similar observations:

> They are for the most part very naughty children, paying [parents] little respect, and hardly more obedience; for unhappily in these lands the young have no respect for the old, nor are children obedient to their parents, and moreover there is no punishment for any fault. For this reason everybody lives in complete freedom ... Bad example, and bad bringing up, without punishment or correction, are the causes of this lack of decency.[93]

In reality, it is likely that the Wendat perceived children "as developing individuals, [they did] not see or hear themselves being told how to think and behave by people invested with arbitrary powers, or by a system. Instead they simply [had] access to the abundant source of wisdom available to all, which comes from the ancient spirit of the people. Children [could] draw on it when and how they [wished]."[94] This does not necessarily mean there were no limitations on children's actions; Champlain and Sagard's observations most likely reflected the contrast between French and Wendat child-rearing practices. The Wendat did not traditionally send their children for formal training; in addition, public humiliation was highly frowned upon and corporal punishment did not exist.[95]

This changed once the Wendat relocated to Quebec. At Notre-Dame-de-Foy, the Wendat observed the French children who attended a school built within the walls of the Wendat village. Here, French children were frequently punished if they did not abide by the rules. Schoolmasters and matrons customarily conducted public displays of reprimand.[96] Understanding the need for Wendat children to conduct themselves as "good" Christians, the Wendat began rounding up all the Wendat children and publicly chastising them for their faults. Parents then took the children to the resident priest to explain once again these faults. After hearing the confessions, the priest would allocate appropriate punishment.[97] This conduct reshaped the Wendat childhood experience. Thoroughly impressed with the outcome, the Jesuits exulted that "such exemplary Punishment has made the little savages so well-behaved that one can now do with them whatever he wishes."[98] In other words, through European forms of punishment, the Wendat were able to quell the previous "freedom" of their youth and force them to conform to Christian perceptions of appropriate behaviour. Eventually they would be seen as surpassing the French in piety. In fact, it was the Jesuits' opinion that "there [was] much more modesty and decency among The huron youth than among The french."[99]

While parents played a major role in implementing punishment for Wendat children, several different people and groups regulated the Wendat community at large in ways that suggest continuity with traditional cultural forms. Individual leaders, for instance, played a major role as both models and enforcers. In 1668 the Wendat headman Ignace addressed a council in order to express his displeasure with the conduct of his fellow citizens. Ignace found the lack of Wendat religious offerings dissatisfying. It was part of Christian tradition and he was angry the Wendat were not adhering to this mandatory religious act. He asserted, "I am ashamed to see that [the French] make offerings to God, and that we have not yet done anything of the kind. That is why I beg you to consent to imitate the example of the French in future, by making some present to the Church. As for myself, I am going to begin first by making my offering of this Collar." In the end, Ignace succeeded as the council resolved that all the young men of the village would make a contribution in their own capacity when they returned from the hunt.[100]

Elders' councils also served as a governing body concerning personal conduct and regulations. This body could both punish and forgive transgressors. In the case of drunkenness, citizens could redeem themselves by coming before the council and proving they had reformed themselves. Again drawing on customary practices, representatives of the defendant offered mandatory gifts to the council, which could range from three wampum belts to four thousand porcelain beads.[101] If the reparations satisfied the council, they extended their forgiveness. A 1672 case indicates that this amalgamation of traditional communal institutions, community oversight, and new Christian mores generated some success stories. An accused Wendat alcoholic concluded his remarks to the council by stating:

> My uncles, I beg you to believe that I have not been angry that my Cabin was burned, and that afterward I was compelled to live in the midst of the Fields; for I am convinced that I well deserved such a punishment. And if out of consideration for ... my advocates, you are pleased to grant me mercy, I promise you that I will Never relapse into my past misdeeds. If I do not keep my word, I beg you never have pity on me again."[102]

According to the Jesuits, he never drank again.[103]

Overall, the Wendat used French templates to create social order within Lorette while incorporating them into their own social structures. The most influential governing body was the entire community. The village itself acted as a conduit for unified peer pressure, ensuring conformity. If a transgression took place, all the Lorettans knew about it. From elders to children, everyone participated to some extent, which engendered a sense of shared ownership of the new values and behaviours the Wendat had incorporated.[104] Yet even as the Wendat brought this collective pressure and exclusionary policy to bear on individuals who violated a set of rules that had not existed in their community decades earlier, they did so within centuries-old frameworks of community governance. The communal pressure on the individual linked the policy on drinking and theft to a customary sense of collective responsibility for the individual; the public had to make amends for the individual. If a person committed an offence against someone else, the entire community was equally held responsible.[105]

Continuity

Despite the rigorous guidelines of Lorettan society and their overt need to demonstrate conversion through changes in cultural practices, cultural continuity persisted among the Eastern Wendat. Syncretism between Christian teachings and Wendat traditions, and between French and Wendat social goals allowed for some Wendat customs to remain intact. The most pervasive example of this was the Wendat's continued emphasis on charitable donations, shared property, and community welfare.

Gift giving formed an integral part of Wendat society before the dispersal, and this practice did not desist with the relocation east. Just as the headman Ignace had stated, offerings became essential elements of Wendat demonstrations of Christian devoutness. The community committed considerable energy to collecting gifts for the salvation of Wendat relatives caught in purgatory. This became an obsession among the Lorettans. Many individuals were known to go without food or clothing in order to accumulate items for this cause. In addition, Wendat hunters traded furs for wampum that was held in reserve by the community for this purpose.[106] When the headman Ignace died, his wife gave four thousand wampum beads and a moose skin, explaining this was to ensure "at the earliest moment, my husband's entrance into Paradise."[107] This type of gift giving, although infused with Christian rhetoric, also maintained the Wendat tradition of making presents for the deceased to help them on their journey in the afterlife.

Lorettans embraced charitable donations because they fit Wendat notions of community welfare and the responsibility of leadership. Similar to rituals of property distribution in Wendake, the Wendat continued the tradition of shared land and provisions in the East. Ignace, for instance, received a substantial amount of land when the Wendat left Île d'Orléans. Instead of keeping it for himself, he distributed it among community members, the majority to widows and poor families. Wild game was distributed in a similar fashion after a hunt, and the Wendat shared food freely with one another.[108] If a family was struggling, for instance, a council would direct more stable members of the community to contribute offerings of sustenance for the family. This type of Wendat charity extended to poor French families as well. During a year of particularly bad harvests, for example, one Wendat woman donated ten bushels of corn from her personal reserve to help French families.[109]

Christian missionaries and teachings supported these activities. Jesuits constantly praised the charitable nature of the Lorettans and asserted that the Wendat surpassed the French in terms of their devotion to such causes. Commenting on the actions of a particularly charitable Wendat woman, a Jesuit exclaimed, "It is a pity that this charitable soul has not so much wealth as our great Ladies in France. Ah, how many monasteries and hospitals would she not found! How many thousands of Poor would she not assist!" This same Wendat woman later commented on how Christianity influenced her actions. She asserted that her new faith had shown her more fully the benefits of relinquishing an attachment to the material world. "I no longer envy the rich," she stated, "I rather feel compassion for Them, because they place Their affection in things that are of no use to them after a brief moment of this life."[110]

The Eastern Wendat also incorporated Wendat tradition into Christian rituals. Although perhaps less obvious than the ways in which the Western Wendat mixed Native and Christian customs, the Lorettans practised a similar form of cultural matrix. Funerals provide one of the best examples of this phenomenon. After the death of an individual, a headman of the village took charge of letting the rest of the community know. He then made the arrangements for the burial ceremony. Relatives dressed the deceased in their finest clothing and covered them in a red blanket. Clergy came to view the body and make the appropriate blessings. At the funeral, the headman made a speech and was responsible for distributing three sets of gifts. The first was a large wampum belt given to the church in order to ensure that prayers be made on the departed person's behalf. The second included three to four presents that usually consisted of the belongings of the deceased. These were given in thanks to those people in charge of burying the body. Finally, the last set of gifts was given to the closest relatives of the deceased. Following the gift-giving ceremony, the group laid the body to rest in a grave lined with layers of bark on all sides. An additional layer of bark was placed over the body before it was covered with earth.[111] For the most part this ritual satisfied Christian burial requirements, yet also retained aspects of Wendat custom, such as the distribution of wampum and gifts during the funeral. Further, the bark-layered tomb was not a French custom, but a reflection of Wendat burial practices. These remnants of Wendat culture melded with, rather than contradicted, the Christian nature of a funeral and were therefore endorsed by both the Lorettans and the Jesuits.

The "Holy Savages" of Jeune Lorette, 1697

By the time the Eastern Wendat made their final move to Jeune Lorette in 1697, their community had been transformed. They were no longer the starving, fearful victims of Iroquois raids, but the prosperous and pious Wendat nation of Lorette. Settled on some of the most fertile soil within the French colonies, the Wendat continued to produce crops and cultivate a successful entrepreneurial tradition as canoe, snowshoe, and moccasin manufacturers.[112] In fact, the Jesuits believed "all the other missions of Canada [were] by no means as fruitful as this one."[113] This strict policy of Christianization, orchestrated by both the French and Wendat, helped make the community a success. The Lorettans had ensured by the end of the seventeenth century that the French still saw them as their closest and most loyal Native allies; they retained value in French eyes despite their changing role. To be sure, the Lorettans' main advantage in maintaining a preferred status with the French in comparison to other Native nations was their Christian piety. This was no small feat as Iroquois and Anishinaabe communities began to welcome Jesuit missionaries on a more frequent basis, threatening the Wendat privileged position and resulting in a Wendat need to become not only Christian but the *most* Christian.

The French viewed Christianity in the same light. It was the Jesuits' opinion that religion was the only tie that bound the Natives to the French and without it the relationship would disintegrate, undermining the entire French colonial enterprise. Father Louis d'Avaugour reiterated these circumstances, noting, "Once this link is broken ... all [would be] over for the colony of the French in Canada."[114]

The tactic seems to have worked. Whereas in the west the Wendat became role models in trade, the Eastern Wendat took on the role of spiritual leaders, supported by their Christian reputation. They became the middlemen for the "Frenchification" of other Native targets of French policy, including the Iroquois. Their status as "the holy savages" among French and Native countrymen was one of the reasons the governor solicited Lorettan warriors to be his personal bodyguards and sentinels when out on military expeditions.[115] This honour testified to the prestige of the Lorettans and became an assumed position by the turn of the century. In one instance, the Eastern Wendat received news that the French governor was in the midst of gathering two thousand troops to attack the English. The circumstances were cause for alarm because the Lorettans had not been invited – a transgression in French–Wendat relations. Taking this as a sign of disrespect, and perhaps instigated by an additional internal insecurity over their position with the French, a Wendat headman confronted the Jesuits about the matter. Just as he finished his angry speech about this, a messenger arrived with a personal invitation from the governor to join the war party. This appeased the headman and his fellow Lorettans, and restored their faith in their special place among French and Native allies.[116]

Most importantly, exemplary Christian piety played a pivotal role in the Wendat ability to continuously find and negotiate space for relocation in the vicinity of Quebec City. Since their very first settlement at Île d'Orléans, the Jesuits and their land were the only means by which the Wendat were able to organize villages, create a community, and establish themselves within the region. This relationship was reciprocal. The Wendat received land and maintained their status as privileged French allies while the Jesuits used the Lorettans as a symbol of the success of their missionary work, a testament to the potential for Christian conversion among Native Americans and a source of legitimacy for the Jesuit presence in North America. It was due in large part to the proliferation of Jesuit reports on the subject and the widespread reputation of the Eastern Wendat that Father Vaillant, Superior of the Residence of Montreal, praised Father d'Avaugour for the success of the mission. After affectionately embracing d'Avaugour; Vaillant enthusiastically exclaimed, "My Father, congratulate thyself, for thou hast as many saints as thou hast Hurons at Lorette."[117] There is no indication that Vaillant visited Lorette himself; thus, it was on reputation alone that d'Avaugour and the Lorettans received such high praise.

The Lorettans managed to evade destruction through their dedication to Christianity. By 1701, they were seen as loyal and committed friends to the French, who would protect French interests, and promote French culture for generations to come.

7
Iroquois Country
Wendat Autonomy at Gandougare, Kahnawake, and Ganowarohare

Although the Wendat orchestrated the relocations to the west and east in conjunction with allied nations such as the Anishinaabeg and French, at least two thousand people (or 20 percent of the Wendat population) either chose or were forced to move into Iroquois country in 1650. This exceeded the numbers of Wendat at Michilimackinac and Lorette.[1] In the early stages of the dispersal, most of the Wendat who moved to Iroquois country were war captives or single families who decided to cast their lot with the enemy. As the years progressed, however, large-scale relocations of hundreds and even whole villages took place.

By the mid-1660s, the Iroquois occupied a precarious position. The English conquest of the Dutch colony New Netherland threatened their sources of European weaponry; even though Dutch traders remained in the Hudson River Valley, they no longer enjoyed the regular supplies that had formerly flowed from New Amsterdam (now New York). This made the Iroquois more vulnerable to attacks from the Mohicans, New England Algonquin, and the Susquehannock (who had their own supply of guns). The English colonies represented a potentially formidable counterforce on the Iroquois eastern front. The Iroquois now suffered from the epidemics that had earlier afflicted the Wendat, which restricted their ability to engage in multiple battles at once, as they had done decades earlier in Wendake. These troubles emboldened the newly energized French administration, which had undergone its own process of consolidation and reorganization when New France became a royal province in 1663. In 1665, King Louis XIV decided to address the Iroquois problem by sending twelve hundred veterans of the continental wars to "exterminate the Iroquois."[2]

The adoption of the Wendat into Iroquois society helped the Iroquois deal with these circumstances. The Iroquois viewed Wendat relocations to Iroquois country as a means to "requicken" their population and extend the political league to additional people.[3] Although this strategy included the adoption of other indigenous groups, such as the Anishinaabeg, the

Wendat represented a unique faction. The Iroquois viewed these Nadowek as former kinsmen, or "ancestral people."[4] Wendat adoption appeared, therefore, as a reintegration of brothers and sisters into Iroquois communities. This could, in turn, quell fighting between the Wendat and Iroquois and aid in the war effort on other fronts as Wendat joined their new Iroquois families in future battles against common enemies.[5]

Despite the existence of a general Iroquois perspective on Wendat adoption, the Iroquois did not operate as a single cohesive unit. Just as the separate Wendat nations of the pre-dispersal Confederacy acted as independent entities, so did the Mohawk, Cayuga, Oneida, Onondaga, and Seneca who constituted the Great League of Peace functioned as autonomous polities. This meant that each nation pursued its own efforts to incorporate Wendat in an occasionally disjointed and even violently competitive fashion. The Mohawk urged the Wendat to consider their geopolitical power as keepers of the eastern door to the Iroquois League's metaphorical longhouse, while the Onondaga argued that their location at the centre of Iroquoia was the more advantageous option.[6] An Onondaga headman underscored the differences between Iroquois nations to the French governor, warning that "a careful distinction must be made between nation and nation; that the [Onondaga] were not faithless, like the [Mohawk] Iroquois, – who cherish, deep in their breast, their rancor and bitterness of heart, while their tongues are uttering fair words."[7] Although some scholars suggest this disunity resulted in a tenuous alliance, others contend that the Confederacy's flexible factionalism allowed for a cohesiveness between the Iroquois nations, creating room for independent ambitions as well as common goals.[8] This assessment holds true in terms of Wendat relocation negotiations. The Iroquois were united in aspirations to adopt the Wendat, yet they acted as separate interest groups in their attempts to acquire them.

The Wendat were very aware of the pan-Iroquois desire to incorporate them into their society, and of the other changing geopolitical realities of the region. In 1650, for instance, the Wendat at Gahoendoe were approached by the Iroquois to "take refuge" and "be but one people."[9] Similar invitations to "inhabit but one land" were made in 1653 by the Mohawk, and in 1656 the Oneida declared that the Wendat and Iroquois should be "one cabin and one country."[10] This type of discourse dominated Iroquois–Wendat diplomacy throughout the 1650s and '60s. The Iroquois consistently asserted they would "put a mat in [their] Cabin for [the Wendat];" they emphasized unity and friendly reception in between bouts of violence to convince the Wendat to join, rather than fight, the Iroquois.[11] This incessant pressure ceased only when large numbers of the Eastern Wendat agreed to move to Iroquois country in the middle of the decade.

Scholars speculate that Wendat motivations for relocation to Iroquois country came from a desire to reconnect with Wendat kin who were already among the Iroquois and wished to maintain their culture and traditions. The basis for this interpretation is the ethnic similarities between these two groups, in contrast to the Anishinaabeg or French. Similar in lifestyle, cosmology, and governance, the adopted Wendat could remain culturally Nadowekian to some extent while experiencing "cultural corrosion" as they assimilated into Iroquois society.[12] Certainly, this was the reality for many Wendat, especially those who relocated in small numbers or were taken captive.[13] Yet, assimilation was not always the rule; in fact, the Wendat experiences in the Iroquois villages of Gandougare, Kahnawake, and Ganowarohare suggest that Wendat strategies among the Iroquois differed very little from those they pursued at Michilimackinac and Lorette. Rather than being absorbed into Iroquois communities, they acculturated, and maintained their autonomy by establishing separate villages, retaining unique leadership roles, and adopting Christian rituals to differentiate themselves from their Iroquois hosts. The Iroquois accepted this compromise because they viewed it as a means to appease Wendat requests for autonomy as well as a way to entice Jesuit priests to the community and gain access to French trade networks.[14] It may have also been a way for the Iroquois to distract the Wendat and French from their Anishinaabe allies, who continued to launch successful raids on Iroquois villages in the 1660s.[15] Ultimately, this strategy allowed the Wendat to remain Wendat rather than Iroquois during the seventeenth century.

Iroquois Persuasion

By mid-century, the Iroquois pursued an aggressive military campaign against the Wendat. Their ability to conquer village after village and capture thousands of Wendat during this period served a dual purpose of not only dispersing the Wendat but also incorporating them into their polity. This strategy did not desist with the 1649 victories in Wendake. The Iroquois pursued Wendat both east and west. Despite their distance from the Iroquois homeland, Michilimackinac became another site of bloody conflict. After only a few years of refuge, the Iroquois attacked the Wendat in their settlement on Mackinac Island.[16] There is very little known about this battle, but considering the timing of the conflict (only a few years after the dispersal from Wendake) the Iroquois likely sought the acquisition of captives and potential adoptees.

A Mohawk victory against the Eastern Wendat at Île d'Orléans in 1656 was a more overt attempt to force the Wendat to integrate. The invasion of the island signalled to the Wendat that if they did not choose to go with the Iroquois voluntarily, they would be forced militarily.[17] The tactic worked; survivors reconsidered their initial refusal to join the Iroquois and subsequent discussions of relocation ensued.

Diplomacy was key to Iroquois persuasion. Although warfare gained compulsory adoptees, preferably, the Wendat would join the Iroquois of their own accord. Iroquois diplomats delivered numerous speeches and presented a number of valuable gifts to entice the Wendat. The Mohawk tried to make amends for the actions at Île d'Orléans, and sent a delegation of thirty Iroquois to Quebec to meet with the Wendat. On this occasion, an Iroquois headman spoke to the Wendat in the following way:

> My brother, it is to thee that my words are addressed. Four years ago, thou didst beg me to take thee by the arm, to raise thee to my country; thou didst sometimes withdraw it when I wished to comply with thy request; that is why I struck thee on the head with my hatchet.[18]

The Iroquois justified the 1656 attack on the grounds that the Wendat had betrayed them by promising to move to Iroquoia four years earlier, but then refusing to leave once settled at Île d'Orléans. Warfare represented the Iroquois solution to this rift in Wendat–Iroquois relations. It demonstrated that if the Wendat did not follow through on their promises, the Iroquois had the means to make them do as they wished. At the same time, the speech also indicated Iroquois desires for an amicable resolution. It was not that the Iroquois wanted to fight the Wendat, but rather that they were forced to fight because of the actions of the Wendat. The Iroquois headman continued:

> Withdraw it no more; for I tell thee in earnest to get up. It is time for thee to come ... Fear not; I no longer look upon thee as an enemy, but as my relative; thou shalt be cherished by my country, which shall also be thine.[19]

The dialogue here was meant to be both convincing and sincere. The headman asked the Wendat to forget past conflicts and see Iroquois country as a place of refuge and security. He assured them that the Iroquois would welcome their relocation, and that their people would be treated well. The Oneida made similar speeches that drew upon the common Nadowek cultural heritage between the Wendat and Iroquois. An Oneida ambassador argued:

> I take thee by the arm to lead thee away. Thou knowest, thou huron, that formerly we comprised but one Cabin and one country. I know not by what accident we became separated. It is time to unite again ... I put a mat in my Cabin for thee. I give thee some land for raising Indian corn ... I lift thee from the ground.[20]

In this case, the Oneida asked the Wendat to remember the compatible Nadowek traditions that might serve as a bond between the two groups. They maintained that the Wendat would not only be welcome among the Iroquois but also given land to raise crops. Overall, the Oneida's reference to "lift thee from the ground" demonstrates their belief that this type of agreement was a means to help the Wendat recover from their losses and rejuvenate the population.

Gifts were another traditional tactic the Iroquois used to persuade the Wendat to join them. Presents usually consisted of wampum belts and beaver skins and formed a collection of gifts, each with their own symbolic meaning. The Oneida, for instance, delivered a series of seven presents to the Wendat in their 1655 negotiations for removal. The ceremonial presentation struck customary notes of metaphorical rhetoric. To begin, the Iroquois headman invoked the sun "as a faithful witness of the sincerity of his intentions, and as a torch that banished the night and the darkness from his heart, to let in a veritable light upon his words."[21] He then gave out his gifts, designed to make amends for past acts of aggression against the Wendat and their allies. His explanations were as follows:

> The first one was given to wipe away the tears that are commonly shed upon hearing of the brave warriors killed in battle. The second was intended to serve as a pleasant draught to counteract whatever of bitterness might remain in the hearts of the French, because of the death of their people. The third was to furnish a piece of bark, or a blanket, to put over the dead, for fear the sight of them might renew the old-time dissensions. The fourth was to bury the dead and tread down the earth very hard over their graves, in order that

> nothing might ever issue from their tombs that could sadden their relatives, and arouse any feeling of revenge in their bosoms. The fifth was to serve as a wrapping for packing away the implements of war so securely that they would never be touched again in the future. The sixth, to make clear the river, stained with so much blood. The last, to exhort the Hurons to accept whatever decision Onontio the great Captain of the French, should choose to make concerning peace.[22]

These gifts emphasized the need for the Wendat and Iroquois to move beyond their past conflicts and resolve to make peace. For the Iroquois, this meant a relocation of Wendat to their country. The last present's reference to Onontio, or the governor of New France, also demonstrates the important role the French played in these negotiations. French officials often attended these councils and took part in rituals, as did Anishinaabe diplomats. Thus, the Iroquois understood the significance of the relationship between the Wendat and their allies and made sure to include them in their diplomatic discussions.

Kinship played a major role in the ability of Iroquois spokesmen to convince the Wendat to join them. The Wendat experience of migration coupled with the loss of captives among the Iroquois meant that many families experienced painful separation and the loss of powerful kin networks. The Iroquois invitation to settle within Iroquois country gave the Wendat an opportunity to reconnect with kinsmen. Although this topic was never really broached directly by the Iroquois in discussions, it was common knowledge and many Wendat would have added this to their reasons to be persuaded by the Iroquois.[23]

Wendat Reservations

Despite the skillful diplomacy of Iroquois ambassadors, many Wendat remained skeptical of relocations to Iroquois country. Several Wendat headmen voiced their opinions on the matter, demonstrating that the Iroquois were still perceived as the enemy and untrustworthy. One Wendat man, named Aaoueate, encountered an Iroquois war party that gave him news of peace negotiations between the Wendat and Iroquois at Quebec. Aaoueate felt confused by their overtures and reacted defensively, but the Iroquois tried to assure him: "Thou art neither a captive nor in danger of death, ... thou art in the midst of thy brothers." The Wendat responded, "You are faithless rogues, ... your hearts are full of venom, and your minds of knavishness; if you talk of peace, it is only to employ a treachery more baleful both for us and for the French."[24]

A Wendat headman at Quebec expressed similar sentiments. He participated in the negotiations and heard the Iroquois promises of respect and sincerity, yet he refused to believe them; he perceived the journey to Iroquois country as a river "bristling with long and great teeth," believing he "would put [himself] in danger of being bitten" were he to leave with them.[25] Certainly, the idea of making a long and isolated journey to join a former enemy would have daunted even the most committed Wendat. Some tried to address this issue by suggesting they travel with a French escort. When the Iroquois resisted this Wendat strategy, the Wendat replied it was not reasonable for them to embark in a war canoe (an Iroquois canoe), and that they must wait for a peace canoe (canoes escorted by the French). If this was permitted, they assured the Iroquois: "From that moment I am at your disposal."[26]

The reluctance of the Wendat to accept Iroquois invitations arose from personal intuition as well as past incidents that pointed to an Iroquois plot to break their promises of friendship. The Wendat recalled, for instance, the death of thirty-four Iroquois on Gahoendoe Island who had tried to fix a similar invitation to Iroquois country. In the end, the true nature of the Iroquois and their desire to wage war on the Wendat came to light. The Wendat also remembered a potential Mohawk plot to avenge the murder of their headman Torontisati at Trois-Rivières two years before. Given these precedents, many Wendat believed the current negotiations at Quebec seemed like yet another scheme to obtain revenge for the Wendat foiling former Iroquois plans to wage war.[27]

The rivalry between the Onondaga and Mohawk to attain Wendat refugees presented another set of challenges. On the one hand, the Wendat did not want to create any friction between the two Iroquois nations, yet groups lobbied the Wendat to join them in their respective villages. By choosing one over the other, the Wendat would create animosity, but if they chose both, they would be forced to split up their community even further. Refusing the offers outright was not an option. According to the Wendat, the Iroquois' "hope, being disappointed, [would] turn to despair, and, seeing themselves both alike deceived, they [would] conspire to effect our ruin." As the Wendat saw it, there was no winning; leaders summarized their situation by stating, "We see plainly ... that those two Iroquois nations, in spirit of mutual envy, wish to win us each to its own side. Whatever plan we adopt, we are equally confronted with misfortune."[28]

Wendat Refusals

These concerns led some Wendat, both individuals and groups, to reject Iroquois overtures. The headman who did not want to get "bitten" by the journey to Iroquois country refused to join any expedition of that nature, stating if he ever did agree to relocate "it would be for another time."[29] Similarly, the majority of Eastern Wendat, who identified as the People of the Cord, agreed almost unanimously that they would not leave Quebec and wished to remain close to the French. This resolution met with serious consideration and influenced discussion among the rest of the Eastern Wendat. Despite Iroquois initiatives, councils, and Wendat pressure, the Cord refused to change their minds. The Wendat leader whom the French called Le Plat delivered the resolution publicly. A headman from the Bear nation offered an explanation to the French and Iroquois. According to this leader, he considered those who remained at Quebec "better than I am."[30] Putting this into context, it may not have been that the Cord were really seen as "better" than those leaving with the Iroquois, but rather it was important that the French perceive the remaining Wendat as superior, thus ensuring a French desire to have them remain. Put another way, the Cord's refusal to join the Iroquois became a diplomatic manoeuvre to gain favour with the French and demonstrate that at least a portion of the Wendat would not abandon the French for the Iroquois.

The Western Wendat also made a collective decision to avoid the Iroquois and their attempts at incorporation. The nature of Iroquois–Wendat relations in the West was based less on skillful diplomacy and more on military might and strategy. Thus, when the Iroquois attacked the Wendat at Michilimackinac in an attempt to try to persuade them to surrender and move east, the Western Wendat responded with a military offensive, as a way of expressing their rejection of Iroquois adoption.[31] When the conflict ended, the Western Wendat did not engage in negotiations with their enemies; rather, this group decided to move farther west, to evade similar incursions from the Iroquois. This successful removal essentially shut the door on further Iroquois campaigns of this nature in the West, while simultaneously putting more pressure on the Iroquois to conduct successful negotiations in the East.

Wendat Acceptance

In the end, many Wendat succumbed to Iroquois tactics and agreed to a so-called "voluntary defection" to Iroquois country.[32] The terms of removal were not merely an Iroquoian construction, however; the Wendat made demands that shaped the process and nature of resettlement. Those who chose to live among the Seneca demanded that the Iroquois incorporate large numbers of both the Deer and Rock people in such a fashion that would allow them to live with each other and distinguish themselves from other Iroquois villages.[33] In addition, the Wendat asked the Seneca to agree to wage war on the Mohawk. The Seneca agreed to create a village for the Wendat and discuss the Mohawk attack further. They also offered to send a canoe with Wendat and Seneca representatives to Quebec City to inquire into the extent to which the French might support a military campaign against the Mohawk.[34]

The Wendat made similar demands in terms of removal to Onondaga and Mohawk territory. Members of the Bear nation desired to relocate among the Mohawk, while the Rock would join the Onondaga. The Wendat asserted these moves were only possible if the French agreed to support them and protect the remaining Wendat in Quebec, and reiterated that the Jesuits needed to accompany them to Iroquois country and install missions among them.[35] The Wendat did not agree to an immediate relocation as the Iroquois requested, but would wait until there were French boats available at Montreal to take them to Iroquois country. In the words of a Bear nation headman, the Wendat would congregate in Montreal and "as soon as some Canoes belonging to the French who are in [Iroquois] country come down here, I am at [the Iroquois'] service, and [they] mayst take me wherever [they will]."[36] Finally, the Wendat decided they would send Atsena, a headman of the Bear nation, ahead with a number of Iroquois, as a test of the extent of Iroquois friendship. Atsena outlined this strategy to the Iroquois: "It is decided; I am at thy service. I cast myself, with my eyes shut, into thy Canoe, without knowing what I am doing ... I do not wish my cousins of the two other Nations to embark this time with me, in order that they may first see how thou wilt behave toward me."[37]

French support was crucial to these negotiations. French authorities viewed hostilities with the Iroquois as the biggest impediment to the success of New France. Jean Talon, the first Intendant of New France, explained that peace with the Iroquois was the only way the colony could begin to prosper.[38] French administrators sanctioned Wendat requests to have Frenchmen and missionaries accompany them to Iroquois country because of this belief. They agreed to send Jesuits as safeguards or hostages, hoping to dissuade future Iroquois attacks on French settlements.[39] The Jesuits viewed the initiative as a means to gain access to other Native groups, while governor Pierre Dubois d'Avaugour believed it would appease the Iroquois so they would remain loyal in future wars with the English.[40] Both groups perceived the proposed move as providential.[41]

Preparations began once the terms of removal were agreed upon. During the day, the Wendat and Iroquois arranged their canoes and personal belongings, while at night the Wendat hosted farewell feasts that included the French, Iroquois, and Anishinaabe nations. One of the main purposes of the feasts was to provide a public forum for Wendat farewell speeches, the majority of which were directed at the Iroquois and French. In one case, a headman beseeched the Iroquois to take good care of his close friend Atsena. He gave the Iroquois gifts in order to ensure that Atsena "not fall into the Mud in disembarking." He continued:

> Here is a collar to make the earth firm where he will set foot on it. When he disembarks, do not allow him to sit on the bare ground; here is something wherewith to make a Mat for him on which he may rest. And, that thou mayst not laugh at the women and children when they weep at seeing themselves in a strange country, here is a handkerchief that I give thee to wipe away their tears, and the sweat from their brows.[42]

On another occasion a headman (probably Atsena) addressed the governor and Jesuits who remained at Quebec.[43] He was obviously reluctant to leave, yet his words express a determination to fulfill his end of the Iroquois bargain. "I leave you," he began, "it is true; but my heart does not leave you. I am going away, it is true; but I leave my cousins, who are better than I am. And, to show you that Québec is ever in my country, I leave you the large kettle, which we use in our greatest rejoicings."[44] This ceremonial kettle was both a material and symbolic gesture of Atsena's desire to maintain relations and a connection to the land and people of Quebec. The kettle represented the Bear nation, unity, and a desire to return for future feasts between the French and Wendat. The kettle also served as a material reminder to the French that the Wendat who relocated to the Iroquois had once lived among them and would continue their close relationship with them as in times past.

Farewell feasts served as a final Wendat attempt to control the ways in which the removals took place. They included celebrations, a meeting ground, and a forum for speeches and appeals. Gifts were exchanged to remind participants, and in particular the Iroquois and French, of Wendat expectations for the future. The removal was not an abandonment of the

French or an inevitable assimilation into Iroquois society. The Wendat believed this relocation was a geopolitical move that would benefit their community as a whole in stopping Iroquois hostilities and appeasing French desires for peace.

Gandougare

In 1651, approximately nine hundred to twelve hundred Wendat joined the Seneca at their village of Gandougare.[45] As the most populous of the Iroquois nations, the Seneca had led the decisive attacks of 1649 in Wendake and represented the majority of the warriors during those battles. It is for this reason that they took charge of the first large-scale adoption of Wendat.[46] For the most part, while there were also Wendat from other villages, the refugee population at Gandougare was comprised of both the Deer and Rock nations, who came from the villages of Scanonaenrat and Contarea in Wendake.[47] By 1672, there were at least two hundred families, or two thousand people living there.[48] Gandougare was unique in that it was made up of three autonomous enclaves of non-Seneca people, although situated within Seneca territory. Despite their common Nadowek heritage, the towns were divided along ethnic lines. The first town was made up of the Onnontioga, the second of the Neutral, and the third of the Wendat.[49] A French presence was not felt until 1669, when the Jesuits established a permanent mission at Gandougare. The Wendat at Gandougare were both Christians and traditionalists. When Father Jacques Frémin arrived over ten years after the Wendat initial relocation, he found only forty converted Wendat adults within the village.[50] Over the summer of 1672, thirty-three children and twelve adults were baptized, thus indicating a large number of non-Christians within the community but simultaneously a shift towards conversion after the establishment of the mission.[51]

The Wendat and Seneca lived in peace at Gandougare. The Wendat continued in "Huron style."[52] For the most part, scholars argue that the Wendat of Gandougare retained their identity and traditional mode of life for the latter half of the century.[53] However, this interpretation fails to specify what "traditional" meant at the time of relocation; in 1649, the Wendat had already experienced numerous cultural transformations due to epidemics and warfare, and Christianity had changed the social dynamics of Wendake. Scanonaenrat and Contarea were both villages that had missions (St. Michel and St. Jean Baptiste), so the Wendat of Gandougare, although not entirely Christian, had nonetheless been exposed to European and Christian teachings during the pre-dispersal period. An examination of the actions of those Wendat living within the Seneca village reveals that they functioned as an acculturated people; they maintained Wendat customs while rivalling the Lorettans in terms of Christian conduct and piety. Notwithstanding their continued practice of Wendat customs, and particularly their curing rituals, these Wendat simultaneously created a new identity as Native Christians.[54] This was so widespread that the Seneca and other Native groups in the area referred to them as "The Believers" or "The Faithful."[55] This reputation created a unique position for the Wendat within Iroquois country, as the Iroquois, Onnontioga, and Neutral were less familiar with Christianity.[56]

Considering that the Gandougarians had little contact with Jesuits from the time of their removal to 1669, the preservation of Christian teachings was a significant achievement. It indicates there were Christians who deemed it important to keep the faith throughout this period. They continued to pray among themselves, despite criticism from non-Christians, and discussed the teachings of the missionaries from Wendake without the guidance of a priest.[57] One of the community's oldest Christians proved the extent of his memory and devotion to Christianity by reciting all the prayers by heart for those Wendat who would listen, essentially acting as an interim priest.[58] The Jesuits were so impressed with this performance once they arrived that they asked him to act as an Officer of the Faith and teach the congregation in the Wendat language at Sunday Mass.[59]

With the establishment of the mission, the Gandougarian Wendat re-engaged with the European and Christian world. They embraced the opportunity and welcomed the Jesuits in earnest. This friendly policy became more and more popular as the years progressed. Wendat elders supported the attitude, in stark contrast to the circumstances that had earlier prevailed in Wendake. Father Frémin observed, "Even the old people, who had despised the light of the Gospel while their country was flourishing, now anxiously sought it, and earnestly asked for Baptism."[60]

The younger generations looked for guidance and information concerning Catholicism from their elders.[61] François Tehoronhiongo was one of these elders. Tehoronhiongo was originally from Ossossane and received his Christian education from Father Simon Le Moyne. During his twenty-seven years at Gandougare, he continued his prayers on a daily basis, and also conducted prayer sessions specifically geared towards a request to have the Jesuits live among the Seneca. Tehoronhiongo was especially anxious that he might die without receiving the proper sacraments. When he heard the Jesuits had arrived at Gandougare, he welcomed them, saying, "At last God has heard my prayer, hear my Confession."[62] This man was responsible for the conversion and instruction of his wife and children; he also organized meetings of both Christians and non-Christians to discuss Catholicism. These meetings focused mostly on the New Testament, which he was particularly fond of.[63] Through such respected intermediaries, the Wendat continued to engage with Christianity on a frequent basis.

Rather than dividing the society as it had before 1650, Christianity in these new settings fostered a sense of community and culture unique to the Gandougarian Wendat. Tehoronhiongo's children grew up hearing about the Bible, and they in turn passed on that knowledge to their friends. It was common practice for Wendat Christian youth to encourage their friends to attend sermons and visit the Jesuits. Many children gave in to this peer pressure, which led to their non-Christian parents attending as well.[64] The result of this tactic was an increase in conversions among the Wendat, including both old and young portions of the population.

Certain events also encouraged the Wendat to convert. In 1672, for instance, a prominent Christian elder received notice that his only son had been killed in battle. The elder was devastated, but kept no secret that he found solace in prayer and justified the death as God's will. Days later, new information came that his son had survived his wounds and was being carried back to the village by his comrades. The entire village went to the elder's house to see for themselves. After this incident, many villagers saw the elder and his family as an example of the power of the Christian faith, as well as models of loyalty and virtue for the community.[65]

Christianity offered psychological comfort and coping mechanisms for Gandougarian Wendat still traumatized by the events of the previous decades. Many Wendat families had lost loved ones from the wars and famine and many of the deceased were baptized. Prayer brought hope to those who survived that they might rejoin their family members in the afterlife. This was most certainly the case with Tehoronhiongo, as most of his family had died as Christians. When he was asked how he was able to deal with these losses, he replied, "Why should I mourn them? My mother died immediately after Baptism, Almost all my nearest kin expired in the arms of the Fathers who had made them Christians; they are all happy in Paradise, and I hope soon to go and find them." His only living child was currently at war, but Tehoronhiongo believed his son would be fine if he died, because the priest gave him confession before he left.[66]

The Christian nature of Gandougarians evolved from the informal teachings of elders to the systematic adoption of Christian customs throughout the village. After the missionaries arrived, the Wendat frequently attended Mass and requested meetings with the Jesuits.[67] They also adopted Christian marriage customs. This included refraining from premarital sex, an aversion to divorce, and guarding young girls more closely, since their Christian virtue became a major priority to ensure successful marriages.[68] This last innovation is more significant in light of the fact that these Wendat unions were between two Native people. Unlike Christian marriages in the west and east that involved Wendat women and French men, Natives entered Christian marriages at Gandougare by choice, not out of a need to appease a French spouse.

The community at Gandougare was perceived as just as pious as their Wendat kin at Île d'Orléans.[69] This was a new development as far as Wendat customs were concerned. The Wendat relocation to Seneca country predates the Wendat removal east and the policy of Christian conformity at Lorette. Thus, Christianity was a key factor shaping Wendat dispersal strategies from the very beginning, whether west, east, or among the Iroquois. Beginning in Wendake, Wendat Gandougarians retained Christian traditions as well as Wendat ones throughout their relocation. This allowed them to maintain their group identity and differentiate themselves from their Seneca hosts and other Nadowek refugees in the area.

Kahnawake

Because segregated Wendat villages like Gandougare were not typical features among the other Iroquois nations, Christianity continued to play a role in the ability of the Wendat to avoid immediate assimilation in more integrated communities. Jesuits considered the predominantly Mohawk village of Kahnawake as a place where "the faith was embraced with more constancy, and there Christian courage manifests itself more strikingly, than in any other place." They viewed it as the "first and Principal mission" among the Mohawk.[70] This reputation arose from the community's overt support for Christian teachings, a reality shaped by missionaries and a Wendat refugee population.

Kahnawake, originally called Kentaké, began as a mixed community of Iroquois and French settlers near Montreal. The amicable relations between these groups and its close proximity to Montreal created a strategic centre for trade as well as a buffer zone between the French population and Iroquoia. By 1667, the Native population had diversified; only one-third was Iroquois and the remaining two-thirds were Wendat and Anishnaabe refugees.[71] Out of these numbers, about 240 to 320 people were

Wendat.[72] In 1673, the Iroquois leader Kryn led approximately two hundred Mohawk to the village, which gave the community an overtly Mohawk identity from that point forward.[73] Soon after Kryn's immigration, Jesuits became frustrated with the lack of conversions despite the mingling of Native and non-Native populations, and in 1676 they persuaded the Native population to segregate themselves and relocate a few kilometres west.[74]

Within the Wendat population, there were many who had received baptism before their dispersal and remembered the teachings of Father Jean de Brébeuf and other missionaries who resided in Wendake. This contingent received the first Jesuits at Kahnawake. The missionaries sought out the Wendat, requesting an opportunity to meet with them in private and separate from the other villagers. Almost immediately, the Wendat congregated in a longhouse and were subjected to a lengthy appeal from the Jesuits to help them spread Christianity to their Mohawk hosts. It is unclear how the Wendat responded, but if the Christian character of the village that developed in the following years is any indication, it seems the Wendat took up the task.[75]

The conversion process of a twenty-five-year-old Iroquois woman demonstrates the extent of Wendat influence on the community and their pivotal role as evangelists. During one of the Jesuit visits, this woman asked if she could stay and listen to the teachings normally reserved for the Christian Wendat. The group welcomed her, and after subsequent visits she expressed a desire for baptism. The Jesuits, however, planned to travel to another village and left before any such act could be accomplished. After two weeks, the woman visited the missionaries at a neighbouring village and requested baptism again. The Jesuits remained unconvinced she had received all the required teachings, but the woman explained that a Wendat woman had educated her about Christianity. She then recited the prayers and principal rites she had learned. Still skeptical, the Jesuits returned to Kahnawake and approached the Wendat community and in particular the woman who had taught the Iroquois. They questioned the young woman's Christian conduct while the Jesuits had been away. The Wendat assured the missionaries that not only had the Iroquois woman practised her daily prayers both day and night, she had also prolifically articulated her devotion to others within the community. Convinced, the Jesuits baptized the woman.[76]

It is likely that this was not an isolated case, but rather an indication of a patterned process that began in earnest with the establishment of a mission in the area. Much like those at Gandougare, the Wendat at Kahnawake preserved Christianity in the years before the Jesuits arrived. In the end, it seems the strategy proved beneficial because they assumed the role of Christian educators and leaders within the village. The Wendat from Lorette heard of their kin's success and sent a wampum belt acknowledging the importance of the community to the spread of Christianity. Their message encouraged Kahnawakians to continue to embrace Roman Catholicism.[77]

Lorettans and Jesuits viewed Kahnawake as *the* example of missionary success in Iroquois country, yet its Christian character was but a means to an end for the Iroquois themselves. The concerns of French civilians who feared the close settlement of potentially aggressive Native populations were assuaged, or at least balanced. Certainly, the Mohawk and other Natives who came to Kahnawake did so for complex reasons beyond access to Christian teaching: Iroquois had access to the French and their trade networks through the missions. Kahnawake furthered this strategy because of its proximity to Montreal and its status of liaison between the French and the English at Albany. One scholar describes this as a "peaceful response to colonization," suggesting friendship, while at the same time staking a rival claim to the St. Lawrence trade.[78] Scholar Gerald Alfred, a Mohawk from present-day Kahnawake, argues that this gave Kahnawakians a quasi-autonomous status in the colonial balance of power. According to Alfred, "they were compelled to develop a fiercely independent ideology because of their precarious position on the geographic and cultural margin of both their traditional culture group and Euro-American society."[79] Despite Kahnawake's isolation from their homeland and seemingly autonomous nature, non-mission Iroquois viewed it as integral to the Confederacy. They saw it as a "listening post" for news, goods, and people.[80] As a result, Kahnawake gained a powerfully unique position among Natives and non-Natives alike. In 1701, for instance, notwithstanding imperial policies that forbade trade between French and English colonies, a secret agreement (the Schuyler-Callières Agreement) was signed allowing the safe passage of Kahnawakians between New York and Canada.[81] A key factor to the success of this community was their Christian character. Although rooted in Iroquois desires to expand their geopolitical and economic influence, as well as Jesuit hopes for Iroquois conversions, neither of these goals would have been possible without the relocation of the Christian Wendat to Kahnawake.

Ganowarohare

Not all the Wendat were incorporated into villages that endorsed Christianity to the extent of Gandougare and Kahnawake. For many Iroquois, conversion incited cultural corrosion and a European conquest of their lifestyle. Indeed, resistance to baptism had been a consistent strategy for most Iroquois in the seventeenth century.[82] Despite these overt rejections of the Christian practices, Christianity continued to play a role in Wendat attempts to preserve their autonomy. The Oneida village of Ganowarohare provides an example. Comprised of both Wendat and Iroquois, villagers at Ganowarohare shared residence and for all intents and purposes acted as one collective community. One of the ways that Ganowaroharians became more interrelated was through marriage, which resulted in a significant number of children who identified as both Oneida and Wendat.[83]

Although Jesuits had been present since 1667, the Wendat and Oneida hesitated to adopt Christian practices in their entirety. Whereas at Gandougare there were up to forty-five baptisms per month and Christian conduct was coveted, Ganowarohare baptisms averaged fifteen per month and these did not necessarily lead to a pious life.[84] Father Jacques Bruyas complained, for instance, that out of all the adults he baptized not one of them had entered into a Christian marriage.[85] Ganowaroharians also refused to adhere to Christian rules concerning premarital sex and divorce.[86] Although Father Bruyas mentioned the existence of polygamy (and his abhorrence for it), it is unlikely this was what he witnessed. Rather, both the Wendat and Oneida came from a Nadowek tradition that encouraged young people to explore various relationships before dedicating themselves to one person. After children were born, however, most parents entered into a monogamous relationship for life.[87]

Ganowaroharians also struggled with alcoholism. In contrast to the extreme rejection of alcohol consumption at Lorette, these villagers frequently indulged in bouts of drunkenness that resulted in numerous violent acts. To the Jesuits' disapproval, their fellow citizens treated neither action as a severe offence.[88] In some cases, conflicts led to murder, which could have led to devastating blood feuds, but these transgressions were eventually forgiven. One Ganowaroharian justified this policy after murdering a fellow neighbour by saying, "What wouldst thou have me do? I had no sense, I was Drunk."[89]

The Jesuits saw the frequent intoxication and lack of Christian marriages as the foremost impediments to full conversions within the community. Indeed, these factors indicated a resistance to adopting French customs in the latter half of the seventeenth century. Yet, there was a small contingent of Wendat, and perhaps their offspring, who continued to identify as Christians throughout this period. Jesuits made mention of the conversion of Wendat children whose parents had been baptized in pre-dispersal Wendake.[90] In addition, the practice of intermarriage between the Wendat and Oneida may have converted more Ganowaroharians than the records indicate.

It makes sense that the Wendat continued to use these conversions as a means to create unique relationships with the French and remind them of their continued loyalty, thereby differentiating themselves from the Iroquois. At the same time, they needed to appease their hosts and did so by maintaining Nadowek traditions of marriage and ignoring Jesuit requests for abstinence and sobriety. This tactic ensured both autonomy and amity at Ganowarohare.

Foreign Relations

The Wendat removal to Iroquois country changed not only Wendat lives but also the politics of the region. Through this process the Wendat recast themselves as middlemen, becoming essential to French–Iroquois relations. As Christians, the Wendat fostered close ties with the Jesuits and the French colonial administration. Both the Iroquois and missionaries took advantage of this. Before the Wendat moved to Iroquois country, the French were as unwilling as the Wendat to send people to engage with the Iroquois. Yet, the French needed envoys to the Iroquois for effective diplomacy. Governor Jean de Lauzon commented on the irony of the French position in 1650: "It was necessary to perish in order to not perish; and to expose oneself to dangers of all kinds, in order to avoid all dangers."[91] This anxiety eased to some extent when the Wendat relocated to Iroquoia. Jesuits found comfort and security among the Wendat, especially in communities disinclined to welcome the French. A missionary related his personal experience as he ventured to Iroquois country: "Except for our good Christian Hurons, who were my only refuge, I met with nothing but a cold reception everywhere."[92] This explains the missionaries' actions at Kahnawake, and their immediate need to convene with the Wendat when they arrived. The Wendat were seen as allies and could help in smoothing out potential conflicts that might arise from the initial presence of French men within these communities.

The Wendat also influenced their hosts. The Iroquois communities encountered Christian teachings through their Wendat adoptees, which set the stage for further Wendat leadership roles when missions were established later on. Iroquois conversions were thus a result of combined efforts by the Wendat and Jesuits to persuade the Iroquois towards baptism. In essence, the French privileged the Christian Wendat and depended on them to further their initiatives in Iroquois country.

French favouritism towards the Wendat did not go unnoticed by their Iroquois hosts. This was one of the main reasons the Iroquois began to convert in the first place. In the negotiations for removal the Iroquois presented a wampum belt to the French explaining they wished the Jesuits to join the Wendat in Iroquois country and "build a new Sainte Marie [mission], like that whose prosperity [they] formerly witnessed in the heart of the Huron country."[93] Well aware of the advantage the Wendat possessed, their invitation to the Jesuits was a way to even the playing field in terms of French relations. Still, the Wendat reputation was not easily usurped. René Cuillerier, a French captive among the Iroquois, said, "Out of all the nations we [the French] have in this country, it is the huron who continue to surpass in spirit."[94] At Gandougare, the Seneca complained to the Jesuits that they "[preferred] the hurons to Them." This led to a persistent campaign on the part of the Seneca to get the Jesuits to write to their superior for additional missionaries, a strategy employed to prove themselves just as devout Christians as the Wendat.[95]

The Wendat relocations brought communication between the French and Iroquois to a new level, and helped foster peace initiatives between both groups. When the Iroquois approached the French in 1653 to discuss a truce, contemporaries viewed the proposal as a Seneca invention. Significantly, this shift in Seneca policy came after the Wendat of Gandougare established themselves among the Seneca for two years;[96] thus, it is not beyond reason to speculate that the Wendat played a role in this endeavour. As for the French, Seneca demonstrations of amicable Wendat relations would have only strengthened the Seneca appeal to the European allies of the Wendat during this time. Thus, the migration of hundreds of Wendat to Iroquois country had a fundamental impact on international relations, shaping not only Wendat foreign affairs but also Iroquois–French interaction.

Conclusion

For many Wendat, removal to Iroquois country proved daunting. For years the Wendat and Iroquois had a tumultuous and violent relationship, rife with abuse and mistrust. In the wake of the dispersal and compounded by incessant Iroquois persuasion tactics, Wendat reactions varied. Those in the west avoided invitations by moving out of reach of Iroquois expeditions, while the Eastern Wendat faced extreme geopolitical pressure and had little choice but to succumb, at least partially, to Iroquois demands. Still, they managed to shape their relocation in ways that preserved important elements of their culture. Aware of their precarious state, the Wendat created a secure and autonomous experience. The French were a major component to this strategy, and so Wendat strategy often involved a shift towards Christian conversion.

The majority of Wendat in Iroquois country were not necessarily Christian when they arrived, but developed their Christian practices in the aftermath of relocation. The converted Wendat evoked pre-dispersal knowledge of the Catholic faith on their own initiative, hoping that the French would recognize their devotion and take particular interest in them. Moreover, by adopting a Christian character, either overtly such as at Gandougare and Kahnawake, or less obviously such as at Ganowarohare, the Wendat differentiated themselves as a unique portion of the Iroquois population. This situation was similar to the experiences at Michilimackinac and Lorette. The Wendat communities consistently retained traditional Wendat customs while recognizing the advantages of cultural compromise and conformity in terms of Christian conversion and French alliance making. Christianity was a diplomatic power source for these Wendat as well as a coping mechanism to help them overcome the obstacles resulting from their dispersal.

A Wendat elder explained the nuanced perspective of Christian Wendat survivors. At ninety years old, this eastern leader had significant perspective on the circumstances at hand. He was in his fifties when the epidemics swept through Wendake; he had perhaps even observed the deaths of Taretande and Aenon. A decade later, he witnessed the emergence of war chiefs in civil affairs and an increase in Iroquois attacks. By the time of the dispersal he was seventy years old and a potential impediment to effective migrations stretching from Wendake to Gahoendoe and beyond Anishinaabe villages to the east. Despite these obstacles, he managed to survive and witnessed the complex negotiations of the Wendat relocation to Iroquois country at Quebec. Certainly, there would have been moments of doubt. Yet upon reflection, he viewed the Wendat evacuation from the homeland as a success. This, in his opinion, was due in large part to his Christian faith and the Wendat's continued inclination towards conversion. He saw the French faith as a form of protection that gave strength to all the Wendat, even to those who lived among the former enemy.[97] For this elder, relocation had been essential to the survival of the Wendat.

At an Easter celebration in 1672, convinced of the bright future of the Wendat, the elder made a public speech: "Courage, little remnant of the Huron Nation! Your stock is not yet withered; it will send forth fresh branches; Jesus, risen again, Will make it revive and bloom anew."[98] He continued:

> Yes, Jesus Will restore it and render it more populous than ever, provided we are always faithful to him and to the blessed Virgin, and are firm in the resolution that we have adopted never to give any entrance to sin into this village, – least of all, to impurity and intemperance, the vices that are likely to destroy the charity and unity existing among us.[99]

There was hope for the Wendat people. Despite numerous relocations, the danger of living among an enemy, the chance of assimilation, and the ambiguity of the future, the Wendat did not give up as they continued to employ simultaneous strategies of cultural renewal and preservation throughout the post-dispersal period.

PART 3

Diaspora

DISPERSED FROM WENDAT country and forced to create new homelands, the Wendat more or less accepted their situation and made the best of it. Moving past the isolated micro-histories of specific post-dispersal Wendat communities, this final section connects the Eastern and Western Wendat through the prisms of leadership, women, and power. These three themes not only illustrate the persistence of Wendat culture and identity but also highlight how and why the Wendat drew on former social, political, and economic networks to maintain a unique Wendat diaspora. Functioning in similar ways to the Confederacy, post-dispersal Wendat men and women cultivated a complex system that incorporated members from Michilimackinac to Quebec City. Combined, these chapters summarize the consequences of seventeenth-century Wendat relocations and clarify the ways in which the Wendat survived the Iroquois conquest in 1649.

8
Leadership
Community Memory and Cultural Legacy

In his 1918 publication *Indian Heroes and Great Chieftains,* Charles Eastman (Ohiyesa) declared, "Every age, every race, has its leaders and heroes. There were over sixty distinct tribes of Indians on this continent, each of which boasted its notable men. The names and deeds of some of these men will live in American history, yet in the true sense they are unknown, because misunderstood."[1] Wendat history in the seventeenth century supports Eastman's assertion. Individuals such as Aenon, Taretande, and their successors shaped the Wendat world in important ways during this time of social and political uncertainty. Their policies of pro- and anti-Jesuit sentiment rippled throughout the community, creating divisions, conflicts, and alliances. Their deaths, along with many other civil leaders, created new positions of leadership as war chiefs took on alternative roles in the wake of the epidemics.

The dispersal, with its various migrations and resettlement strategies, reorganized the Wendat world again. Vast changes in geography, demography, and community took place; yet, the nature of Wendat leadership remained relatively intact. For the most part, roles and responsibilities remained the same, with some exceptions such as the Officer of the Faith. Leaders were typically men (although women played an important advisory role) and in the post-dispersal period most headmen became Christian converts.[2] Despite the assertion that leaders during this period began to act on their own regardless of community desires, the examples in this chapter demonstrate that Wendat leaders relied on collective decision making, and continued to be accountable to councils and the Wendat community at large.[3]

To speak of specific Wendat leaders in the latter half of the seventeenth century is to point to only a handful of men. Individual stories are almost as rare as in the pre-dispersal period, making the few references we do have important pieces in reconstructing the experiences and events of the dispersal and relocation. An online search for Wendat chiefs in the

Dictionary of Canadian Biography database highlights five names for the period between 1650 and 1701. These include the Eastern headmen Pierre Atironta, Étienne Annaotaha, and Louis Taondechoren, and the Western headmen Kondiaronk and Michipichy.[4] Historian Gilles Havard's study *The Great Peace of Montreal of 1701* gives similar biographical information on the Western Wendat involved in the French–Native treaty negotiations of 1701 in his appendix; he mentions Kondiaronk and Michipichy, as well as Le Baron.[5] In-depth biographical depictions remain rare, as most of these individuals are highlighted through abstract glimpses in larger discussions of seventeenth-century North American geopolitics.[6] This chapter contributes to the work on Wendat historical biographies in the post-dispersal period by beginning with an overview of both the leaders we know (who are represented in literature) and the leaders who have remained hidden in the sources to date. It traces these individuals, as well as other leaders, within the context of their communities and the diaspora. The dispersal did not affect the nature of Wendat leadership, and leaders continued to have significant influence on Wendat communities for generations.

Western Leaders

Wendat leaders from Michilimackinac have received the most attention by scholars and in many respects are some of the most well-known Wendat of the seventeenth century. This is due in large part to their high-profile visibility during the Great Peace of Montreal in 1701. It was these men (all Christian converts) who crafted the treaty, leaving notable traces of their actions and personalities in the colonial records of the negotiations, totems on the treaty itself, and memoirs of those who attended.

Kondiaronk (Gaspar Soiaga, Souoias, Sastaretsi), also called "Le Rat" by the French, was born during the initial years of the dispersal in Wendake and was roughly fifty years old at the time of the 1701 treaty negotiations. By 1682, Kondiaronk was acting as a leader for the Western Wendat; he gained the title of Sastaretsi, a hereditary name associated with prominent leadership. Throughout his life he maintained friendly personal relationships with French leaders such as governor Louis de Buade de Frontenac and his replacement Jacques-René de Brisay de Denonville, meeting with both men on several occasions.[7] Contemporaries widely acknowledged Kondiaronk's reputation as a stealthy diplomat. Father Pierre François Xavier de Charlevoix remarked, "He was naturally eloquent ... Nobody could ever have more influence than he."[8] Claude-Charles Bacqueville de la Potherie also called attention to Kondiaronk, declaring, "He had the sentiments of a beautiful soul, and was a savage only in name."[9] Kondiaronk's initiatives during the late seventeenth century focused on maintaining the Wendat status as middlemen among the geopolitical domain of the upper Great Lakes and the St. Lawrence. He expressed constant paranoia over being left out of Iroquois–French peace talks. Kondiaronk died in the final days of the peace negotiations on 2 August 1701. It is unclear whether any family members survived him, although he had at least one son, who died in 1696.[10]

The Wendat leader Le Baron was a contemporary of Kondiaronk and at times was also called Sastaretsi.[11] Aside from the hereditary name, Le Baron and Kondiaronk shared similar relationships with the French governors and conducted diplomatic campaigns on behalf of the Wendat of Michilimackinac.[12] Le Baron had a reputation as a controversial figure; Grosse-Tête, an Anishinaabe (Ottawa) headman, often questioned this Wendat leader's integrity. At one meeting, Grosse-Tête publicly declared, "Le Baron makes things up ... he is an artificial man who does not show his true feelings."[13] Several failed initiatives to create a separate alliance with the Iroquois attest to Le Baron's tricky personality. Because of this, the French viewed him as a "dangerous person."[14]

Michipichy, also called Quarante Sols by the French, was a key player within Western Wendat foreign policy in the late seventeenth century. It is believed he was originally an Iroquois captured by the Wendat who rose to the rank of headman.[15] This assertion is ambiguous, however, especially in light of his fairly persistent stance that the Iroquois should not be trusted, and because of the Anishinaabe sounding prefix of *mishi*.[16] While his suspicion of the Iroquois eventually led him to warn Kondiaronk to stop Iroquois peace talks, he eventually supported the initiative and became one of the signatories in 1701.

This group of charismatic Western Wendat leaders went to great lengths (and distances) to meet the needs of their people. Their policies changed and developed over time. In some instances they concluded agreements in favour of the French; other times they neglected the French and privileged the Iroquois. It is a misconception that any one of these leaders was consistently pro- or anti-Iroquois or French. Dichotomies such as this distort our understanding of the alliance-making process during this period. Although the Wendat tended to favour the old coalitions of the Anishinaabeg and French, they were open to talks with any group who might secure and strengthen their position within Great Lakes power systems. If anything, Kondiaronk, Le Baron, and Michipichy were in favour of promoting the best policy for the Wendat and in particular those of the west.

Eastern Leaders

Historians have given less attention to the Eastern Wendat leaders of the post-dispersal period. This obscurity is not due to a lack of information on them, however, as the *Jesuit Relations* are replete with character sketches; more likely, Lorettans and their leaders did not take on highly publicized roles at the Great Peace of 1701 and thus have been eclipsed by Le Baron, Michipichy, and especially Kondiaronk in the historiography. This is not to say that the East lacked in leadership. To be sure, important figures guided the eastern community through passionate religious conviction and Christian value systems.[17]

Atsena, or Le Plat, was a leader of the Bear nation who had sacrificed himself to the Iroquois as a test case before other Eastern Wendat moved to Iroquois country in the mid-1650s.[18] He was a powerful man within his community, a quality exemplified by his loud and eloquent speeches. He was well liked by his people and upon his departure several other headmen made long addresses and presents to the Iroquois to demonstrate how much Atsena would be missed. Even the Jesuits expressed fondness for Atsena; Father Simon Le Moyne made the following farewell address: "My brother, my heart is sad at seeing thee depart; ... As for thee, take courage; thou shalt see me at every stage of thy journey, in every place where thy cabin will be erected, at every spot where thou wilt disembark."[19] Le Moyne was referring to the proliferation of the Catholic faith in Iroquoia and the strength that Atsena might draw from it upon his journey there. This is the last time Atsena is mentioned in the records; his fate after his departure remains unknown.

Ignace Saouhenhohi, called "The Vulture" by the Jesuits, was considered one of the "foremost [headmen] in the [Wendat] colony," as well as a man of "fine qualities" committed to his people, his faith, and the French.[20] He was also critical to the success of Wendat removal out east. When the Wendat relocated to Île d'Orléans, for instance, Saouhenhohi redistributed the land given to him personally by the local French to all the widows and poor people of the community. Similarly, when he went hunting he shared hides and meat with Wendat and French who were undernourished and struggling. On many occasions Saouhenhohi acted as a mediator for community disputes, a role he consistently received praise for.[21] Actions such as these allowed him to become a Lorettan headman, a tenure he held for three years. Among his other contributions, he strongly influenced Iroquois conversions; he made many speeches in councils with the Iroquois, encouraging them to accept Christianity, and the French credited him with several conversions of Iroquois headmen who testified that Saouhenhohi inspired them.[22] Ignace Saouhenhohi died on 21 February 1669, two decades after the initial dispersal from Wendake. His wife and two children – a twelve-year-old daughter and three-year-old son – survived him.[23] The funeral took place in Quebec City at the bishop's personal request. The ceremony began with a funeral procession from Lorette, accompanied by all members of the Wendat community as well as many French inhabitants. His body was also buried at Quebec.[24]

The Wendat considered the war chief Thaovenhosen a "model of Christian integrity." In the Jesuits' eyes "[h]is mind [was] broad and elevated, [conceiving] nothing base, nothing unworthy of an honest and wise man ... To the French as well as to the [Natives], he [was] an incentive to live well and fight well."[25] One of his most notable achievements was his position as the head of the Lorettan bodyguard for the French governor. In this role he had many military victories, including several over the English.[26] In addition, he led an overt campaign against the customary "mourning wars," arguing that the vengeful taking and torture of captives violated Christian principles. In one case, he chastised a council deliberating on the fate of a prisoner. He reminded the councillors "to remember that they [were] Christians and citizens of the village of Lorette; that dire cruelty [was] unbecoming to the Christian name; that this injury [could not] be branded upon the reputation of the Lorettans without the greatest disgrace."[27] They acceded to his request. Thus, Thaovenhosen, because of his reputation as a successful war chief, paved the way for shifts in Wendat customs while also saving a life.

Other leaders were able to push similar agendas inspired by the Catholic faith. Pierre Atironta spent six years as a Wendat headman after his escape from the Iroquois in 1666.[28] He was a devoted Christian before his capture, but became even more dedicated after his return to the Wendat. As a result he was admitted to the Jesuit-created confraternity of the Holy Family,[29] which gave him a public platform to promote several of his outstanding goals for the community. Atironta supported peace with the Iroquois (despite his years in captivity) and led community opposition to alcohol consumption and sales. In 1672, Atironta became ill and despite the care of doctors at the French hospital, he died on 16 December. At least one niece survived him.[30]

Jacques Onnhatetaionk made similar headway in terms of anti-alcohol campaigns and Christian conversion. He originally volunteered himself as an aide to Father Le Moyne in Mohawk country, and with his family (which numbered at least ten) travelled there with the hopes of spreading the Christian faith to the Iroquois. To his dismay, the task was not an easy one and after a brief stay, he returned to Notre-Dame-de-Foy and the Wendat. Upon his return and his reinstatement as headman, Onnhatetaionk preached daily about the evils of alcohol. In fact, the Jesuits attributed the high level of temperance in Wendat society almost completely to Onnhatetaionk's persuasion. A young man who agreed to abjure drinking explained, "Would I pay so Little heed to the words of my captain, who so often dissuades us from that sin, as to Allow myself to fall into it in future?" Even more significant, an entire group of Wendat hunters were persuaded to abstain from drink after hearing Onnhatetaionk's talk. Through these demonstrations of influence in spiritual affairs, Jacques Onnhatetaionk reclaimed his reputation as an effective leader who achieved his goals and those of his community.[31]

These brief details highlight the achievements of Eastern Wendat leaders. Although they did not participate in the Great Peace of 1701 or gain the fame of their Western Wendat brothers, their influence on the local Eastern Wendat community had significant and long-lasting effects. In the end, the widespread use of Christianity by leaders allowed them to foster strength in times of fear and alter old traditions such as the mourning war and new problems such as alcoholism.

Iroquoised Wendat[32]

Not all Wendat leaders lived among the Wendat. In some cases captive Wendat took on leadership positions within Iroquois country, due in large part to their Wendat identity. The Wendat language was still the primary lingua franca in the post-dispersal period and the Iroquois engaged in numerous diplomatic ventures with the Wendat diaspora and their allies. Having a Wendat spokesperson furthered the Iroquois' diplomatic effectiveness because Wendat leaders brought other skills, including familiarity with the French and Anishinaabeg as well as their Wendat kin. The Wendat and their allies trusted Iroquoised Wendat leaders more than other

Iroquois leaders, and expected them to conduct agreements that would not only appease the Iroquois but also favour their Wendat kin.

Treaty negotiations between the Iroquois and Wendat in 1656 illustrate this type of leadership. The Iroquois presented gifts to the Wendat at the end of deliberations and an Iroquois headman made a final speech. A Wendat, who became a headman in the aftermath of his capture by the Iroquois, delivered a wampum belt. As he approached the Wendat, he explained that the belt was a personal gift from *him* to his Wendat family. In brief it was a seal of *his* pledge and "to assure them that they were not deceived" by the Iroquois.[33] This personalized gift was to some extent a collective present, since his Iroquois community elected him to this position and his role within the negotiations. The individualized presentation can be seen as an Iroquois tactic; it was public, yet at the same time a sidebar exchange where the former Wendat used his identity and kin connections to quell any uncertainty about Iroquois intentions. The Iroquoised Wendat acknowledged this reality in his speech:

> My brothers, I have not changed my soul, despite my change of country; nor has my blood become Iroquois, although I dwell among them. My heart is all Huron, as well as my tongue. I would keep silent, were there any deceit in these negotiations for Peace, thus I am talking to you. The proposal is honest, embrace it without distrust.[34]

The Wendat received the exchange with gratitude and the negotiations concluded on amicable terms. The extent to which this Iroquoised headman played a role in the success of the meeting is unknown, but one can speculate that his presence, the wampum belt, and his speech helped smooth the talks. Moments like this would have served to encourage the Iroquois to continue this strategy. After the dispersal, the Iroquois had hundreds of captured Wendat to use to their diplomatic advantage. Similarly, the Wendat used their identity as a means to not only survive in Iroquois country but also re-establish themselves as influential citizens within their new community.

Martyrs

The status of the Iroquoised headman before he came to live among the Iroquois is unknown. He was probably not an established leader among the Wendat prior to his capture, because the Iroquois preferred to torture and kill captive Wendat leaders as a warning for those who chose to resist their attacks. It may have also been a calculated Iroquois strategy to deprive the dispersed Wendat of leadership during this period.[35] In particular, the Iroquois targeted prominent Christian leaders for harsh treatment, suggesting that all parties realized the link between Christianization and Wendat systems of power in exile.

By the mid-1650s, the Iroquois had increased pressure on the Wendat to voluntarily relocate to Iroquois country. A number of notable Wendat resisters met untimely deaths at the hands of their enemy during this period. In 1656, the Iroquois took eleven Wendat captives. Among them were the Eastern Wendat leaders Jacques Oachonk and Joachim Ondakont, who both received death sentences. Each would serve a distinct symbolic purpose because of his status and reputation among the Wendat.

Oachonk was a prominent Christian leader within the community. He served as the prefect, or key administrator, of the Catholic congregation. His dedication to the faith did not waver upon capture; instead, he consoled other Wendat, encouraging them to maintain their belief in God no matter how difficult the circumstances seemed. Instead of making the customary war cry song, Oachonk chose to sing a Christian prayer during his torture. Repeatedly, he chanted, "Do not pity me, do not consider me unfortunate; I shall be happy in heaven. I fear not fires which my blood can extinguish; I fear the fire of hell which never dies out. This life is nothing to me, when my thoughts carry me to Heaven." This song was so loud it was heard for over a kilometre.[36] In the end, Joseph Oachonk met his death with the simple, yet calculated message, "JESUS, have pity on me."[37]

Joachim Ondakont was a different kind of Wendat leader. Notwithstanding Oachonk's influence within the Wendat community, out of the eleven captives taken, Ondakont was the most prominent leader among them. He had gained this status through his achievements as a respected war chief. His past incursions with Wendat enemies had won him a widespread reputation as a skilled warrior and brave man. It was for these reasons that he made a fitting companion to Oachonk in death; both were brought to the scaffold at the same time. Ondakont was burned up to the waist, his fingers were cut off, and his entire body was covered in blood. Seeing there was no end in sight, his comrades calmed him with a chant inspired by his Christian faith, even though Ondakont had accepted Christianity only half-heartedly before his capture. We know this because Ondakont evaded his death sentence, breaking free from his bonds while his captors slept. He walked for fifteen days until finding his way back home, where he divulged the details of his fortunate escape.

Information about the loss of men like Oachonk, as well as the gruesome details of their torture, filtered back to the Wendat community via escaped comrades such as Ondakont or purposefully through Iroquois envoys. This Iroquois "message" conveyed the death of Wendat leaders by the hands of the Iroquois as a demonstration of their power and strength, and it made clear that resisters to Iroquois incorporation policy would be executed. Finally, the message expressed that the Iroquois were not Christians and the majority did not support conversion. As a result, captive Wendat leaders who promoted Christianity became particularly vulnerable to future Iroquois assaults. Certainly, this Iroquois strategy affected both Wendat captives and the rest of Wendat society. Now that Wendat leaders, more than any other Wendat, were targets for Iroquois capture, leadership roles carried higher risk than in years past, risks that might have deterred some individuals from taking on the task. Mortality threatened the consistency and effectiveness of Wendat foreign policy. Despite this danger, men like Oachonk and Ondakont continued to lead their people.

Accountability

The exigencies of Wendat circumstances during the dispersal called for proactive and innovative leadership. Wendat leaders still remained accountable to their constituency, whether it was their family, village, nation, the east, the west, or the diaspora at large. As during the pre-dispersal period, leaders had to give voice to group initiatives, rather than self-interested ventures. Some served a single Wendat nation with remarkable longevity; Atsena, the leader of the Bear nation, maintained his position during the dispersal, migration east, and the early years of settlement at Quebec.[38] In other cases, leaders represented different groups at different times. Michipichy was the spokesperson for the Wendat at Michilimackinac in 1689, while Le Baron represented the Western Wendat in 1695.[39] Yet in 1701, Michipichy spoke almost exclusively for the Wendat of St. Joseph River, Le Baron spoke for those at Michilimackinac, and Kondiaronk acted on behalf of all the "allied nations."[40]

The Wendat shared clear ideas about the responsibility of the leader to represent the group's will, and the community punished headmen who transgressed this ideal. Michipichy delivered a long oration to this effect when a member of a treaty council misrepresented the desires of his people.[41] The headman's legitimacy depended on this link between representatives and nation. Put another way, a Wendat leader's main role was to deliver messages on behalf of his constituents, to express the desires of the group at large. Several post-dispersal cases illustrate this point. In the summer of 1682, for instance, Western Wendat headmen arrived at Montreal to speak to the French governor on behalf of their people. They had been charged with resolving the problem of alcoholism among their youth and sharing the miserable state of their community because of it.[42] Similarly, the death sentence of the Wendat traitor Louys may have been carried out by the Eastern Wendat leader Henheonsa, but the act was done on behalf of the entire community. To this end, while Henheonsa delivered the two hatchet blows to Louys's head, another Wendat leader, Outarahon, made a long speech to French witnesses to justify Henheonsa's actions "and to guarantee that his nation would thoroughly approve all that was done."[43]

Approval also remained an important component of legitimate leadership. The escaped captive Jacques Onnhatetaionk did not resume his status of Eastern headman automatically with his return from Iroquois country. Rather, numerous feasts and ceremonies took place, as well as many campaigns by the Wendat asserting their support for his leadership. In the end, only after a council convened and consented to his reinstatement could he gain back his "voice." He gave a wampum belt to signify the council's resolution.[44] All of these requirements signalled that the traditional custom of community endorsement for leaders persisted almost unchanged in the post-dispersal period.

Councils remained the central conduit for Wendat decision making. Leaders both participated in and were held accountable by these assemblies. At Michilimackinac, the Wendat held a council to decide whether to accept the Jesuits and support their efforts in conversion. Upon resolving to do so, the council gave the Jesuits a large wampum belt. Subsequently, a single headman rose and delivered a speech explaining the council's intent. He asserted, "[The Jesuits] alone should govern their Cabin. As regards [to] those with whom [the Jesuits] [are] not Satisfied, if [the Jesuits] manifest by a single Word that [they are] not pleased with Them, they at once [will] come of their own accord and bring the inmates of their Cabin to prayer."[45] Although it is unlikely that the council resolved to have the Jesuits "govern" them, it does seem that, through this leader's speech, they wished the Jesuits to understand that they had decided to support the Christian missionaries in their endeavours at Michilimackinac.

The fate of prisoners of war also fell under council governance (although women initiated the deliberations). In 1688, the Western Wendat captured fourteen Iroquois warriors. As soon as they returned to Michilimackinac, they held a council. After some deliberation, the group confirmed that twelve would remain among the Wendat. In addition, one captive would be given to the French commander Jean Juchereau de Maur, and the last prisoner would go to the Ottawa.[46] Deliberations such as these reflected a persistence of collective decision making when it came to war captives. Adoption and death were fates allocated by consensus because not one individual but the group at large owned them.

In 1665, twelve Eastern Wendat headmen held a council to discuss their feelings towards the French and their relocation to Quebec. Upon conclusion, a representative was sent to explain to the French governor, Onnontio, the council's sentiments. The long and detailed oration required a highly skilled diplomat to deliver it successfully. The oldest leader of the council was charged with the task. The speech was as follows:

> Great Onnontio, thou seest at thy feet the wreck of a great country, and the pitiful remnant of a whole world, that was formerly peopled by countless inhabitants. But now thou art addressed by mere carcasses, only the bones of which have been left by the Iroquois, who have devoured the flesh after broiling it on their scaffolds. There was left in US nothing but the merest thread of life; and our limbs, most of which have passed through the boiling caldrons of our foes, had no more strength – when, raising our eyes with extreme difficulty, we saw on the river the ships that were bringing thee, and, with thee, so many soldiers ... Thereupon the Sun seemed to shine upon us with brighter beams, and to illuminate our fatherland of old, which had been so many years overcast with clouds and darkness. Then our lakes and rivers appeared calm, and without storms or breakers; and, to tell thee the truth, I seemed to hear a voice issuing from thy vessel, and saying to us, from as far as we could discern thee: 'Courage, O desolate people! Thy bones are about to be knit together with muscles and tendons, thy flesh is to be born again, thy strength will be restored to thee, and thou shalt live as thou didst live of old ... I see thee, O brave Onnontio; I hear thee; I address thee. Be welcome, and receive this little present from the emptiness of our land, as a sign of the

> joy we feel at thy fortunate coming, and the homage we render to the greatest of all Onnontios on earth, who has taken pity on our wretchedness and sends thee to deliver us therefrom.[47]

He concluded the speech by giving the gift of a painted moose skin to the governor. The use of "I" in this oration was a formality, as the headman was not speaking on his own volition but for the council and thus the Wendat community. Through metaphoric language and French praise, this leader wove together a sympathetic story of Wendat dispersal, and their desperate situation, while clearly stating the main design of the council, which was for the Wendat to stay near Quebec and the French.

War/Civil Headmen

The shift in Wendat leadership in the 1640s, with war chiefs taking on civil responsibilities, complicated the roles of these individuals. The lines dividing these two types of leadership amalgamated in later years, making it more common to have headmen acting in both capacities, rather than having one dedicated to war or civil affairs. Kondiaronk clearly acted as a civil leader in his participation in diplomatic ventures, while at the same time he could raise armies and conduct military expeditions. In 1688, for instance, it was Kondiaronk who led an assault on a group of Iroquois ambassadors and killed one of their main deputies.[48] The French traveller Louis de Lahontan corroborated Kondiaronk's dual position when he stated that this leader was both "a war chief and a member of the huron council."[49] The Wendat leader Le Baron took on similar roles. La Potherie attested that although Le Baron was "less about trade and more about politics," he was nonetheless responsible for rallying "young warriors" on numerous occasions.[50] In some cases, Le Baron wore both hats. In 1695, for example, he met with the French governor to discuss foreign policy. Talks turned to war, however, and Le Baron returned to his community upset because he had "wanted peace, but [the governor] wanted war."[51]

Not withstanding examples of dual-roled individuals such as Kondiaronk and Le Baron, the position of war chief did not totally disappear during the post-dispersal period. At Michilimackinac, Lahontan remembered meeting the "war chief Saentsonan" who was on his way to Fort Niagara on a military expedition.[52] Similarly, the Jesuits introduced Thaovenhosen as a "warrior chief."[53] Thus, we have war chiefs throughout the diaspora – Saentsonan was from the west and Thaovenhosen was from the east. Both communities still faced frequent encounters with the Iroquois, so it may have been relevant to maintain the position of war chief in order to offset the responsibilities of the men charged with civil affairs. Whatever the case, it is clear that not all war chiefs took on civil tasks, but civil leadership often incorporated military leadership in the latter half of the seventeenth century.

Community Memory and Cultural Legacy

Although Wendat leaders were still subject to traditional checks and balances of Wendat society – selective leadership positions, appeasing their constituents, and respecting the authority of council decision making – this framework did not restrain headmen from making their own unique mark on their community. Leaders not only played integral roles but also influenced the Wendat for generations. These individuals served as points of reference for later Wendat, who kept careful genealogies that preserved hundreds of years of ethnic and cultural heritage. Leaders, and the memories of their character and actions, are often among the first distinguishable symbols within a collective community; in the case of people subject to forced migrations, these so-called heroes and chieftains are even more important in maintaining and creating bonds between the migrants. The loss of Wendake and other material and territorial references for identity meant that the Wendat, like other diasporic peoples, had to draw on less tangible points for cultural continuity.

Naming was one way the Wendat maintained the memories of ancestors and in particular significant leaders of the past. In a 1747 census of what Jesuit Father Pierre Potier called "Les 3 Bands huronnes avec Leurs anciens at Leurs anciennes," the names Aenon and Taretande reappear.[54] Like his namesake of the 1630s, Nicolas Taretande, also known as "le bedeau" by the French, belonged to the Bear clan. Similarly, the name of another eighteenth-century Bear clan member, Pierre Enons, is thought to be a different rendering of Aenon. Both of these individuals had connections to the Eastern Wendat and Lorette.[55] In the same census, the Western Wendat name held by Kondiaronk (Sastaretsi) rematerializes in the person of Mathias Sastaretsi. It is possible that Mathias met or knew Kondiaronk as a child, as he was probably around fifty years of age at the time of the census.[56] Mathias was at the end of a long line of Sastaretsis, a Wendat tradition that may date back to the pre-dispersal period. Indeed, there is reason to believe that at the same time that Kondiaronk held that title, a Wendat leader at Notre-Dame-de-Foy was also called Sastaretsi.[57] The title does seem to suggest that it was the name for the "one who leads the clan, the phratry and the nation."[58] Louis de Lahontan, during his travels among the Wendat in the late seventeenth century, questioned his companions about the name and its significance. His Wendat interpreters replied that it was the name of their leader and that it was well over seven or eight hundred years old.[59]

By transposing past names onto living individuals, the Wendat retained a tangible reference and reminder of people like Aenon, Taretande, and Sastaretsi. Poitier's 1747 census also reveals the mobility of these names. Unlike material culture or geographic fixtures, names were easily transportable throughout the diaspora. They were not easily lost along the road or left behind, yet in terms of cultural baggage they were heavy. Names designated more than just the people who use to represent them; they functioned as maps to family lineages, symbols of ethnicity, and also communicated traditional Wendat ideals of bravery, leadership, and behaviour to future generations.

Legends of Wendat heroes, both cultural and historical, served a similar purpose. These mythicized figures, based on real people, reflected Wendat customs and embodied the aspirations and ideals of the society. These could be passed down as lengthy stories – like legends, or more simplistic wives' tales. They often illustrated to the audience not only the heroic actions of a historic leader but also the standards to which the Wendat should strive.

In 1872, ethnographer Horatio Hale visited a Wyandot reservation near Detroit. There he interviewed several community members, including Joseph White. It was during these discussions that White told Hale about the legend of King Sastaretsi.[60] He explained that the people's memory of the migration west towards Michilimackinac was still intact and that they refer to this particular legend for its details. According to White, King Sastaretsi was a great Wendat leader who dated back to the predispersal period. In the wake of the Iroquois attacks, Sastaretsi agreed to act as a guide for his people in order to take them west. Upon their departure, the king warned his fellow Wendat that "this would not be the end of their wandering."[61] He kept his word and travelled to the far edges of Lake Huron, where he died. The legend concludes with the Wendat building a statue in Sastaresti's honour where he was buried. It was said to point them in the direction of the journey.[62] Within White's rendition of this legend, we come to understand Sastaretsi's role in the migration. He was trusted and influential, to such an extent that his memory was encapsulated within both material culture (the statue) and collective memory (the legend).

Other leaders from the dispersal period have been incorporated into the Wendat dialogue in less overt ways. The pious death of Ignace Saouhenhohi entered Lorettan folklore as the death of a Wendat saint. Indeed, it was common many years after his passing for Wendat to exclaim, "Oh, may I die like Ignace!"[63] This phrase underscored the influence of Ignace within his community and demonstrates how later generations drew upon his reputation as a model Christian to shape their own actions. Simple phrases like the one referring to Ignace also changed over time. In 1911, Claire Picard-O'Sullivan, a Wendat woman from Lorette, shared her community's memory of the great war chief of the 1640s Ahatsistari. Her account was recorded as follows: "/She/ remembered that Ahatsistari was a great Indian warrior whom everybody dreaded. He was called 'The reaper of scalps.' Whenever someone, in former days, was found dead and scalpless in the woods, the people would say, 'Ahatsistari has been here.'"[64] In this case, "former days" refers to the historic period when Native Americans still employed scalping as part of their military customs. When this tradition ended, there was no place for a phrase such as "Ahatsistari has been here," yet Ahatsistari remained in the minds of his Wendat descendants. Claire Picard-O'Sullivan explained that it became common practice for women at the turn of the twentieth century to scare the children of her village by saying, "Look out! Ahatsistari is coming!"[65] The phrase and context in which Ahatsistari was remembered had changed, but the communal knowledge of his heroic feats and reputation as a notable Wendat leader had not.

Through the continued use of Wendat leaders' names and the successful retention of Wendat heroes, the post-dispersal Wendat communities were able to reflect upon a common ancestral heritage. This history, with individual leaders as flash points, connected the Wendat across time and space. Heroes were stored in the Wendat communal memory, serving as proud reminders of the individuals who gave their people hope, strength, and guidance in the past.

Conclusion

The title "King" Sastaretsi is misleading. Not only was there never a King Sastaretsi, but there were never *any* Wendat kings. Positions of inherited grandeur and power, autocratic rule, and notions of nobility were not part of the Wendat world. Kingships required subservience, supreme authority, and luxurious prestige. Wendat positions of leadership, in contrast, demanded compromise, consensus, and accountability. There was no *single* leader in this case, but *many* respected headmen who were collectively responsible for executing the goals of a variety of factions throughout their constituency.

In the west, the actions of Kondiaronk, Michipichy, and Le Baron resulted in some of the most important global diplomatic initiatives of the century. In the east, the local initiatives of Ignace Saouhenhohi, Atsena, Pierre Atironta, Jacques Onnhatetaionk, and Thaovenhosen quelled the abuse of alcohol and furthered Christian conversions. Because of their high profiles and Christian character, all Wendat leaders risked being the targets of Iroquois torture and Wendat martyrdom. On the other hand, Wendat men in general had the opportunity to survive among the Iroquois, and to rise to the ranks of headmen because of their Wendat origins.

Relocation in the aftermath of the dispersal from Wendake had little effect on the nature of Wendat leadership. Leaders functioned as spokesmen for the Wendat, representing different sets of people at different times and places. Councils continued to be the main source of authority within Wendat communities and their support was fundamental in putting forward any policy. Further, the division between war chiefs and civil headmen continued to be ambiguous, as individuals such as Kondiaronk and Le Baron acted in both capacities, while Thaovenhosen and Saentsonan maintained a separate and distinct role as warrior chief. Finally, although the Wendat may not have had kings, in the words of Charles Eastman, they most certainly had "heroes."[66] Their contributions were recognized by their contemporaries as well as Wendat descendants centuries after their time. Through their mythicized legacy, leaders served as cultural capital inherited by all the Wendat. It is difficult to judge the success of these individuals and their policies, yet if the survival of the Wendat people, their culture, and their collective memory is any indication, these men left their mark.

9
Women
Unity, Spirituality, and Social Mobility

LEADERSHIP TOOK ON MANY different forms within the seventeenth-century Wendat diaspora. While men dominated the public sphere, women led their community in other ways. The experience of dispersal and resettlement and its connection to dislocation and land were intimately linked to women's traditional responsibilities within Nadowek society. Women cultivated the land to sustain their families; it was also the landscape on which homes were built, and therefore a space under the authority of mothers, daughters, and wives. This fostered a unique connection between land and people, making removal a particularly difficult situation for women.[1] In 1817, for instance, in the midst of comparable forced migrations in the United States, Cherokee women gathered together to voice their perspective on dispersals, land, and women's roles. Speaking to the men of their community, they began, "Our beloved children and headmen of the Cherokee nation[,] we address you warriors in council. We have raised all of you on the land which we now have, which God gave us to inhabit and raise provisions." A year later, the women maintained their perspective: "The land," they said, "was given to us by the Great Spirit above as our common right, to raise our children upon, and to make support for rising generations."[2] The Wendat had expressed similar sentiments during their relocations a century earlier. During the eastern resettlement, a concerned friend acknowledged the legitimacy of a disheartened woman's sadness over moving again. In much the same language as the Cherokee women, the Wendat friend acknowledged, "I see very well that your regret at changing your village comes from The love that you bear to the Fields which you have here, and which you cannot transport so far."[3] The consistent and persistent notion that Nadowek women held a distinct relationship with the land in contrast to their male counterparts is just one reason the experience and effects of forced removals on Native women represent a unique avenue of research. Whether the more familiar Cherokee Removals of the 1830s or the lesser-known Wendat relocations of the 1650s, '60s, and '70s, uprooted Native communities orchestrated their migrations in correspondence to the roles of their women.

In the case of the Wendat diaspora, scholars generally frame the results as detrimental to the status of women and their overall well-being. In the east, they argue, Christianity eroded women's power; in the west, they faced Anishinaabe patrilineal structures; while in Iroquois country, a lack of representation in the council meant that the "political power of the transplanted [Wendat] women was eliminated."[4] These arguments are perhaps extensions of the dominant historical interpretation that Native women lost power due to Christian influences, even with their avid attempts to counteract the work of missionaries.[5] While Christianization did change women's status in the pre-dispersal period, during the latter part of the seventeenth century Christianity did not constrain Wendat women, but instead provided a vehicle for unity, spirituality, and social mobility. The process of diminishing political and social status among Wendat women did not happen immediately, and it does not reflect the numerous ways women continued to project their influence in the post-dispersal period. Women instigated planning and decision making in the early stages of diaspora formation, while at the same time the dispersal created unique new opportunities for women. Women's active participation in resettlement negotiations, continued collective group activity, and their roles as mothers, wives, and daughters significantly impacted individual women and Wendat society as a whole.

Relocation Negotiations

The Wendat decided to relocate from Wendake to Gahoendoe, Anishinaabe communities, and later to the east and west through a drawn-out process based in consensus and councils. No single person orchestrated these strategies, and although men seem to have dominated the scene, women participated in the process. Many Native societies perceived a transfer of land as "unethical" without the input of women. After European contact, however, discussions of territory and land distribution rarely incorporated women.[6] This was not the situation for the seventeenth-century Wendat. Although less obvious than the public displays made by men, women remained central to decision making, and negotiators used them as leverage in persuading the French to accommodate Wendat refugees at Gahoendoe as well as in the east.

The decision to allow Jesuits to move with the Wendat to Gahoendoe would not have happened if not for the women. Among the numerous discussions taking place in the immediate aftermath of the attacks in Wendake, Wendat women gathered together to discuss the circumstances and strategize. Although the Jesuits did not record the details of the meeting, the resulting wampum belt made by the women themselves and the message delivered by the headmen at an evening council make it clear that a women's council took place.[7]

After three hours of intense speeches by the headmen, the Wendat presented the Jesuits with ten large wampum belts representing the voice of the "women and children."[8] According to the headmen, the purpose represented by these symbolic gifts was not only to ask the Jesuits to take compassion on the widows and their children but also "to revive in [the Jesuits] the zeal and the name of Father Echon (the name which the Hurons have always given to Father Jean de Brébeuf); ... that [the Wendat] hoped that his example would touch [the Jesuits], and that [their] hearts could not refuse to die with them, since they wished to live as Christians."[9]

In other words, it was the women's desire that the Jesuits support the Wendat decision to move to Gahoendoe in light of the fact that there remained a high number of struggling widows and orphaned children who, in return for assistance, would accept Christianity and serve as a willing population for future conversions. This last presentation to the council helped convince the Jesuits. According to the missionaries, it was "the disposition of their souls, and the reasons which nature could supply them [that] conquered us."[10] Shortly after, the Jesuits agreed to relocate to Gahoendoe.

The reference to the unique suffering of women as both widows and single mothers resurfaced on a number of occasions within resettlement negotiations. In the case of Gahoendoe, the Jesuits officially agreed to the Wendat requests out of a desire to protect and support the women and children. In the east, the removal to Île d'Orléans met with similar notions of sympathy from a woman who could relate to the Wendat women in ways that the Jesuits could not.

Éléonore de Grandmaison was the seigneuresse, or landlady of the land, at Île d'Orléans.[11] At the time of Wendat settlement negotiations, the twice-widowed Madame Grandmaison had just recently married a third time, to Jacques Gourdeau de Beaulieu. She had five daughters and one son, and was also the first and only white woman living on the island during the Wendat relocation.[12] Grandmaison's life experience almost certainly affected her decision to rent her land to the Wendat refugees. Throughout the negotiations she expressed pity for the women and children, possibly because she knew what it was like to mourn the loss of a husband while simultaneously trying to raise children.[13] The fact that the Eastern Wendat consisted mostly of women may have assuaged the fears of Grandmaison and other French civilians, who might have opposed the arrival of a large number of Native men in the area; a group of struggling Wendat women might have seemed less threatening. The bonds between these women – Wendat and French – transcended ethnic boundaries, as their gendered experiences as wives and mothers connected them on a different level. Part of the negotiated terms, for instance, included that Wendat women bring food and supplies to Grandmaison on a regular basis. Holding true to the agreement, four to six Wendat women frequently visited Madame Grandmaison throughout their stay on the island, which fostered deeper bonds with the seigneuresse.[14]

Councils

Collective decision making and initiatives continued to be a part of the Wendat women's activities in the post-dispersal period. The Women's Council at Notre-Dame-de-Foy, for instance, petitioned and supported the reinstatement of Jacques Onnhatetaionk, the former Iroquois captive, as headman. This required several separate manoeuvres. First, the clan mothers brought him gifts of Indian corn. The quantity differed greatly; while some delivered chests full of harvested corn, others declared that their entire field was his for the taking.[15] Next, each clan mother gave Onnhatetaionk a wampum belt, testifying their support for him. The belts were delivered during several feasts held in Onnhatetaionk's honour. All this was done before the former headman was officially reinstated.

Onnhatetaionk recognized the influence of these women in his speeches and with his gifts of gratitude. In addition to hosting a feast and thanking the Jesuits and headmen of the village, Onnhatetaionk offered wampum belts to the priests to support Mary and the Catholic Church, to governor Frontenac as a request to maintain friendly ties with the French, and most significantly to the clan mothers as a promise to meet their request to unite the Wendat and continue to "kindle a Common fire for Them."[16] Thus, Onnhatetaionk acknowledged the power of these women within his society and respected their goals as leaders of the community. It is unlikely that Onnhatetaionk could have regained his position as headman or maintained his office afterwards without the support of the women and had he not met their demands for unity.

This traditional group organization and decision making among women at Notre-Dame-de-Foy served as the basis for similar associations created in the wake of the dispersal. In 1653, the Jesuits created the Catholic confraternity of the Holy Family – the same association the leader Pierre Atironta later participated in.[17] Although not a gender exclusive society, the Jesuits differentiated the men from the women by speaking specifically of the "Women of the Holy Family." For these Wendat Christian women, the group functioned as a sisterhood and a means to instigate social reform and security. They created projects, for instance, that directly affected the community, and expressed their continued responsibility to raise and nurture generations of Wendat. The Women of the Holy Family supported entire Wendat families for months during some of the most difficult times of their relocation and a women's council determined the manner and extent of support, deciding on a general contribution that the women collected at the end of the council and delivered to needy families. The Women of the Holy Family gave corn to poor French families as well, further cementing ties with the civilian community they lived near.[18]

The traditional women's councils and the Women of the Holy Family functioned in similar ways. Although the Holy Family was a Jesuit creation, the Wendat made it their own and used it as a vehicle to better their society. These women made collective decisions to assist weak and poor Wendat in order to strengthen the overall community. Thus, rather than diminishing a woman's ability to maintain her role as the primary caregiver and social welfare authority, this Christian organization delivered an additional means to organize and execute plans.

Converts

Women accepted Christian conversion hesitantly during the initial years of missionary work. In Wendake, Jesuits commented on the overrepresentation of men in the congregation, a circumstance explained partially by the conversion of war chiefs and headmen's desires to appease the French.[19] Yet, as the years progressed, women became some of the most avid supporters of the Christian faith. The stark contrast from the pre-dispersal to the post-dispersal period did not go unnoticed by the missionaries. One of the clearest demonstrations of this shift was the change in the way women mourned the loss of warriors in battle. Before, it was customary for widows to gather for several days and cry and wail aloud, lamenting their lost loved ones. In 1660, however, when the news of a great defeat reached the Wendat village in the east, "prayer took the place of lamentation" and the women gathered in the chapel for consolation from the priests.[20] Moreover, the congregation at Sillery consisted of only women.[21] Conditions in the west were comparable; the Jesuits mentioned an entire group of women who demanded a simultaneous group conversion after witnessing the parhelia at Michilimackinac.[22] Western clan mothers who could not visit the Jesuits on their own because of their age asked the missionaries to continue the teachings they learned in Wendake. A blind woman explained this request saying she had not forgotten the teachings of Father Brébeuf, which she witnessed personally, and that she desired to continue instruction so she might not "die without grace."[23]

This widespread turn to Christianity arose in part from the desire to seek out coping mechanisms to deal with the hardships they faced from the dispersal. Death was a common phenomenon for most Wendat, but women struggled with the aftermath of losing a husband, brother, father, or son in battle. Women traditionally channelled the mourning obligations of the entire community, and Christianity offered a new way of dealing with these losses. After coming to the realization that her young daughter was about to die, a Wendat mother declared, "I used to be inconsolable, in the past, when any of my near relatives died; but, since I have become [the Holy Virgin's] daughter, and know that, to please [her], one must wish what is God's will, I am content to see my dear child die."[24]

Aside from mourning, Wendat Christian mothers and wives found comfort in the idea they could rejoin their children and husbands in heaven, one of the most important aspects of Catholicism for many Wendat converts. Even during the pre-dispersal period, reports of people travelling to the Wendat Land of the Dead served as a means to persuade traditionalists to convert. On one occasion, for example, a man returned from the afterlife and told his fellow Wendat, "Rejoice ... for I have returned from the country of the souls, and I have found none there any longer; they have all gone to Heaven."[25]

In addition to spiritual succour, the extra material support that Jesuit missionaries provided to converts also appealed to Wendat women. Without husbands and sons, these women lacked the protection customarily provided by Wendat men. They looked to the Jesuits as viable replacements for the father figures missing in their children's lives. On one occasion a dying father called out to his wife to take pity on his children, who would soon be fatherless. The wife, seeking to not only calm her husband but also reassure herself, replied, "Do not weep, my dear husband; our children will not remain fatherless after your death. The Fathers who instruct us will be the fathers to them, so long as our children are good Christians; and I will take all possible care to make them become so."[26]

Conversion of mothers and wives ultimately led to further conversions within the Wendat community. Matriarchs convinced their husbands and children to follow their lead. The children of Marie Gentehaon received baptism in light of her Christian beliefs. Despite being held captive in Iroquois country for twenty years, Gentehaon passed on her faith to her daughter Françoise Gannendok and Françoise's husband. Both mother and daughter died at the same time and received Christian burials.[27] Often this was the case within families in the post-dispersal period. If the daughter was a Christian, it was likely that her mother was also a convert.[28] This type of familial conversion extended to unborn generations as well. Upon hearing that the Jesuits were coming for a visit, a Wendat woman exclaimed, "Our smallest children are so rejoiced that they begin to grow before our eyes; and even those not yet born leap with joy in their mothers' wombs, and wish to come forth at the earliest moment, to be blessed."[29] Women, as mothers and wives, held the power of persuasion. Despite the dispersal, women continued to dominate the household and maintain their influential role as matriarchs within Wendat society. It was not until women began to convert that Christianity became more widespread.

The Seminary

Wendat Christian women and girls enjoyed unique educational opportunities. In 1639, the widow Madame de la Peltrie sailed from France with three Ursuline nuns to establish one of the first institutions of learning in North America under a royal charter signed by Louis XIII. The Ursuline Seminary at Quebec offered refuge, education, and vocation to women and girls who desired it. Mother Marie de l'Incarnation, who was a widow herself for ten years before joining the Ursuline order, ran the seminary. Unlike the Native residential/boarding schools of the nineteenth century, these seventeenth-century schools were voluntary. Students could come and go as they pleased and parents were allowed to visit.[30] Native girls generally bore extra responsibilities in comparison to the French girls, such as working in the kitchen or conducting household tasks.[31] The nuns taught primarily in the Wendat language and French, but eventually expanded to incorporate the languages of the Anishinaabeg, Innu, and Iroquois.[32] Because the seminary enrolled both Native and French girls, students socialized across ethnic lines on a daily basis.[33]

The nuns involved themselves immediately upon the arrival of the Eastern Wendat to Quebec. They tended to the sick and hungry, taking in a number of Christian families, while the Wendat began to organize their resettlement in the region.[34] In addition, they welcomed a number of young Wendat girls into their classrooms; these girls received lessons on Christianity as well as food and shelter.[35] Marie de l'Incarnation made it clear in a letter written in the spring of 1650 that she hoped the Wendat would take advantage of the nuns' generosity and "that the [Wendat] would establish themselves close to them."[36] Several months later, she continued to accept the Wendat who came to her seminary because its buildings were strong and secure in comparison to the Wendat half-built houses.[37]

Over and above the security and education presented by the Ursulines, young girls found opportunities for vocational positions through the seminary. The daughter of a Christian Wendat woman named Jeanne went to live with the nuns for almost two years and received training in the French language. During that time, she excelled in her studies and surpassed many of her French counterparts in reading and writing. Jeanne's daughter became an interpreter at the affiliated hospital, Hôtel Dieu.[38] However, this young woman's choice to remain within the domain of the French Ursulines was not a rejection of Wendat culture or society, as she continued to visit the Wendat community and engaged with the Wendat on a frequent basis at the hospital. Rather, Jeanne's daughter used the opportunities made available to her through the seminary to maintain her personal well-being (both spiritually and physically) while contributing to her Wendat kin through her vocation as interpreter.

Wendat seminarians could also become nuns themselves.[39] Arriving at the seminary in May 1650, Geneviève-Agnès was one of the first Wendat to enter the convent; she was between eight and nine years old at that time. The daughter of one of the most respected Wendat Christian headmen, Geneviève-Agnès was skillful in languages and mastered French within her first year. She joined the choir and gained a reputation as one of the loveliest voices at the seminary. Geneviève-Agnès also worked in the kitchen, a daunting task for any young girl, but the work did not seem to dim her devotion to the seminary. Perhaps one reason for her attachment to the institution was her relationship with her peers. She was notably well liked by the French students, which after seven years of living among them would have only strengthened her desire to remain within the convent's walls.[40]

Geneviève-Agnès demonstrated her loyalty to the seminary in a number of ways. On different occasions, her parents would visit and ask if she would like to rejoin them at the Wendat settlement; they missed her and wanted her to live with them again. Notwithstanding this appeal, the young seminarian refused her parents' requests. In another instance, after being brought before a disciplinary council for bad behaviour, Geneviève-Agnes was asked to choose between leaving the convent or receiving a physical reprimand. The girl broke into tears as soon as they mentioned leaving and chose the latter option. The nuns decided that her commitment to the Order was so profound they could not go through with any form of punishment and let the upset girl return to her classmates.[41] Finally, Geneviève-Agnès demonstrated her personal attachment to the seminary through her request to join the Ursuline religious order, and in particular to become a hospital nun. She obtained her request at the age of fifteen, becoming the first Native sister in New France in 1657.[42] She had little time to enjoy her position, as she died shortly after. Supported and witnessed by her fellow Wendat, Sister Geneviève-Agnès was buried in her holy garb alongside the other nuns at Quebec.[43]

Several reasons likely lay behind Geneviève-Agnès's adamant attempts to stay within the jurisdiction of the Ursulines. First, at the age of fifteen, she was impressionable and vulnerable. Having experienced a period of warfare and social crisis, the seminary would have been the only real home and stable environment for the young Wendat girl. The unfamiliarity of the new Wendat settlement versus the recognizable perimeters of the convent served as additional comfort. Beyond sanctuary, the desire to dedicate a lifetime of service to the Christian faith cannot be discounted. After spending her childhood and adolescence in prayer and religious devotion (the basis for which the institution that nursed her to health was founded) Geneviève-Agnès may have wanted to return the favour. For her, the life of a nun would facilitate an ability to help other people in similar situations.

A contemporary of Geneviève-Agnès expressed similar notions of attachment and sanctuary. At the age of ten, this young girl received a visit from her parents, who were making plans to relocate to Iroquois country in the wake of a temporary peace. They explained that they felt comfortable with the decision, as many of their relatives were already there. They wanted to know if she would consider leaving the seminary and joining her family. The girl's initial reaction was emotional and confrontational; she asked, "What? Are you not ashamed to wish to leave the country of prayer, and go to a place where you will be in danger of losing the faith?" She reprimanded her parents' lack of dedication to the Christian faith. In the end, she held fast in her attachment to the seminary and replied, "Go, if you will, to that wretched country, but I shall not follow you; I will never leave the holy maidens if you forsake me."[44] Her parents departed shortly after. This decision suggests that Geneviève-Agnès's attachment to the Ursulines was not an isolated incident. Some Wendat girls, at least, from a very early age, felt a connection to the seminary, which persuaded them to remain there rather than rejoin their families.

The seminary presented opportunities for non-seminarists as well. Cécile Arenhatsi, a twenty-three-year-old Christian widow approached the Ursulines for work. She presented her case to the Mothers, stressing her widowed status and her need to support her six-year-old daughter, Marie. She had heard, while still in Wendake, the Jesuits talk of the "holy virgins" (the Wendat title for the Ursulines) and their generosity. It was this, she contended, that inspired her baptism and devotion to the Christian faith. After their removal to Quebec, she made it a priority to seek out the nuns and see if they could not help her from this desperate state. The Ursulines agreed to engage Arenhatsi as a servant and to enroll Marie at the seminary.[45]

The Wendat woman's dedication and gratitude did not end once she gained employment and Marie was taken care of. Despite a few unforeseen obstacles, including the fact that she rarely got to see her daughter because of her service to the nuns, as well as being the witness to and victim of a dangerous fire that burned down most of the seminary, Arenhatsi maintained she had made the right choice and continued to respect and admire the Ursulines. As she explained in the aftermath of the fire, "I offered my life to God ... I thought of him alone; and I feared also that my sins had caused [the fire] to happen to virgins so holy, of whose company I am so unworthy."[46] Arenhatsi used her status as a woman and Christian to gain access to the opportunities presented by the seminary. This strategy also extended to her daughter, Marie, who, depending on her disposition, would have the same if not more choices than her mother because of her position as a seminarist.

Iroquois Captives

If Wendat women refugees saw Christianity as an additional source of strength and security in the aftermath of the dispersal, Wendat women captives among the Iroquois used it as a necessary means for survival. The obstacles faced by these women were horrific in both the physical and psychological sense. Not only did they have to bear the torments personally, but they also had to witness the loss of family members and beloved children. The Wendat woman Gannendio watched the murder of her children while held captive by the Iroquois, and afterwards received nine knife wounds at the command of her adopted family.[47] She survived, despite assaults, and lived through the experience with the pain of not only mending flesh but also the memory of her slain children. Marthe Aatio had a similar experience, albeit deadlier. After watching the deaths of both her brother and son, she continued the long journey to Iroquois country escorted by her captors. She managed to save the lives of her infant twins, carrying the babies on her back. Unfortunately, this made her slower than the rest of the group, and after a short while the twins were killed in front of her in order to quicken the pace. Soon her knee became infected and she could only drag herself along the ground. Her captors deemed her too weak and ended her misery with a hatchet to the head.[48]

In the face of such dire circumstances, Wendat women depended heavily on their Christian teachings to gain comfort and solace. Before Aatio's death, she practised her faith during her captivity. Every morning and night, as well as before every meal, she said a prayer. Although mocked by her captors (and even some Wendat), she made the sign of the cross over her two twin children before nursing them. In response to chastisement, Aatio explained, "You think of nothing but the earth, and our thoughts are of Heaven."[49] The focus on heaven certainly made sense because of her circumstances; with her family gone, her only hope was that through death she might rejoin her lost relatives. Indeed, death, for Christian captives, was a better alternative than remaining alive. The Wendat woman Thérèse pleaded with her captors for death in the aftermath of an unofficial confession, saying that it would do her the greatest service if they ended her life so that she could attain a Christian salvation. Ironically, her captor was so impressed by her boldness that he would not let her die.[50]

Another captive, Gandigoura, lived six years among the Iroquois before escaping. She recalled her concerted efforts to be "careful not to forget a thing which she held dearer than life."[51] Some escapees attributed their survival entirely to their maintenance of their Catholic devotion. One woman, after escaping the Iroquois and hiding in the woods for six days with her two children, was asked how she managed to overcome the obstacles she faced. "I lived on prayers," she said. "When I grew weak, I said my Rosary, and I at once felt my strength return and continued on my way." She continued, "At night, I put my children to sleep; and, as I could not sleep myself, I passed the nights almost entirely in prayer and in saying my Rosary." She concluded, "It is the blessed Virgin alone who has saved my life, and whom I wish to serve with all my heart until my death."[52] This belief, whether true or not, secured these women, allowing them to focus on ways to overcome their captivity.

Those who did not escape were no less dedicated to maintaining their Christian identity in both private and public settings. Because of Iroquoian resistance to Christianity, many Wendat felt threatened if they practised their faith openly. Public chastisement and ridicule also made meetings difficult to conduct. Wendat women addressed this issue by organizing secret gatherings outside of the Iroquois villages or in Wendat homes. Among the Mohawk, for instance, a number of Wendat clan mothers established "flying and hidden Churches." During these meetings, one woman, usually a prestigious elder, would recite prayers from memory and the audience would repeat them back.[53] These gatherings unified Wendat Christian women and served as an added source of support – as well as facilitating the maintenance of an independent Wendat identity – throughout their captivity. This tactic also gave them the ability to retain the Christian teachings of the past and set them apart from the Iroquois women.

Despite Iroquois resistance, some Wendat women even used their Christian knowledge to gain favour with those Iroquois interested in learning more about the Jesuit teachings. The Ursulines publicized the fate of a former Wendat seminarist who was captured at the age of fourteen and who lived among the Iroquois for ten years. She married an Iroquois and became head of her household. Over time, she persuaded all the members of her family to pray.[54] Jesuits noticed the public work of women such as this and remarked on the spread of Christianity throughout Iroquois country: "The Captive women have kindled this fire which is burning in the hearts of the Iroquois."[55] By the mid-1650s, the Jesuits rejoiced that due to Wendat Christian women, the Iroquois had "heard so much about us, and have been told so often of the great blessings of the Faith, that, in spite of their ignorance of it, it commands their esteem; and they love us in the hope that we will become to them what we have been to the Hurons."[56] The Iroquois perspective demonstrates the success of Wendat women in promoting their Christian strategy. By maintaining their faith, they stood out among their captors and gained favour with the French. This allowed them to acquire positions of power and persuasion within Iroquois country.

Cécile Gannendaris

Cécile Gannendaris exemplifies many of the themes in this chapter. As an Eastern Wendat woman living in the post-dispersal period, she exercised matriarchal authority over her family, participated in women's organizations, and acted as a leader on social matters within the community. As a Wendat Christian, she gained additional access to support groups, positioned herself as an expert and enforcer of moral conduct, and received comfort from her belief in a Catholic afterlife.

Gannendaris was first and foremost a wife and mother. She married twice to traditionalists who converted to Christianity at their wife's insistence. The first husband was completely devoted to her, and expressed his love, affection, and respect for the matriarch of his household. His conversion was an easy transition in that he already adhered to many of the teachings. The couple had at least four children before he died of an unknown disease.[57] Not long afterward, Gannendaris married again to a man who was just as devoted to her. For him, conversion to Christianity was more difficult. Having lived a lifetime under the regulations of traditional Wendat codes of conduct, the strict and different regime of Catholic rules was not easily obeyed. In light of his relationship with Gannendaris and her strong inclination to have him convert, however, he endorsed the Christian teachings and received baptism. His "salvation" was "particularly dear to her," as he became "one of the best Christians in the Colony."[58]

Gannendaris's children also became Christians because of their mother. She taught them and convinced them of the benefits of heaven. Gannendaris employed different forms of corporal punishment, a practice rarely used by the Wendat but endorsed by her understanding of Christian doctrine. She justified herself to her children, "Ah, my Child, how wouldst thou bear the strange tortures of the demons, if thou canst not bear so light a punishment? Take good care not to fall again into this fault for which I have just chastised thee, for fear lest thou be condemned to sufferings that never end."[59] In other words, Gannendaris reinforced the severity of hell through physical displays of punishment so that her children understood how baptism would help them avoid these circumstances in the afterlife.

Gannendaris paid particular attention to her two daughters, especially when the girls became deathly ill. Already devout Christians, according to the Jesuits, their mother went to great lengths to ensure their salvation in case they died. When her twelve-year-old daughter could no longer walk due to a debilitating disease, Gannendaris wrapped the child in a moose-skin robe and with the help of another Wendat woman carried her to the church during Easter to receive communion. Her other daughter, at the age of seven, was instructed by her mother to continue to say her rosary throughout an illness that eventually took her life. The child took this to such an extreme that she insisted on adhering to her mother's instructions even when she had lost the ability to speak. Much as she had formed her husband's religious training, Gannendaris also shaped her children's spiritual beliefs.[60]

Gannendaris's influence did not stop with her family. The Wendat community viewed her as a leader and expert on matters of social welfare and etiquette. The Wendat sought advice from her on a regular basis, asking questions that ranged from personal conduct and morality to spirituality. As one of the most knowledgeable clan mothers, Gannendaris often led women's meetings. During these assemblies she used her own experiences to entice Wendat women to follow the Christian code of conduct. This did not waver when she became ill. In fact, Gannendaris took the opportunity to gather a number of Wendat women and continue her teachings. She addressed them:

> My Sisters, I was formerly regarded among you as fairly good-looking, and now I am hideous to look at. I used to love cleanliness, and now my body is a mass of corruption. I was not the poorest person in our Village, and today I get no help from my possessions. That is the condition in which you will find yourselves some day. Do many good deeds during your lives, for from them only will you receive any consolation in the hour of death.[61]

As a member of the Women of the Holy Family, she gave similar exhortations and attended meetings focused more specifically on Christian doctrine. For Gannendaris, her association with the Holy Family was an extremely important aspect of her life, so much so that she left her most prized wampum belt of six thousand black beads to the organization in her will.[62]

In addition, Gannendaris extended her role as a teacher to both the Jesuits and Iroquois visitors. She instructed missionaries in the Wendat language and explained Christian teachings to Iroquois pupils over the course of several days. Throughout this time, she made a concerted effort to demonstrate her passion and devotion to the faith in order to inspire these potential converts.[63]

Aside from the spiritual benefits and respect gained from Christian adherence, women found other benefits as well. Gannendaris, for example, gained access to food and health care for her family. When she became ill, the Quebec bishop sent food to her home to help sustain her household. Wendat women and "persons of quality" brought additional provisions to the hospital where she was treated. This support was crucial. Without a mother and wife, Gannendaris's family would have struggled to provide these necessities.

During her illness, Gannendaris drew strength and comfort from her faith in terms of dealing with the prospect of death. Much like many other Wendat, she believed for a long time in heaven out of a wish to rejoin her loved ones in the afterlife. This belief consoled her through at least three deaths, one of which was her first husband and the others a daughter and son. She only became more steadfast as her illness worsened. When asked by her second husband if she had any doubt about the afterlife, she responded, "No, no, I cannot doubt what our Fathers tell us of the good reception given to Christians in Heaven."[64] A few days before her death, she told of how she had been awakened by a sweet voice calling her name. When questioned by the Jesuits about the experience, she said, "I think it is the voice of my daughter who died last year and who came in this way to call her little brother, some days before he died."[65]

Cécile Gannendaris died on 6 February 1669. Customary procedure took place: a Wendat headman announced the details of the funeral but added that in light of the piety of the deceased all Wendat within five kilometres of Quebec should say their rosary as a sign of respect. Upon receiving the news, the Quebec bishop ordered the parish bells to ring and requested that the funeral be held at his church. Several weeks later, Gannendaris's brother held a feast in her honour and presented a wampum belt to the Elders' Council so that her memory would remain fresh within the community.[66]

Unlike that of Wendat leaders such as Kondiaronk and Ahatsistari, Gannendaris's legacy was lost within a few generations. She was not the subject of folklore and wives' tales and there was no statue made in her honour. Yet, during her time, she became one of the most influential members of the Wendat community: a consultant and authority concerning the Eastern Wendat policy of cultural and Christian conformity; a source of information and inspiration for groups of women and potential converts; and a matriarch to her family's spiritual salvation.

Conclusion

Wendat women exerted power as keepers of the land and people in the post-dispersal period, but also to meet personal goals. They instigated and influenced relocation negotiations at Gahoendoe and Île d'Orléans through their continued use of collective decision making and councils, despite their lack of public attendance at these deliberations. They made their presence felt through wampum belts, headmen's speeches, and the records of Madame Grandmaison's sentiments. This kind of collectivity fostered unity among Wendat women, and created bonds essential to promoting their causes and securing their futures outside the borders of Wendake.

For many, spiritual conversion to Christianity acted as an additional safety net after the dispersal. The continued influence of mothers on their children and wives on their husbands expanded this spiritual network throughout the diaspora. Wendat, whether they lived in the east, west, or Iroquoia, created a fundamentally Christian identity due to the influence of these women. In the east, women found new opportunities to come together through the Holy Family and the seminary, while in the west the memory of Brébeuf's teachings in Wendake strengthened the bonds between the older generations, inspiring them to pass on the knowledge to the younger women. In Iroquois country, Wendat women united to "kindle the fire" and spread Christianity to Iroquois traditionalists.

Wendat women's continued unity and newly inspired spirituality allowed them to create opportunities that did not previously exist. Recall the old woman Anne, from Chapter 1: her baptism in the 1630s created a devastating situation in which the anti-Christian Wendat ostracized and abandoned her. Despite Anne's effort to fulfill obligations to her infant grandchildren, she was unable to tend to their needs, which resulted in their untimely death. This situation stands in stark contrast to that of

Cécile Gannendaris in the 1660s. Rather than being a reason to abandon Gannendaris, her Christian character was the very thing that gave additional support to her family during her illness. Certainly, they received vital supplies and food from within the community, as well as from the bishop, because of her devotion to the faith.

Circumstances changed after the dispersal. Christianity was a source of power for the Wendat in general, but for Wendat women in particular. During this period, social mobility extended far beyond the customary women's councils (which still existed) to new roles as teachers, interpreters, seminarists, hospital nuns, and Ursuline sisters. This shift allowed women to maintain and expand their influence throughout the diaspora and for the remainder of the seventeenth century.

10

Power

Sources of Strength and Survival beyond the Dispersal

At the heart of the notion of diaspora is the image of a journey. In most cases this is not one migration, but multiple relocations with diverse experiences, people, and landscapes.[1] For the seventeenth-century Wendat diaspora, the journey from Wendake to Michilimackinac and Lorette represented both a physical and psychological experience. Not only did they overcome obstacles of travel, having to clear and plant fields, build longhouses and palisades, but they simultaneously reconstructed their society, identity, and economic networks.

A Wendat headman reflected on the dire circumstances of the Wendat situation during the early stages of dispersal. He introduced his Native delegation to the French governor by saying:

> Thou seest at thy feet the wreck of a great country, and the pitiful remnant of a whole world, that was formerly peopled by countless inhabitants. But now thou art addressed by mere carcasses, only the bones of which have been left by the Iroquois ... and our limbs, most of which have passed through the boiling caldrons of our foes, had no more strength.[2]

Certainly the odds were against them. The weak and "wrecked" Wendat implemented strategies to overcome these obstacles, but the outcome remained undetermined. By 1665, the time of this headman's reflection, he could see beyond the desolation. After fifteen years of journeying, he proclaimed things already looked better. "The Sun," he asserted, "seemed to shine upon [the Wendat] with brighter beams."[3] This final chapter examines the details of the Wendat journey from a "pitiful remnant of a whole world" to a people rejuvenated and actively engaged with the new world created in the wake of their dispersal. It does not view the communities of Michilimackinac and Lorette as separate relocation projects. Rather, it connects them to a diasporic process through the prism of power.

Power can be used as an indication of strength and prosperity as well as a sign of societal struggle and disadvantage. The ways people gain, use, and lose power is often a reflection of their social, economic, and political standing. Diaspora communities, for instance, are forced to renegotiate their collective power as a result of their dispersion.[4] The Wendat drew from a range of sources to survive their plan of resettlement. In turn, these sources translated into multi-dimensional systems of power based on long-standing relationships, reformulated to meet the needs of the Wendat post-1650. The headman was right; the metaphorical sun began to shine on the Wendat diaspora, since power did not wane during the post-dispersal period, but was gained and maintained.

Sources

The Wendat actively sought out sources of power after their exodus from Wendake, strengthening their social status and overall chances of survival. The Wendat, whether they were headmen, women, elders, or others, drew upon five main repositories.

Cultural Capital

Previous notions of Wendat culture and heritage shaped the behaviours and beliefs of their post-dispersal community. The Wendat reorganized many customs in response to diaspora conditions, but they maintained specific links to lifeways before their move. Migrants packed these traditions into their cultural reservoir and transmitted them from one generation to another. In the west, the Feast of Squash, Bear Dance, and formal Wendat headmen's regalia worn by the "three kings" demonstrated these traditions just as in the east the continued practice of gift giving at funerals, communal use of land and food, as well as the skill of canoe, moccasin, and snowshoe manufacturing expressed a similar continuity.[5] The Wendat used these displays of cultural capital to remind both themselves and others that their traditions were not left in Wendake and their customs remained useful and relevant in the post-dispersal period. The Wendat continued to influence diplomatic initiatives in part because their language remained the lingua franca of regional foreign relations for Natives and Europeans. Commenting on its widespread use by non-Wendat nations in the 1630s and '40s, New France citizen Pierre Boucher testified that most of the people of the region spoke Wendat, especially the Anishinaabeg, Petun, Neutral, and Iroquois.[6]

Its continued use by Anishinaabe, Iroquois, and French ambassadors in the latter half of the seventeenth century indicates an already established etiquette. In a 1665 assembly, including French, Anishinaabe, and Wendat representatives, the Wendat spoke first, "in their own language," to explain the meaning behind their gifts of wampum and to clarify the discussions of the assembly.[7] This was then translated into French for the governor, as the attending Anishinaabeg would have understood it perfectly. Another example of the prevalence of Wendat language occurred during a peace treaty the following spring. Despite the fact that the meeting was between the Wendat, French, and Iroquois, the negotiations were conducted exclusively in the Wendat language. The meeting concluded with a signed treaty outlining the major points of the agreement – and the entire document was in Wendat.[8] This custom privileged the Wendat in terms of diplomatic initiatives, especially because Native diplomacy emphasized the representatives' ability to eloquently articulate their constituents' desires. The French often felt inadequate because of their failure to master Wendat, let alone the Native rhetorical use of metaphor.[9] The Iroquois were also at a disadvantage, although they were likely more comfortable with this Nadowekian dialect than the French.[10] Pragmatic reasons likely dictated the decision to use Wendat for this and other negotiations; not only did all three groups understand Wendat, but it had been a long-standing tradition to conduct diplomacy in that language. Further, the interpreter for this particular proceeding was the French Jesuit Pierre-Joseph-Marie Chaumonot, a missionary who was probably trained in Wendat rather than Iroquois.[11] This practice allowed the Wendat to influence the region through the appropriation of their language by non-Wendat people. It made it a useful tool for diplomacy and set the Wendat apart from other Natives in the region.

Kinship

Kinship connections remained central to Wendat organizational strategy in the post-dispersal period. Their relocations to Anishinaabe communities and their settlement patterns east and west expanded these relationships. The continued intermarriage of the Wendat from the various diasporic communities sustained the Wendat diaspora. The Wendat Jacques Otratenkoui took advantage of the distances and differences between Wendat villages, as well as marriage customs, in order to facilitate relocation within the sphere of Wendat society. Otratenkoui first married a Lorettan woman from an influential Christian family. He remained with her for some time, but eventually decided that the Christian piety of the east was too much. He packed his belongings and told his family he wanted to head west to conduct trade. In reality, his journey to Michilimackinac became permanent, resulting in the abandonment of his Lorettan wife and his marriage instead to a western traditionalist.[12] Considering the importance of Christianity at Lorette, his first marriage gave him access to the influence and high profile character of his wife's family. His second marriage also served as a source of advantage. By marrying a Wendat from the area, he became part of her family and gained security from the community at large when they adopted him.

The diasporic Wendat also continued to marry their Anishinaabe neighbours, with similar effects. It is likely, for instance, that an Eastern Wendat trader named Louis Ouakouts married an Ottawa woman in the 1680s.[13] Although living in the east (it is not clear whether they were Lorettans, but they definitely lived between Montreal and Quebec City), this couple maintained contact with their relatives in the west. In particular, Ouakouts's wife sent messages and wampum to her Ottawa relatives at Michilimackinac.[14] Kinship connections between the Ottawa wife in the east and the Ottawa community of the west facilitated this type of communication; marriages like this allowed the Wendat to maintain their close relationship to Coalition members.

Similarly, Wendat marriages to the French expanded access to goods, protection, and powerful friends in French civil society. In the pre-dispersal period, inter-ethnic relationships rarely existed, because it was mostly French missionaries and nuns who were in contact with the Wendat, but the influx of French immigrants in the 1660s as well as the relocation of the Wendat to the predominantly French settled areas of Michilimackinac and Quebec City in the 1670s changed these dynamics.[15] It was more common for Wendat women, rather than Wendat men, to take French spouses. French reports from the west frequently discuss Wendat women partnering with French soldiers and high-ranking officials.[16] Notarial records from the east list Wendat women who married French habitants, merchants, and traders from Quebec City.[17] Marriage to these men connected the Wendat to the French by "real" kinship relationships, extending the familial branch to their children. As wives and mothers of French children, Wendat women and their families gained from their personal connections because instead of being the metaphorical "children" of the French "Father," they literally and biologically became the uncles, aunts, cousins, and grandparents of French people.

The Wendat continued their belief and practice of so-called fictive kinship relations as well. Just as the Wendat maintained their perception that the Anishinaabeg remained part of their "same cabin," or family, Wendat involvement in the Holy Family deepened their ties with the French.[18] Through this organization they became members of a selective Christian network, a spiritual family with God as the "Father" and the French and Wendat members their spiritual kin.[19] In fact, the Jesuits first contextualized the organization in terms of Wendat kinship practices, explaining that all Wendat Christians should be considered part of the "heavenly family" or "lineage of believers."[20] Through this rhetoric, the Wendat expanded their membership to a Euro-Christian celestial family.

Homeland(s)

Among the many psychological repercussions of forced migrations for refugees, anxiety over forgetting their geographic origins would have been a common and painful phenomenon for most Wendat migrants.[21] Many Natives continued to reference past villages long after their exodus from Wendat country. Both the Wendat and non-Wendat peoples identified diaspora members by their villages in the homeland of Wendake. Before 1649, Wendat taken captive by the Iroquois identified themselves by their former homeland, and specifically their town of origin. In 1653, a list of captives included the Wendat Onta,annaoche, from Scanonaenrat, and Ochhend, from Ationnontetsia.[22] Other examples omitted a Wendat name all together and merely identified them as "formerly from St. Francis Xavier."[23]

The Wendat created profound connections with their new "homeland" to compensate for the loss of Wendake. It is common for migrants to enlarge their former concept of homeland by adopting new homelands and incorporating them into their nascent identity. This process, experts contend, "contributes to an expansion of rootedness by allowing people to incorporate a whole new landscape learning experience into the one they already have."[24] The Wendat from the east and west adopted this strategy wholeheartedly. They shared ancestral links to Wendake, while identifying as Lorettans and Wendat from Michilimackinac. Contemporaries identified those from the east as "hurons de Lorette," "Sauvage de Lorete," "gens de Lorette," "huron Christians de Lorette" and the "Lorettans"; and those from the west as "Hurons de Michilimackinac," "Huron Village at Michilimackinac," "Indiens de Michilimackinac."[25] Along these same lines, a hand-drawn map of the communities at Michilimackinac in 1698 clearly differentiates the "Huron Indians" from other groups such as the Illinois and Miami.[26] Homeland(s) empowered the Wendat by giving them a sense of place and permanence. Lorette and Michilimackinac were established communities with identifiably Wendat characteristics, effectively expanding the cultural borders of Wendake into new regions. Far from being the far-flung remnants of a disappearing nation, the Wendat from these communities became recognized citizens of that land and location.

Aside from using Lorette and Michilimackinac as points of reference to their Wendat identity, the homeland(s) also situated the Wendat in a privileged geographic location. In the east, the Wendat were close to French guns and supplies, Montreal diplomatic meetings, and the St. Lawrence trade routes. In the west, Michilimackinac developed as a hub for economic activity, French military strategy, and Anishinaabe support. Together, the Lorette–Michilimackinac corridor extended the sphere of Wendat geopolitical influence in comparison to the more limited borders of Wendake.

Wendakeronon Identity[27]

Memory of the old landscape of Wendake was accompanied by an equally strong awareness of Wendat identity pre-dispersal. Instead of adopting the character of their Anishinaabe, French, and Iroquoian hosts and neighbours, the Wendat clung to their distinct ethnic roots as Wendakeronon.[28] Despite their loss to the Iroquois and their dwindling population, the Wendat perceived themselves as the ancestors of a powerful people – a legacy used in the post-dispersal period to assert that their status had not changed since the exodus in 1650. A focus on common ethnic heritage served to bond the Wendat across the diaspora, and enabled them to gain favour with future and former allies.

Wendakeronon connections remained the key to using this strategy effectively. Their long-term engagement with the French privileged them in terms of gaining access to Jesuit guidance, land, and protection. When a Western Wendat woman at Michilimackinac requested special meetings with the Jesuits, she gained their attention by explaining that she had been a pupil of Brébeuf's in Wendake.[29] The woman's reference to Brébeuf qualified her as a former Wendakeronon, a people whom the French viewed as having decades of exposure to Christian practices and a particular affinity for it.[30] In reality, the Wendat had been the "first" for most French–Native relations. The French saw them as the first Christians, their first allies, and their first trade partners.[31] Dating back to Samuel de

Champlain, the Wendakeronon set the stage for their diaspora descendants in terms of French relations.

Wendat reputations as diplomats, eloquent orators, and political strategists fortified their Wendakeronon identity. Commenting on Wendat characteristics, Claude-Charles Bacqueville de la Potherie summarized the Wendat as generally "very politic, treacherous in their movements, and exceedingly proud." He continued, "They have more intelligence than the other Indians. They are generous, and show much delicacy in their conversation. They are good speakers, insinuating in their manners, and are rarely taken in by anyone."[32] Louis de Lahontan made similar observations as he recorded his impressions of them in the 1680s. According to Lahontan, the Wendat were "brave, entrepreneurial and spiritual." This was in comparison to the Anishinaabeg, whom he deemed "ugly," and the Iroquois, whom he described as "tricky."[33]

Wendat self-articulations of Wendakeronon identity, in conjunction with the acceptance and perpetuation of such character by contemporaries like the French, sustained a Wendat identity beyond their dispersal. As a result, members of the Wendat diaspora took advantage of their noted reputations as intelligent, articulate, and calculating individuals by merely affiliating themselves with their Wendat heritage.

Christianity

Christianity certainly offered a major source of power for the Wendat in the post-dispersal period. Leaders used conversion to gain political and economic privileges with the French, and women leveraged their piety to acquire additional opportunities. In Iroquois country, Christianity helped the Wendat sustain their distinct identity, which not only set them apart from their captors but even qualified them for roles as teachers and leaders within their new communities. On the whole, the Wendat from across the diaspora embraced baptism as a means to cope with the obstacles created by their dispersal. It supplied new forms of comfort, cosmology, and security during a time of social crisis.

Not all Wendat were convinced conversion was a logical resource for their survival, however. Late into the 1650s, some Wendat still projected resistance, echoing the arguments of Taretande in the 1630s. Individuals continued to "attribute to the Faith all the wars, diseases, and calamities of the country." They explained that "their change of Religion [had] caused their change of fortune; and that their Baptism was at once followed by every possible misfortune."[34] Traditionalists distrusted not only

Christianity but the French alliance in general. They often pointed to the Dutch as a potential alternative ally because the Dutch did not typically press for conversion and allowed the Iroquois to "live in their own fashion."[35] Notwithstanding the importance of this vocal minority, or their potential influence on the Wendat communities, the overall character of the Wendat diaspora became increasingly more Christian as the century progressed. This suggests that the traditionalists became a marginalized faction in the post-dispersal period as Christians dominated the policies and culture of the majority.

Systems

Scholarly attempts to describe Native North American activity and connectivity have shaped our understanding of the nature of these relationships today. Most often, scholars define human interaction in terms of political organization and motivation. Dominating these narratives about the seventeenth-century Native world are what the *Handbook of American Indians North of Mexico* calls "confederacies" and "looser alliances."[36] This paradigm of Native political organization, with confederacies at the forefront, has distorted our view of Native North America in general and Native polities in particular.[37] The terminology in many ways reconfigures the character of Native alliance making, giving more weight to centralized sedentary societies and disregarding links that do not fit the typical European notions of alliance. As we have seen, the pre-dispersal Wendat participated in numerous systems, some of which fit the concepts of confederacy, while others, such as their relationship with the Anishinaabeg, placed them outside the standard scholarly paradigm.

Another way to understand Wendat human actions and connections is as "systems of power," which helps reconceptualize these Native networks from a Wendat perspective.[38] Wendat alliances, both within and outside the Confederacy, functioned as systems of "social power, whether economic, political, cultural or military, that we can describe functionally and spatially."[39] In the aftermath of 1649, the Wendat used their repository of various power sources to continue to create and work within a world of multiple systems of power. Wendat systems were rooted in tradition and persisted despite the dispersal, even as they were transformed by it.

The Coalition

The Coalition broadened its scope in terms of kinship ties, geography, and political influence after the dispersal. As a system, it projected its power overtly in diplomatic meetings, trade negotiations, and military ventures. Its influence was felt throughout the Great Lakes and St. Lawrence Seaway; from Lorette, Sillery, Ekaentoton, Sault Saint Marie, to the country of the People of the Sea, and Michilimackinac. This, in turn, enlarged the geographic boundaries of the Wendat world. To a great extent the Coalition influenced the west the most, because the Wendat relocated among predominantly Anishinaabe communities. The Wendat worked within this system to achieve settlement strategies in their first wave migrations. They often called upon the Coalition to exert military strength against the Sioux, the Iroquois, and the English, and combined to pressure the French into supporting Coalition projects.[40]

The Wendat constructed this system over decades, even centuries, not within a political or military framework, but rather through more traditional Wendat sources of power, with specific emphasis on kinship, homeland(s), and Wendakeronon identity. Kinship, such as the relationship between the Eastern Wendat trader Louis Ouakouts's wife and her Anishinaabe kin in the west, fostered a close relationship between Coalition members. The adoption of a homeland also deepened this association. In the east, the Lorettan Wendat maintained bonds with Anishinaabeg at Sillery through visits between the two villages, whereas at Michilimackinac the connection became more obvious. Located in villages directly beside each other, the Wendat and Anishinaabeg shared the experience of relocation as well as space. The Wendat relied on new and old Anishinaabe friends to legitimize the move and entice their new neighbours to allow them to stay. Similarly, the Wendat clung to their Wendakeronon identity, and reminded their allies of past participation in Feast of Souls ceremonies and their reputations as formidable middlemen, agriculturalists, and diplomats before the dispersal.

A number of scholars question the resilience and stability of this system, especially in the late seventeenth century.[41] They base this assessment almost entirely on the Western Wendat experience and a scandal surrounding Le Baron's alleged attempt to confirm a secret peace treaty with the Iroquois.[42] The French trader Nicholas Perrot remarked on a similar rumour that included Kondiaronk, contending, "We know very well that the Hurons have always wanted to destroy the nations of the Pays d'en Haut, and that they have never been strongly attached to the French."[43] In light of the numerous examples of successful Coalition initiatives, Perrot's assertion has little weight. Kondiaronk reiterated this perspective, saying, "We have one cabin and one fire, and we should have the same spirit as well."[44] In reality, it was not until the Wendat removal to Detroit at the turn of the eighteenth century that internal conflicts presented themselves on a more frequent basis and the Wendat–Anishinaabe alliance system began to collapse.[45]

The French Connection

If the Western Wendat were more inclined to engage with the Coalition's system of power, the Eastern Wendat participated more fully in a power structure orchestrated around their relationship with the French. Although not nearly as well defined as the Coalition by 1649, what began as intermittent interaction with French missionaries and trade expeditions to Montreal developed into an intricate web of political, economic, military and social relationships for the rest of the century – the dispersal strengthened it. Jesuit Jean de Lamberville confirmed this development observing that, "these poor people [the Wendat] owe all this great Change in their customs to the loss of Their country and Their Transmigration into ours." Further he confided, "Formerly I wept at the overthrow and destruction of the hurons by The Iroquois, and now I Praise God for it; for I see clearly that, if the nation had remained flourishing as it was of old, we would not in a hundred years have gained so much ascendancy over Them."[46] The destruction of Wendake facilitated the need for the Wendat to create more intimate ties with the French.

The Wendat relocations and French immigration to North America formed the contours of this system's geographic boundaries. For the most part, the Wendat and French simultaneously established themselves at the same key geopolitical outposts in the seventeenth-century post-dispersal period. With Lorette/Quebec City on one end and Michilimackinac on the other, the French–Wendat allegiance intersected and connected people within the same geographic sphere of influence.[47] This system benefited both parties. Aside from gaining military allies and trade partners, the French acquired potential Christian converts and access to Anishinaabe furs. The Wendat, on the other hand, profited from what the Wendat Ignace Saouhenhohi termed "the power of protection."[48] The kind of protection Saouhenhohi talked about rested in guns and the growing French population. Frenchmen now outnumbered the Wendat; therefore, Wendat migrations to predominantly French settlements increased their odds against enemies such as the Iroquois.

The Wendat nurtured their French connections by tapping into cultural capital, kinship ties, Wendakeronon identity, and Christian sources of power. The French had a better grasp of the Wendat language and customs than of other Native groups. This gave the Wendat an advantage during meetings and encouraged the French to "prefer them" above all others.[49] Proximity to French settlements and frequent interaction with settlers and soldiers resulted in marriages that made the Wendat and French part of the same family. The Wendat also recalled their historical relationship with the French dating back to Samuel de Champlain, illustrating Wendat hospitality and persistent loyalty to the French. Finally, widespread Wendat Christian character provoked the French to continue their affiliation with the Wendat in the hopes of achieving their goals of the "Frenchification" and "salvation" of North America's Native people. These sources of power connected the French to the Wendat for decades and created an essential system of social security for both groups after the Wendat dispersal.

The Confederacy

There is no doubt that the pre-dispersal system known as the Wendat Confederacy underwent significant change. Yet, it did not disintegrate in its entirety, as many suggest.[50] Rather, former confederates transformed the system into a flexible, expanded version of their former political organization, retaining old components as well as creating new ones. In Wendake, the Confederacy fit the familiar framework of a Native political league. It was more or less "designed for defense or offense of two or more autonomous nations who engaged in a compact or formal statement of principles to govern separate and collective action."[51] Typically, it acted under one supreme council that included representatives of the contracting nations who ceded to the league various powers and rights they previously exercised individually. After the dispersal, however, the Wendat faced obstacles of distance and disconnectedness. No longer living within close proximity, Lorettans and the Western Wendat reconfigured the Confederacy into what can most appropriately be described as a "diasporic polity."[52] In brief, the Wendat engaged in a far-flung network of people to whom local authorities granted self-governing privileges. These groups were often associated with trading and financial networks, and many did not have an autonomous territorial base where they were the majority.[53] Moreover, members of diasporic polities were often prohibited from controlling land, in exchange for the right to live and trade among other nations.[54]

The Wendat united through their common sources of power. Cultural capital, kinship, homeland(s), as well as their Wendakeronon identity and Christianity played significant roles in sustaining the former Confederacy as a diasporic polity. Communication was also key in the process. Although some believe that the Wendat maintained limited interaction between the east and west, the numerous accounts of Lorettans and those from Michilimackinac conversing, trading, marrying, and conducting diplomacy together deliver an alternative interpretation.

The Wendat discussed the possibility of reconnecting the diaspora by having one of the communities join the other. In 1660, the trader Pierre-Esprit Radisson met with a number of Eastern Wendat and asked them if they wanted to join his expedition to the west, "to see their owne nation that fled there."[55] After some consideration, the Wendat declined the offer. In 1669, a number of the Western Wendat travelled to Quebec to discuss French military aid against a "powerful enemy."[56] The Eastern Wendat, along with the Jesuits, took this opportunity to invite the hundreds of Wendat living out west to relocate permanently to Lorette. It seems that the Western Wendat did not outwardly reject this offer, as the Jesuits believed that at least a portion of the Western Wendat would move the following spring.[57]

Delegations from one corner of the Wendat world to the other persisted into the 1670s. In 1672, the Eastern Wendat felt the need to promote a common Christian character when they travelled to Michilimackinac. They publicly declared that all meetings should be conducted with the utmost respect for the Christian faith and that if they became aware of any suggestion of offence, the Eastern Wendat would leave immediatly.[58] There is no indication that the Lorettans left or did not participate in the meetings, which demonstrates a western adherence to the east's requests. There was a similar acceptance of Christianity at Michilimackinac.

Trade also connected the diaspora. Marie Félix du Bocq and Louis Ouakouts set out from Lorette in 1682 to Michilimackinac for trade. Among the goods belonging to du Bocq were: 18 combs, 132 "big knives," a packet of arrow heads, 2 gross of awls, 7 half large muskets, 21 leather knives, 12 strike-a-lights, approximately 10 pounds of lead, 140 musket balls, 7 to 8 pounds of powder, 7 large double mirrors, a "heap" of blue beads as well as black, red, and white beads, and cosmetic powder.[59] Du Bocq also acted as a Jesuit courier, delivering letters from Michilimackinac to the Jesuits at Quebec.[60] These letters most likely contained important updates concerning the Jesuit Order and the Wendat living in close proximity to them.

Although motivated by economic pursuits, interactions between the Eastern and Western Wendat resulted in exchanges concerning information about each respective community.

Marriages continued kinship links throughout the diaspora. The Eastern Wendat Jacques Otratenkoui took the opportunity to take a Western Wendat wife. Through this act, Otratenkoui created familial ties at Michilimackinac, and his daughter consequently possessed ancestral bonds to both her community in the west and her father's homeland of Lorette.[61]

Lastly, former confederate members worked within their diasporic polity to conduct diplomacy. On many occasions Western and Eastern Wendat initiated policies and agreements autonomous from each other, but there is reason to believe they were represented collectively at the Great Peace of Montreal in 1701. Although the Eastern Wendat did not have a headman sign the treaty, there is a chance that Kondiaronk represented both the east and west. This theory is supported by the fact that the Lorette Chief Nicholas Vincent possessed a wampum belt in 1825 that he believed to be a gift to an Eastern leader by Kondiaronk in 1701. This verifies that the Lorettans were present at the negotiations, and therefore were likely represented by Kondiaronk.[62] The joint representation of the Wendat in 1701 suggests a continuity of Wendat political traditions post-dispersal. Linked by a common language, families, homelands, heritage, and religion, the Wendat maintained their status as a political entity by continuing to engage in shared diplomatic ventures. Claude-Charles Bacqueville de la Potherie asserted that by the turn of the eighteenth century, those Wendat living at Lorette and Michilimackinac were still from "the same nation."[63]

Conclusion

The hopeful Wendat headman who spoke of "bright beams" at the beginning of this chapter was in many ways correct. Recall his passionate salute to his fellow Wendat: "Courage, O desolate people! Thy bones are about to be knit together with muscles and tendons, thy flesh is to be born again, thy strength will be restored to thee, and thou shalt live as thou didst live of old."[64] The headman hoped that the dispersed Wendat would regain their strength and form a legitimate body politic comparable to the Wendat Confederacy "of old." Yet, despite good intentions, his aspirations were nostalgic, to say the least. By the 1640s and the Iroquois invasion, the Wendat were not in a formidable state. Weakened by disease, military attacks, and internal divisions between pro- and anti-Jesuit factions, the

Confederacy experienced near-fatal degrees of turmoil and flux. Leaders fell, women struggled with new restrictions on their influence, and warfare dominated foreign policies. With the dispersal, these circumstances changed. Rather than returning to a state of social crisis, the Wendat pushed forward and reconfigured their systems of power, overcoming many of their previous problems.

The Wendat people emerged both empowered and disempowered by the dispersal. While some lost their authority, such as Wendat traditionalists, and leaders became targets of Iroquois martyrdom, others, such as Christian women, sought out additional opportunities, and Christian headmen maintained their influence as geopolitical leaders throughout the Great Lakes. Larger systems also shifted direction during this period, but remained rooted in their pre-dispersal origins. Changes in homelands, culture, and politics resulted in a decline but not complete destruction of the Confederacy, while the Coalition and French alliances became more important. Moreover, a study of the processes of Wendat dispersal and relocation in the seventeenth century demonstrates that natural factors such as disease and drought became critical to the success of the dispersal and the nature of the diaspora. The famine experienced at Gahoendoe and the deaths of hundreds if not thousands of Wendat forced confederates to migrate out of Wendake and rely on Anishinaabe and French allies for refuge. It was also during this period that large numbers of Wendat settled among the Iroquois, resulting in closer ties with their traditional enemies and enabling a number of peace treaties between the two, including the Great Peace of 1701. In addition, Wendat culture evolved but remained intact. Taking on both policies of compromise and conformity, the Wendat drew from their reputation as Christians to differentiate themselves as a distinct and favoured people throughout the Great Lakes and St. Lawrence region.

Epilogue

Reconnecting the Modern Diaspora, 1999

On 10 August 1999, the dispersed descendants of the once powerful Wendat Confederacy reunited in a Feast of Souls ceremony.[1] Numbering in the hundreds, participants gathered at a sacred ossuary pit located near the old Wendat village of Ossossane, near what is today Midland, Ontario. This was the location of a Feast of Souls ritual in 1636 and the heart of Wendake in the seventeenth century. The reason for this modern gathering was twofold. It was first and foremost organized to return Wendat bones taken from the pit in the 1940s by archaeologists and placed in the Royal Ontario Museum (ROM) in Toronto. Out of this quest, however, arose an additional goal of reuniting the four modern Wendat nations (located in Quebec, Ontario/Michigan, Oklahoma, and Kansas) in their homeland.[2] Moreover, organizers hoped the gathering would serve as a forum to renew the Wendat Confederacy on twenty-first-century terms. Nearly four centuries after their initial dispersal, disparate groups across North America continued to connect and identify as "Wendat."[3] This present-day Wendat diaspora joined together through the same avenues as their seventeenth-century ancestors, drawing upon the power, traditions, and culture of the Confederacy before its dispersal.

The ROM, located in Toronto, Ontario, houses some of the most important exhibits and artifacts in all of Canada. It is not surprising that nearly five hundred boxes of Wendat bones, discovered and excavated by archaeologist Kenneth Kidd in 1947 and 1948 ended up in the ROM's collection. For forty years, these souls (as the Wendat call them) were kept in the basement of the anthropology department of the museum and were never actually put on public display.[4] As a little boy, Michel Gros-Louis, a Huron-Wendat from Quebec, visited the museum. Through this visit Gros-Louis discovered the location and status of the bones. From that point on, he promised himself he would do whatever he could to return the souls to their proper resting place. He reflected on this goal: "I feel it is my duty to do that out of respect for my ancestors."[5] In 1997, Gros-Louis went to the ROM and made a formal request to have the bones returned. The ROM agreed and plans were set in motion.[6]

The reburial required complex preparations. They included the collaboration of Native and non-Native groups, the communication and organization of numbers of volunteers, and most importantly the involvement of the Wendat diaspora communities and their leaders. Chief Janith English (Wyandot Nation of Kansas) put in many long hours to prepare for the event. Other Wendat leaders (Chief Wellie Picard, Huron Wendat of Wendake; Chief Leaford Bearskin, Wyandotte Nation of Oklahoma; Second Chief Jim Bland, Wyandotte Nation of Oklahoma; and spokesperson Steven A. Gronda, Wyandot Nation of Anderdon) asked Chief English to draft a written agreement reinstating the Wendat Confederacy.[7] The task was daunting; nevertheless, she found solace in the work and completed a copy that reached one page in length. It not only spoke of the contemporary bond between Wendat people but also drew upon ancient concepts of leadership and traditions of unity. The document concludes, "We vow to attempt to work together in a way that the embers of long ago council fires may be fanned into a flame of kinship, culture and love that will warm countless generations of Wendat people."[8] The "embers of long ago" that Chief English sought to reignite came from the remnants of those seventeenth-century men and women who preserved the Wendat identity for future use. In addition to her written work, Chief English created a flag for each of the four nations. The chiefs agreed upon a symbol and she spent three months hand-sewing each flag. According to English, the work was worth it because "they were [her] present to *the* Nation."[9]

Participants from the Wyandot Nation of Kansas began preparations three weeks prior to the gathering by abstaining from alcohol and drugs. This continued throughout the ceremony and for a subsequent week after.[10] Other volunteers began planning well in advance. Despite the importance and relevance of this historic gathering to the broader Canadian society, Heritage Canada and Indian Affairs both denied the Wendat request for financial aid.[11] Consequently, local organizations supported the event, including the Martyrs' Shrine, St. John Ambulance, Wye Heritage Marina, Friends of Sainte-Marie, Sainte-Marie among the Hurons, the Wye Marsh Wildlife Centre, Camp Simpresca, Girl Guides of Canada (Silver Birch Area), Chappell Farms, A&M Superstore of Barrie, and the

Wendat Confederacy flag, 1999. Courtesy of Chief Janith English

Midland OPP detachment.[12] Commenting on the specific amount of work and preparation put in by Pierre Lefave, the manager at the public history site Sainte-Marie among the Hurons, Chief English said, "I was astounded to enter each of the buildings. There was a fire blazing in every fireplace and candles on every mantle of that huge complex. No small gesture of welcome."[13] These intricate details demonstrated the amount of time and energy put in by volunteers.

Eventually the day came, and despite inevitable modern-day alterations to this version of the Feast of Souls, the 1999 event maintained its traditional purpose as a means to unite the Confederacy by solidifying friendships, old and new alike.[14] Preliminary events took place the day before the Feast on 28 August and included the arrival by canoe of four Wendat chiefs, as well as the signing of English's document reinstating the Confederacy. In one fire, each group contributed the ashes of their own nation's fires, symbolizing the joining together of these dispersed peoples.

Accompanying the Wendat chiefs were leaders from local Anishinaabe and Iroquois nations. In particular, Chief Lorraine McRae of the Chippewas of Mnjikaning at the Rama Reserve stood along the bank of the Wye River to welcome the Wendat chiefs formally. It was McRae's people who had accepted the stewardship of the fish weir at Atherley Narrows near Orillia, Ontario, during the time of the Wendat dispersal. "Our peoples met thousands of years ago," remarked McRae, "and I feel so honoured to be sharing in this homecoming." Observers witnessed the procession with solemn respect. Although only eleven years old, Riel Lamarche, a descendant of the famous Métis leader Louis Riel, understood the circumstances. "They have come home," he explained to journalist Roberta Avery, who was among a number of reporters attending the event.

Aside from non-Wendat participants, approximately four hundred Wendat travelled "home" for the ceremony. The five hundred boxes of bones were loaded into a cube van and transported from the ROM to the burial site. Leaders delivered elaborate speeches before each box was smudged with sweetgrass. This was followed by an individual blessing bestowed on the containers by ninety-year-old elder Madelaine Gros-Louis from Wendake, Quebec – the oldest attendee at the ceremony. The boxes were then carefully passed down one by one through a human chain, and opened to reveal the discoloured fragments of human remains. Small child-sized skulls, rib cages, and leg bones were exposed, looking more like bundles of firewood than remnants of human beings. Slowly, they made their way towards the eight-foot ossuary pit that was lined with over a dozen beaver pelts, as well as other customary burial items such as kettles and pots. Michel Gros-Louis then placed the bones in a circle at the bottom of the pit. He explained the personal satisfaction of the moment in the following way: "I feel at peace seeing my ancestors returned to their rightful resting place." For Gros-Louis, this was the culmination of ten years of work. It was the right thing to do not only for his people (past and present) but also for himself – fulfilling the promise he had made years ago when he first became aware of the bones.

Gros-Louis was not alone in his sentiments. The connection between the Wendat and their seventeenth-century ancestors was profound. The Feast of Souls in 1999 became a vehicle for contemporary peoples to meet with their past. Kinship bonds were reaffirmed and new relationships were formed. Jim Bland, Second Chief of the Wyandotte of Oklahoma, was overcome by his personal experience. "My ancestors are here. I feel that," Bland explained. The feast became a meeting ground that on the one hand delivered a window into the ancient world of Wendake, while on the other hand, it inspired a new generation of Wendat. Steven Gronda, of the Anderdon Wyandot, expressed the dual purpose of the event: "The Huron rebirth will come as we return the remains of our ancestors to mother earth." Chief English also commented on the unification process, explaining, "I felt like we were suspended in time and place. I feel a oneness with all my brothers and sisters here with me now, and those who went before."

Beyond a profound connection with ancestors and the revitalization of the Wendat Confederacy, Wendat organizers attempted to address the pain and dislocation experienced by the Wendat because of their dispersal. Although many centuries in the past, the feeling of loss had transferred down for generations. According to Chief English, the emotions and trauma of 1649 persist in the collective memory of the modern Wendat. It is her understanding that "many years ago when our people left this beautiful land on the shores of Georgian Bay, our hearts were heavy, our people were very, very sad." Sallie Andrews, a Wyandotte of Oklahoma, sympathized with the pain of her ancient relatives. The event for Andrews was "an emotional experience of great sadness, it's more than words can say." Despite this sadness, however, a healing process had begun. Chief English saw it as fundamental to creating a strong and vibrant Wendat society. English shared her beliefs with a reporter during the 1999 events, giving "thanks to the creator that this healing has taken place." By drawing upon the experience of 1649, the Wendat regained a sense of belonging and identity from their ancestors. Reflecting on this notion in connection to the Feast of Souls in 1999, Chief English encouraged people to

> remember that the opposite of Love is not hate; it is apathy. Conflict is inevitable when people resolve to reconnect and attempt to define new relationships. For those who love one another, joy is almost inevitably connected with a degree of pain ... This was a very powerful event ... We all tried the best we could to accomplish the seemingly impossible: to soothe the wounds and welcome each other home after 350 years of separation.[15]

Central to this healing process was the concept of place and space. Similar to their seventeenth-century kinsmen, the twentieth-century Wendat looked to the old boundaries of Wendake for comfort and belonging. It represented a location to reconnect in a physical, emotional, and spiritual way to the people and events of their past. Consequently, Chief English foresaw that "this place [would] become a place of peace and healing for all who [visit]."[16] Concepts of homeland and place are frequent points of reference for diaspora people. For the modern Wendat it represented a territory filled with memories of warfare, disease, and the dispersal of their Confederacy; at the same time, it symbolized a source of power as well as a sense of identity and heritage.

The events of 1999 resulted in a number of achievements for the contemporary Wendat community. Since the initial burial, it has become tradition to gather at the site every summer, for members from each nation to reconnect on an annual basis. Moreover, the ROM has handed over the responsibilities for the preservation of the burial pit to the Wendake Band Council. Of particular significance is the founding of the Agondachia Association, which also goes by the name Ossossane Foundation in reference to the location of the burial site. This organization's main goals are "the survival of the Wendat heritage and the traditional ways of the Wendat people."[17] The association, therefore, adopted the initial goals of the gathering to promote those objectives for the future.

Popular support for the Feast of Souls in 1999, nearly four hundred years after the perceived "destruction" of the Wendat, exposes the reality of the situation. The existence of a collective Wendat community today is due in large part to the people who maintained that identity and culture beyond their physical dispersal in 1649 – people like Kondiaronk, Pierre Atironta, and Cécile Gannendaris. Generations have drawn upon the legacy of the Confederacy, their legends, history, and traditions, to create a new cohort of Wendat leaders and communities. These people may have transformed in the wake of wars, colonialism, and relocation, but at their core they are Wendakeronon, the descendants of Aenon and Taretande, and the results of a cultural persistence rooted in the seventeenth century. Chief Janith English believes in the power of the past and its importance to the modern Wendat Confederacy. Her overall perception of the events in 1999 highlight the undeniable conclusion that although the Wendat were dispersed in 1649, they were not destroyed. Thus, English contends, "When I participated in the ceremonies in 1999, I felt as if I had come full circle. The Feast of Souls is the heart of the Spirit of Our Nation. It has assumed a different form; but our Heart never changes."[18] Similarly, the Wendat of today are not the Wendat of the past, but their hearts have remained the same.

Appendix
Sources and the Discourse of Destruction

In his 2007 publication *Words of the Huron,* John Steckley, a highly published Wendat scholar, notes that the history of the seventeenth-century Wendat is a familiar narrative to many. Through class lessons, public history sites, and textbooks, most Canadians have at least some idea of who they were.[1] Indeed, historian Cornelius Jaenen contends that *all* the histories concerning New France mention the "destruction" of Wendake as a seminal event.[2] Richard White's influential book *Middle Ground,* which made waves in terms of the history of European and Native relations, begins by describing his geographic analytical boundaries in relation to "the lands beyond Huronia."[3] White positions the Wendat homeland as a central and symbolic reference to power and politics in the context of seventeenth-century historical frameworks.

For many Canadians, the Wendat legacy remains integral to national and provincial narratives. Writing in the late nineteenth century, Daniel Wilson stated he was interested in the Wendat because "the Hurons are the native historical race of Canada, intimately identified with incidents of its early settlement and of friendly intercourse with *La Nouvelle France.*"[4] Ernest Jackson Hathaway justified his 1915 publication *Story of the Hurons* by saying the history of the Wendat is the "complete first chapter of the history of Ontario."[5] And in 1909 Arthur Jones asserted, "The heroic in our history finds here [Huronia] its home."[6] Persisting throughout the twentieth century, government officials of Ontario's Tourism Department in the 1960s justified the establishment of public history sites dedicated to the Wendat, because Wendake was "often called the cradle of Ontario's history."[7] According to a 1969 survey, 60 percent of the people of Toronto (Canada's largest city and the provincial capital of Ontario) believed that learning the history of the Wendat through the creation of public history sites was an "important part of the history of Canada and Ontario and helped make them better Canadians."[8]

The Wendat are important to American identity and history as well. Kansas historian William Connelly presented a paper in 1918 describing the critical influence of the Wendat people on Kansas City's history and important national events, such as the American Civil War. For Connelly, the Wyandot of Kansas were of particular importance because of their ancestral links to the Nadowekian people who became "supreme in eastern America" in the seventeenth century.[9]

By describing Wendat history as "Canadian" or "American," scholars have taken ownership of a historical period and people. Within this context, the Wendat and their history are no longer autonomous. Instead, they are integrated into these larger non-Native societies; the Wendat historical narrative becomes colonized to meet nationalistic demands geared towards identity formation and state security.[10] Tucking Wendat history into mainstream accounts of exploration, colonization, and confederation also serves to lengthen the early Euro-American national narratives. Yet, Wendat history began long before the establishment of Canada and the United States.

I came to write my first paper on the seventeenth-century Wendat in response to these national narratives and the proliferation of Wendat history. Sitting in a high school Canadian history class, I became fascinated by the textbook descriptions of Wendat society. My paper concluded with explicit disappointment that, according to my research, the Wendat were destroyed over 350 years ago. Understandably, I was both shocked and confused a few years later to hear a professor at the University of Ottawa introduce himself as Georges Sioui, a Huron-Wendat from Quebec. Perplexed, I approached Professor Sioui to gain clarification. "How is it possible," I naively asked, "that you are a Wendat? Weren't your people destroyed in the seventeenth century?" Sioui responded respectfully, "It is a long story, but I can assure you, I am Huron-Wendat and my people were not destroyed."

Since that time I have come to realize the truth behind Sioui's assertion. Far from being destroyed, the seventeenth-century Wendat survived their dispersal to such an extent that there are modern descendants of the former Wendat Confederacy now living in Quebec, Ontario/Michigan, Kansas, and Oklahoma.[11] This final section seeks to uncover the origins of my former confusion and the discourse of destruction that has dominated the Wendat historical narrative for centuries. It is an investigation into the sources that have led to this destruction myth and seeks to understand how it was produced, sustained, and perpetuated up until the present day. Ultimately, although in many cases the information expressed in a wide variety of forums is historically sound, the interpretations include a repetitive discourse infused with the language of demise. This has led to the circulation of a popular misinformed mythology with serious consequences for our understanding of seventeenth-century Wendat history.

Contact Zones: Academic Scholarship

The ways in which people engage with Wendat history, and in particular their dispersal by the Iroquois in 1649, are varied. These "contact zones," between researcher and historical narrative, give way to unique experiences and interpretations.[12] For the most part, these materials are produced by non-Wendats for non-Wendats. The most easily accessed and widely distributed materials are in the written form: primary and secondary reports, articles, manuscripts, and textbooks.

The origin of the "destruction" myth begins with the *Jesuit Relations,* a series of small books that delivered reports on the work of Jesuit missionaries from around the world. *Relations* from the mission in New France (in the area that came to be known as Canada), which began to appear annually in 1632 and lasted to 1673, were widely read in France and circulated to other Catholic European countries. Jesuits working in the field sent detailed letters to their superior in Quebec City, who compiled and edited these letters, copying verbatim in some places and paraphrasing in others, and forwarded the compilations to the Jesuit headquarters in Paris, where further editorial changes were made before the *Relations* were sent to the printers.

Intimately involved in Wendat affairs during the Iroquois attacks of 1648-49 as well as during the years after the dispersal from Wendake, the Jesuits recorded the Natives' trials and tribulations in the *Relations* of 1649 and in the subsequent years. Because the *Relations* are numerous and the most easily accessible primary source for Wendat history, the way that Jesuits wrote about the so-called destruction greatly influenced the interpretations of later scholars.[13] Even though the Jesuits continued to write about the Wendat after the 1649 dispersal, they used language filled with defeat and loss. The edited volumes that Reuben Thwaites prepared, for instance, are littered with rhetoric discussing the "destruction of the Hurons."[14]

Very few publications refer to the Wendat in the years following the end of the Jesuit reports in 1673. Not until the late nineteenth and early twentieth century did an avid interest re-emerge. These "early scholars" – anthropologists, ethnographers, archeologists, and historians – extracted details from the *Relations* and composed them into scholarly narratives available to the academic community. This sphere of scholarship includes works by Horatio Hale, Francis Parkman, and Charles Marius Barbeau, as well as lesser-known historians, theologians, and geographers.[15] Projects also grew out of reports made for such organizations as the Ontario Historical Society and the Bureau of Archives.[16] Non-Native men dominated the field, and generally the works situated the Wendat within the larger context of histories of Native peoples, New France, and colonial North America.

These early scholars took the Jesuit language of annihilation literally. Consistently, they recount the events of 1649 with explicit "destruction" rhetoric. Francis Parkman titled his account of the years leading up to the dispersal as "The Doomed Nation" and proceeded to discuss how "fatuity, not cowardice, was the ruin of the Huron nation."[17] "All was over with the Hurons," he continued, "without a leader, without organization, without a union, crazed with fright and paralyzed with misery, they yielded to their doom without a blow ... The Hurons, as a nation, ceased to exist."[18] Similarly, nineteenth-century historian E.J. Hathaway called the "extermination" of the Wendat "one of the greatest national tragedies in the human race."[19] Writing in 1827, prominent American political leader Lewis Cass delivered a tragic description of the dispersal as "frightful havoc among the Hurons, and the accounts of their sufferings, given by the old missionaries, who witnessed and shared them, almost task the belief of the reader."[20] The *Handbook of Indians of Canada* (1913) summarized these interpretations by describing the circumstances of 1649 in the following way: "After the destruction of the Huron or Wendat confederation and the more or less thorough dispersal of the several tribes composing it, *the people who, as political units, were originally called Huron and Wendat, ceased to exist.*[21]

Later in the twentieth century, a third wave of Wendat scholarship emerged. Although interested in a similar ethnographic focus as their predecessors, this group produced academic books dedicated almost exclusively to Wendat history, rather than to colonial or national narratives. Using the same sources as the early scholars, these "twentieth-century revisionists" situated Wendat history within the first half of the seventeenth century. Indeed, the most well-known scholars of the Wendat, such as Elizabeth Tooker, Bruce Trigger, Conrad Heidenreich, Karen Anderson, Georges Sioui, Roger Carpenter, Gary Warrick, and Erik Seeman designed projects emphasizing the fifty years before the dispersal.[22] Because of this, and despite their tremendous scholarship and contributions to our understanding of Wendake, these ethnohistorians reinforce the notion of a Wendat demise at the hands of the Iroquois through their temporal frameworks. Trigger, for example, opens with the remark, "For a brief period in the first half of the seventeenth century the Huron played a key role in the history of eastern North America." This implies that they ceased to play a role after 1649.[23] Although the revisionists acknowledge the formation of a diaspora Wendat culture, there are few accounts of post-1650 history in their studies.

Overshadowing these same studies are two lines of argument that confuse perceptions of Wendat survival post-1649. Scholars repeatedly connect the Iroquois attacks to the "Destruction of Huronia" (or the historical territory occupied by the Wendat) and argue that 1649 marks the "End of the Confederacy" (or the political alliance between the Wendat nations).[24] Although in many respects they are historically accurate, these interpretations combine to create a theme of eradication. While still acknowledging that the Wendat continued to exist and contribute to North American society, the language and frameworks distort their academically sound narrative. The word choice of "destruction" and "end" cannot help but describe a situation in which the Wendat are portrayed as destroyed. Notwithstanding the importance of these established assertions, they inadvertently suggest that the Wendat as a people disappeared at the same time as they ceased to live in Wendake and identify as Wendat confederates.

Textbook depictions of the Wendat are a testament to this intuitive phenomenon, as the language of "destruction" and "end" is often translated into general works on early North American history. Applying this discourse, editors and authors of modern textbooks have taken the analyses of scholars and transposed them into educational frameworks for students. These texts situate the Wendat within the larger stories of Native American, Canadian, and American histories as well as provincial/state and colonial histories.[25] They are produced for the masses and reach large portions of the population; the complicated analysis of academics is simplified and the narrative understandable to the general public. They are also geared towards a pedagogical end – finding ways to explore historical events and people in a meaningful way. In *The History of Canada* (1891) for instance, the Wendat historical narrative concludes: "As this famine-stricken band occasionally emerged from the gloom of the forest into the clearings where populous villages had been so recently situated, the charred ruins and traces of havoc and slaughter mutely, yet forcibly, *proclaimed the almost general destruction of the Huron race.*[26]

Current history texts continue the tradition. The authors of *The Peoples of Canada* (1992), note "The weakened Hurons were killed, surrendered, or fled ... The next year the missionaries returned to Quebec with a few hundred Hurons – the pathetic remnant of a once-powerful nation."[27] A similar passage appears in an *Origins* textbook (2000) describing the "fall of Huronia," where the "Huron dispersal marked the end of Huronia."[28] Surprisingly, French-Canadian historical interpretations do not differ from their English counterparts, unlike many other areas of research. *L'Ontario français historique* (1980) asserts that the Iroquois attacks of 1649 resulted in "the dislocation of the Huron Confederacy ... the end of the Huron nation."[29] American textbooks are no exception to the trend, either. Describing the Wendat defeat by the Iroquois, the authors of *US: A Narrative History* (2009) assert:

> Reeling from disease and internal division, the Hurons saw their world collapsing. In 1648, well-armed Iroquois warriors destroyed three Huron towns. The Hurons made the wrenching decision to burn their remaining towns and abandon their lands for good. Perhaps 2,000 became Iroquois, either as war captives or humble refugees. Others merged with neighboring peoples, while thousands more fled and starved or died of exposure in the harsh winter of 1649-1650.[30]

These textbooks are the basis for classroom lessons and curriculum programs. Public-school curricula in Canada and the United States provide mandatory units on the subject.[31] Moreover, these curricula are produced by government agencies (the National Endowment for the Humanities oversees the creation of America's national history standards, while the Ministries of Education regulate the Canadian provincial standards), ensuring the widespread distribution and application of the lessons.

In support of these requirements, other agencies have created teaching aids to help educators come up with activities to convey the material. A current elementary-school lesson entitled "Lesson 5: The Jesuit and the Huron," provides teachers with the following narrative:

> Between 1610 and 1640, disease carried by the Europeans killed close to half of the Huron population. Huron shamans accused the Jesuits of bringing disease and angering the gods with their religious practices. When the weakened villages fell into the hands of the enemy Iroquois, the Jesuits were tortured as was Jean de Brébeuf in 1649. Between 1648 and 1650, *the Iroquois nearly decimated the Huron nation.*[32]

In sum, the persistence of the "destruction" myth, spanning hundreds of years of scholarship, has resulted in a wealth of literature to support such misconceptions. By using terminology such as "extinct," "ruined," and "decimated," the interpretation is by default one of defeat and destruction. Little attention is given to the resilience of the Wendat or their ability to overcome complete eradication. Moreover, by centring Wendat history on the pre-1649 period, there is little for the general public to draw on in the years following the dispersal.

Contact Zones: Public History Sites

Beyond academic scholarship, there are many alternative media for those seeking further information on the Wendat. Interactive public history sites, for instance, continue to reinforce this narrative. According to historian Laura Peers, "these sites are not simply value-neutral, 'Objective,' three-dimensional versions of scholarly research or facts," but rather sites of hegemonic power.[33] They tend to uphold Euro-American settler society, marginalizing Native American groups and histories in order to nationalize such histories for the greater nation states. They make particular Native nations into hero/victims, but assume their passing and annihilation. Public sites like the excavated fifteenth-century Wendat village at Crawford Lake Indian Village in southern Ontario enlighten the general public about Wendat modes of life. The Crawford Lake project began in 1971 with an archeological excavation of the area and developed into a tourist and education attraction in the 1980s. It includes three fully constructed longhouses with interior furnishings designed to reflect traditional material culture of the Wendat. Conservation Halton runs this project. Although relatively small in nature, it serves as a centre for school groups, summer camps, and Guide and Scout groups, and provides tours and day-long interpretation programs.[34]

More well known is Sainte-Marie among the Hurons (SMH), which is the most popular Wendat public history site in North America. Promoted as "the finest of the Province's heritage projects," SMH was established by Ontario's Department of Tourism as a reconstruction of the old Jesuit mission set up in Wendake and destroyed as a direct result of the Iroquois wars.[35] Included in the site are thirty-one reconstructed buildings, such as the chapel, carpenter shop, and blacksmith shop, as well as a cemetery and a Wendat longhouse. The popularity of the site has grown considerably over the years. In 1968, 134,442 visitors from all six continents ventured to the site; 44,051 of these visitors were French and English students on educational field trips.[36] In one summer alone, fifty-two thousand people signed the SMH's guest book, including students, camps, women's institute groups, teachers' conventions, newspaper conventions, and religious groups. In addition, the Huronia Historic Sites and Tourist Association, several local newspapers, radio stations, and the Canadian Broadcasting Corporation endorsed the establishment of SMH.[37] "The role [SMH played] in tourism and travel," according to the Minister of Tourism in 1971, "[was] a major one, to the Huronia area and to Ontario as a whole."[38]

Across the border in Michigan, Mackinac State Historic Parks – which includes the sites of Colonial Michilimackinac and Fort Mackinac – provides another avenue for the public to engage with Wendat history. Michilimackinac State Park, created in 1909, covers thirty-seven acres with twenty-one hundred feet of Great Lakes shoreline. Federally recognized as a National Historic Landmark, it was built with the support of the State of Michigan. Although not a central focus of the park's interpretive message, the Wendat relocation to the area from 1671-1701 is highlighted through the historical accounts of the "tribal occupation" of the site.[39]

Information plaques are one way that public history sites like Crawford Lake, SMH, and Mackinac State Historic Park transmit their message. At SMH, visitors are greeted with the following introduction to the events surrounding the dispersal: "By the winter of 1648-49, Huronia was so ravaged by disease and conflict that the Jesuits abandoned and burned Sainte-Marie and with some Huron followers moved to Christian Island. The following year the Jesuits and Hurons withdrew to Quebec.[40]

As passive victims, the Wendat display no agency as they "follow" the Jesuits to safety. Moreover, the plaque neglects details concerning the Western Wendat or those who chose to live with the Iroquois. Describing the abandonment of a Jesuit mission on Manitoulin Island in 1650, another plaque, located at the Ontario mission site, explains that this event followed "the defeat and dispersal of the Hurons by the Iroquois."[41] Similar language appears on a plaque describing the significance of French explorer Samuel de Champlain's contact with the Wendat. According to this plaque, the "expedition increased the hostility of the Five Nations (Iroquois) towards the French and their Indian supporters, which culminated in the defeat and dispersal of the Hurons, 1649-1650."[42] The narrative at Mackinac State Park, although focused in the post-dispersal period, maintains a similar portrayal. The Wendat, who eventually relocated to Michilimackinac, are depicted as "fleeing the Iroquois," following the Ottawa, and being "lured" by the French.[43] These interpretations strengthen the popular notion that Wendat history holds little significance after 1649, and that the Wendat were helpless victims after their military defeat by the Iroquois.

Contact Zones: Museums

Museums have long provided an arena for historical inquiry. From large national projects to smaller locally run institutions, the Wendat and their history are incorporated into the meta-narrative of national as well as indigenous and local histories. On display at the National Museum of the American Indian, in Washington, DC, a Wendat wampum belt is presented to visitors through a glass box. On the exterior, the caption reads, "Culture: Wendat (Huron), Object Name: Wampum Belt, Date Created: 1600-1650."[44] Although the information is limited, the years 1600-1650 serve to reinforce the 1650 benchmark. Clearly the belt was not constructed over fifty years, but it dates to the pre-dispersal period. This information, therefore allows visitors to make their own conclusions, one of which might be that it is a Wendat belt, created by a people who ceased to exist after 1650. The Canadian Museum of Civilization provides a less ambiguous message. In a written description of a Jesuit mortar found at SMH, the caption reads: "From 1645-1655, the powerful Five Nations Iroquois confederacy waged war that destroyed rival Iroquoian nations. Weakened by disease and torn apart by internal strife, the Huron were defeated in 1648 and 1649."[45]

At the Huronia Museum, located near the SMH site, the Wendat dispersal is portrayed as not only the end of the Wendat but also the beginning of their assimilation into the larger "Canadian" society. Contact with the French is the culprit in this case, as "it would ultimately lead to the dispersal of the Huron people between 1647 and 1651, and the creation of new political and social groups that ... now form a large part of Canadian society."[46] Considering Laura Peers's argument that visitors generally visit public history sites and museums not to learn new information but rather to reinforce preconceived notions of a history, the information provided by these museums seems to bolster the defeatist narrative, as well as the pre-1649 timeline, by reconceptualizing the Wendat as "Canadians."[47]

Contact Zones: Popular Culture

The Wendat have inspired North American popular culture as well. "The Huron Carol" is the oldest and most widely recognized piece of this genre. Written by Father Jean de Brébeuf in 1643, this song was originally entitled "Jesous Ahatonhia" and is often described as Canada's first Christmas carol. The song was initially written in Wendat and French and was later translated into English by Jesse Edgar Middleton in 1926.[48]

Poets have used Wendat history in order to describe emotional moments of desperation and death. Adam Kidd's "The Huron Chief" (1830), for instance, was written while he travelled across Canada in a birchbark canoe and was inspired by both the hospitality of Native people he met along the way and his dislike of their treatment by non-Natives. Before publication, Kidd had requests for over fifteen hundred copies. Proposals were drawn up for the collection to be translated into Native languages as well.[49] Around this same time, the Quebec City historian and lawyer François-Xavier Garneau wrote a poem entitled "Le dernier huron" (The Last Huron).[50] It was meant to encapsulate the experiences of the dispersal and conquest by the Iroquois during the mid-seventeenth-century wars. Garneau laments, "Oh people, you will be no more," and calls Wendat warriors to rise to the battle and change the fate of their people.[51]

Brian Moore translated the fear and anxiety expressed in Garneau's poem into a successful novel – *Black Robe: A Novel.*[52] Published in both French and English and distributed throughout Canada and the United States, Moore's novel is a mixture of historical fact and artistic licence. Moore describes the intention of his work as an exploration of Wendat and Jesuit belief systems. In short, he explains, "This novel is an attempt to show that each of these beliefs inspired in the other fear, hostility and despair." For Moore, these factors "[resulted] in the destruction and abandonment of the Jesuit Mission, and the conquest of the Huron people by the Iroquois, their deadly enemy."[53]

Theatrical performances present Wendat history in a similar way. Moore's book, for instance, became so popular that in 1992 it was released as a feature-length film.[54] Although the movie's rendition of Moore's classic attracted some criticism for its portrayal of indigenous culture, it received the Genie Award for Best Canadian Film and positive reviews for its in-depth historical research.[55] The film ends in 1635 during one of the first epidemics in Wendake. Written as a caption within the last scene is the following synopsis: "Fifteen years later, the Hurons, having accepted Christianity, were routed and killed by their enemies, the Iroquois."[56]

Taking another look at the Jesuits and Wendat, James Nichol produced *Sainte-Marie Among the Hurons: A Play.*[57] This play was first performed at the London Theatre in London, Ontario (1974) and subsequently at the National Arts Centre in Ottawa (1977). Main characters include the Jesuit "Blackrobe" and two Wendat, "Broken Rock" and "Sleeping Water." The play has included celebrated Canadian actors Colin Fox and Wayne Burnett. It covers the years 1634-49 and takes place in seventeenth-century Wendake. *Sainte-Marie Among the Hurons* concludes with a 1649 battle between the Iroquois and the Wendat. The scene closes with the Wendat character Sleeping Water speaking to the audience and summarizing the circumstances in the following way:

> The Blackrobes [Jesuits] run before the Iroquois. Our Huron villages smolder black and dead. What am I now, left alone? Not Huron, for they don't exist. Not Christian, for they have fled. The fever has lifted, and like a man who cannot die, captive in my broken land, I breathe, I open my hands and eyes ... I live![58]

Together, these various forms of popular culture present different renditions of the same interpretation. The Wendat ceased to exist after 1649. They were captured, dispersed, and defeated; thus, their stories, poems, and films end there.

Contact Zones: The Internet

Finally, interpretations of Wendat history found on the Internet continue the discourse of "destruction." Although often unreliable, Wikipedia has become the most popular online reference for gaining quick information. It is the second link for a Google search on the Wendat or Huron and explains the dispersal as follows:

> The Iroquois attack caused the Huron to enter a state of terror. By May 1st, 1649, the Huron, in their panic, burned 15 of their villages and fled as refugees to surrounding tribes with about 10,000 fleeing to Christian Island. Most who fled to the island starved over the winter as it was a non-productive settlement

> and could not provide for them. Most who survived were believed to have resorted to cannibalism ... the surviving Huron relocated near Quebec City and settled at Wendake, Quebec. They absorbed other refugees and became the Huron-Wendat Nation.[59]

In this definition, the fear-stricken Wendat react with desperation and social collapse. The post-1649 experience of relocation is brief and simplified. More academically sound websites do not contradict this popular Wikipedia entry. The Ontario Association of Professional Archaeologists, for instance, hosts a number of pages that deliver information on the seventeenth-century Wendat. Their Charity Site excavation page situates the importance of this archaeological project in terms of contextualizing the "demise of the Hurons."[60] This interpretation continues on the Association's pages on the Christian Island excavation. Beginning with the subtitle "The Final Years in Huronia," the circumstances of the dispersal are explained in the following way:

> Realizing the hopelessness of their situation, many of the remaining Hurons abandoned their villages, burned them to the ground so the Iroquois could not use them. This was the beginning of the period of cultural devastation that has since gone unparalleled in this province ... Thus the domination of south central Ontario by the Hurons was over. *In a matter of a few years the Huron Nation was completely dissolved.*[61]

Contact Zones: Wendat Community Traditions

Wendat descendants have additional access to their community's history and oral traditions. Ethnographer Charles Marius Barbeau depicted a dwindling, yet present, tradition of oral history within the modern Wendat diaspora communities at the turn of the twentieth century. He estimated that the Wendat of Oklahoma and Anderdon had a sizable number of storytellers but that in Quebec "hardly any traces of ancient mythology [were] left."[62] Still, people like Anne-Marie Sioui did exist and worked with Barbeau, describing Wendat traditions of song, dance, mythology, and history, proving that a collective memory of past events had been passed down through the generations.[63]

Participants in most diasporas suffer from an anxiety over forgetting their homeland and the process of dispersal.[64] Demonstrating the importance of sharing the past with future generations of Wendat, and the need for modern Wendat communities to remember their ancestors' experiences of dispersal, the Huron Museum, located on the Wendat reserve in Quebec, printed the following message under the title "Memory" in their main exhibit:

> We, the Wendat, keep our history alive in our memory along with the awareness of our roots that are so deeply attached to the land around the Great Lakes and the Saint Lawrence. In every era, this faithfulness to the memory and traditions of the Ancestors renews our sense of belonging and opens new paths to the future for our people.[65]

Although accounts of oral traditions may have been limited in 1900, twenty-first-century Wendat have tried to maintain or rediscover their stories for future generations. The Wendat ability to gain knowledge about their history is an experience reserved for the Wendat community for the most part. It is not merely out of an interest in the history, as the museum states, but a need to connect with the past and understand their place in the world.

With the exception of Wendat community traditions, most people, whether they are Wendat or not, engage with Wendat history through similar avenues of academic literature, classroom lessons, interactive public history sites, museums, popular culture, and the Internet. These media not only determine the narrative but also encourage a widespread and long-standing interest in Wendat history throughout North America. They provide varied "contact zones" between historians (both professional and hobbyists) and histories. Overall, the medium by which Wendat history is transmitted has little consequence in terms of the dominating discourse and themes. Although not always explicitly stating their total demise in 1649, all sources express language and frameworks that emphasize the pre-dispersal period, which has unintentionally led to the popular misconception that seventeenth-century Wendat history ends with the Iroquois conquest.

Wendat Responses

If the general public, like me, reacts to these historical "contact zones" by creating subconscious conclusions about the destruction and the demise of the Wendat, how have the Wendat themselves reacted to the presentation of the conquest of 1649 and their dispersal? Specialists of human conquests and conflict argue that "the manner in which the war is remembered (and forgotten) – derives from the complexity of the interplay between the victors and the vanquished."[66] For the Wendat, the battles of the mid-seventeenth century, as presented by various media, permit certain aspects to be highlighted, while obscuring others. The subsequent relationship between the Wendat and New France officials, along with British and later Canadian and American governments, has led to dominant non-Wendat representations of these events and a colonization of the Wendat past. One of the reasons behind the overabundance of non-Wendat material is that the Wendat themselves continue their struggle to overcome the sense of loss experienced by their communities during their exile from Wendake. As one scholar observes, "The achievements of an exile are permanently undermined by his or her sense of loss."[67] This sense of loss, although seemingly hundreds of years in the past, still remains within the modern Wendat communities. "At the heart of both defeat and war," contends historian Wolfgang Schivelbusch, "lies the threat of extinction, a threat that resonates long past the cessation of hostilities."[68] The themes of loss and futility are therefore understandably accepted as legitimate aspects of the dispersal by modern Wendat.

Although the main themes of the narrative may be accepted and even endorsed by the Wendat, the people overtly reject both the premise of destruction and the non-Wendat misinterpretations of their history. Max "One-Onti" Gros-Louis, former grand chief of the Huron-Wendat nation, has strongly protested the literature written on the Wendat: "There is no shortage of books written about us, written by learned historians (or writers who are recognized as such!). But we reject them because too often they contradict what our ancestors have transmitted to us orally, from generation to generation."[69] For Gros-Louis, the books do not represent a Wendat perspective of the past. And it was the educators who "forced us to learn things that I found outrageous, particularly Canadian history, where my ancestors were judged to be cruel, barbaric thieves, crafty hypocrites, liars, lousy, and I don't know what else."[70] This passage vividly demonstrates his resentment and hostility towards these narratives. Psychologically, the representation of the Wendat as marginalized members of the larger North American society led Gros-Louis and others to reject sources derived from outside the community.

Professor Georges Sioui, another member of the Huron-Wendat nation, has expressed similar sentiments. At barely five years of age, Sioui was enrolled in the Lorette Reserve School run by the Sisters of Perpetual Help. Sioui believes that the nuns' duty was to "implant a system of values and morality that would wipe out every shred of respect we might still feel for our ancestors and for the dignity of their way of life."[71] Sioui recounts from memory one nun's history lessons concerning the circumstances of the 1649 battles and the capture of Jesuits from the mission of Sainte-Marie: "Your poor ancestors were savages ... The King took pity on them and sent missionaries to convert them, but your savage ancestors killed the missionaries.[72] They became our Holy Canadian Martyrs, who died to save the savages."[73] Upset, Sioui ran home to his parents, who attempted to counteract the "savage" interpretation presented by the nun. Similar to that of Gros-Louis, Sioui's response to such a history, whether intended or not, was disillusionment and rejection.

Public history sites can also engender feelings of sadness and resentment for the modern Wendat. Although Sainte-Marie among the Hurons does not portray the Wendat as "savages," it is nonetheless a place that provokes conflicting emotions for the descendants of the seventeenth-century Wendat. Many Wendat, according to one interpreter, visit the site on a yearly basis as part of a pilgrimage. In most cases the pilgrims will introduce themselves as Wendat, although "you can often tell they're Huron before they tell you, they have that look in their eyes," says an interpreter.[74] The "look" according to Laura Peers, is because "rather like visitors to Holocaust museums who have personal ties to their history being represented, Native visitors have a difficult relationship to some historic sites."[75] SMH is a reconstruction of a place that is central to the Wendat destruction myth – the Jesuits tore it down in the wake of the Iroquois attacks and it was from this mission that many Wendat began their relocation out of Wendake.

In the summer of 1999, Chief Janith English (Wyandot Nation of Kansas) expressed her emotional experience upon returning to the territory formerly known as Wendake for the first time. Through the narratives and histories passed down from generations of Wendat descendants, English came to understand that "many years ago when our people left this beautiful land on the shores of Georgian Bay, our hearts were heavy, our people were very, very sad."[76] English gained her perspective from texts, classroom lessons, public history sites, museums, and community oral histories. Her feelings are therefore the direct results of centuries of rhetoric emphasizing loss and desolation rather than survival and strategizing. Thus, many Wendat, like Chief English, have sifted through the biases and retained an understanding of the sad and destructive aspects of the dispersal.

More recently, there have been a number of attempts by the modern Wendat to revise the history. With respect to academic works on Wendat history, Georges Sioui's *Huron-Wendat* is an effort to write an extensive chapter on Wendat society. Its aim, as Sioui puts it, is to "counteract this collective conditioning and restore Amerindian dignity and the right to survival."[77] Indeed, this work goes beyond the usual written documents, applying ethnohistorical approaches and delivering a Wendat perspective on seventeenth-century culture, diplomacy, and politics.[78] Notwithstanding the contributions of Sioui's work, his narrative retains a pre-1649 framework. His third and final chapter on Wendat society, for instance, concentrates exclusively on the years 1615-50. Further, Sioui contends, "In 1634 the Jesuits entered the picture. This was the beginning of the end for the Wendat."[79] The use of such language unintentionally asserts that there was an "end" to the Wendat – an argument that clearly Sioui intends to counter.

An elementary-school textbook published by the Conseil de la nation huronne-wendat represents another attempt to demonstrate Wendat history from a Wendat perspective. This text, entitled *Anontaché* in the Wendat language, meaning "where did it come from?" delivers Wendat history through a conversation between a little girl, "Lucie," and her grandfather. Lucie asks questions about Wendat history and her grandfather attempts to answer her. When Lucie asks why the Wendat left Ontario, her grandfather replies,"Because in 1648, the Iroquois attacked and destroyed their village ... then they took refuge at Sainte-Marie and then Christian Island, where they lived until 1650. Then because of Iroquois attacks and famine they left and went to Quebec."[80] The grandfather then proceeds to list the various locations where the Wendat lived in the east before settling at Lorette, Quebec. This account departs from the textbooks discussed by Gros-Louis, because it gives power to the storyteller and the Wendat within the narrative of their dispersal. It is a history created by and for the Wendat.

Although government institutions and non-Wendat people create most interactive public history sites, the Wendat have established a number of sites for the general public. Located within the Huron-Wendat reserve in Quebec, the Huron Traditional Site, or *Onhoüa Chetek8e* in Wendat, provides a "journey into the heart of Huron traditions, past and present."[81] This site includes guided tours of longhouses and medicine huts, explanations of Wendat cosmology, and several artifacts of other North American indigenous groups. This site is privately owned and operated by a member of the Huron-Wendat nation, Mario Gros-Louis. According to Gros-Louis, his original vision and purpose of the site was to share Wendat history with the larger population. In essence, "The evolutionary path of the Americas has to a certain extent historically tied our people," says the founder. "While visiting our recreated village and by letting yourselves be carried away by our stories, you will discover the hidden faces of the Huron's way of life." Gros-Louis concludes, "We trust your stay amongst us will bring a better understanding of our evolution and culture."[82] In the site's brochure visitors are told:

> Towards the middle of the 17th century, several thousands of people have succeeded to escape from all those misfortunes that even the courage of our ancestors did not succeed to cast away. For this reason we had to find new lands to escape these plagues. Among the survivors, several who were already converted to Christianity, went in the direction of the St. Lawrence River Valley. Only approximately 400 of them arrived in Quebec.[83]

This brief interpretation, although depicting "misfortunes," reorients the general discussion with its inclusion of "survivors," "escape," and "courage."

With a similar mandate in mind, the Huron Museum, located in Wendake, Quebec, focuses its history of the dispersal on the tragic collapse of the seventeenth-century Wendat Confederacy and promotes the decolonization of Wendat history in general.[84] Under the title "The Fall of The Confederacy," a caption reads: "Families, small groups, even entire villages, broke away and scattered the clans and nations to the four winds." Other captions explaining seventeenth-century artifacts assert, "These objects also tell of deep wounds resulting from a tragic destiny that led to the breakup of the Wendat Confederacy."[85] Stories of resilience and survival and describing the accomplishments of nineteenth and twentieth-century Wendat come much later in the exhibit.

The modern Wendat nations use the Internet as another means to present their history from their viewpoint.[86] Interestingly, the Huron-Wendat of Quebec do not include any information on the dispersal; they chose instead to list source references. In contrast, the Wendat nations of Anderdon, Oklahoma, and Kansas, who are the descendants of the Western Wendat, include brief mentions of the dispersal. The Wyandot of Anderdon Nation, for example, includes a chronology of important Wendat events and a brief synopsis of the dispersal between the years 1649-50. The details are as follows:

> 1649: War begins between the Mohawk and their allies the Seneca who are of the Iroquois nation against the Wendat. The Mohawk and Seneca have many guns and scatter the Wendat nation. 1650: Part of the Wendat nation seeks refuge with their neighbors the Petun also known as the Tobacco nation by the French. The formation between the Wendat and Petun become the Wyandot.[87]

The Wyandot Nation of Kansas also uses a chronological timeline that incorporates a discussion of the dispersal. The website uses Larry Hancks's "The Emigrant Tribes: Wyandot, Delaware and Shawnee – A Chronology." This narrative describes how in 1649 "the Huron Confederacy disintegrates. Some flee to islands in Georgian Bay; others seek refuge with the Ottawa, Petun, Neutrals, Erie or French, while still others become adopted captives of the Iroquois."[88] Finally, the Wyandotte Nation of Oklahoma presents a description of the dispersal as interpreted by Sallie Cotter Andrews and the Wyandotte Historical Committee. In this case the narrative is: "1648: ... The Huron nation was scattered. 1649: Huron and Petun are decisively defeated and flee westward to Mackinac Island. 1650: 300 Huron who had wintered on Christian Island go to Quebec accompanied by 60 Frenchmen from the abandoned Huron mission."[89]

Combined, these websites give some insight into the events surrounding the dispersal. The nature of the narrative is factual, although because it is interspersed with the language of "fleeing," and "scattering," the story sadly remains one of haphazard decisions and actions.

Wendat reactions to non-Wendat accounts of their people's history have led to a surge of histories in various forms from a Wendat perspective. This new body of work aims to empower the modern Wendat nations who continue to deal with the repercussions of colonialism and conquest. Not only are these histories crucial to the process of decolonization, but they also serve to create new "contact zones" between the general public and Wendat history. They highlight community insights into Wendat events and people. In terms of the destruction myth, these discourses infuse personal feelings of loss, despair, and victimization. Therefore, the themes presented in the mainstream narrative persist. Although it is evident that the seventeenth-century Wendat were not destroyed in a literal sense, the language of destruction and tragedy holds true and remains hegemonic.

Conclusion

Depictions of Wendat destruction, trauma, dislocation, and violence are not inaccurate portrayals of the circumstances surrounding their dispersal in 1649. The collection of accounts from seventeenth-century Jesuits to the modern Wendat point not to a critique of historical fact but to a patterned discourse that has inadvertently led to public misconceptions concerning Wendat history. The tendency for the literature, classroom lessons, interactive public history sites, museums, popular culture, and websites to employ language that describes "demise" and "decline" insinuates an end for the Wendat people. This unintended conclusion is only bolstered further with the emphasis on the pre-1649 period. Without detailed knowledge of the events taking place during and after the dispersal, the history of the seventeenth-century Wendat is relegated to the first half of the century. With little discussion on the years after 1649, readers, the public, and Wendat descendants are left with illusions of an end to Wendat history, rather than a benchmark. Even with the emergence of Wendat interpretations, information about the fifty years after the dispersal remains relatively absent from the communities' collective memory. As a result, questions of diaspora process and Wendat identity and agency in the early stages of Wendat dispersal still exist. This book is thus an attempt to directly address the destruction myth. It is my hope that the focus on the latter part of the seventeenth century will expand the general narrative and that the language of defeat will become less prevalent as future scholars produce similar projects emphasizing Wendat determination, renewal, and survival.

Notes

Introduction

1 The Wendat/Wyandot/Wyandotte are also known as the Huron. The French gave them the name Huron, which is derived from the word *hure,* meaning "boar head."

2 The original recording of Catherine Johnson's oral tradition was transcribed by anthropologist Charles Marius Barbeau and translated by Mary Kelley. Barbeau, *Huron-Wyandot Traditional Narratives,* 4.

3 Historian Bruce Trigger titled his work on the Wendat *Children of Aataentsic.* For a more contemporary version of the Sky Woman origin myth see Trigger, *Children of Aataentsic,* 78.

4 Some of the Wendat are believed to have migrated from the east during their settlement of Wendake. This at least partly makes seventeenth-century Wendat the descendants of the so-called St. Lawrence Iroquoians (the Stadacona and Hochelaga), who met with Jacques Cartier in the sixteenth century near what are today Montreal and Quebec City. For more on pre-Wendake Wendat migrations see Sioui, *Huron-Wendat,* 12-16.

5 There is some speculation that this group was an independent unit of the Confederacy or a subsection of the Bear nation. Trigger, *Children of Aataentsic,* 30.

6 Warrick, *A Population History,* 11, 23.

7 The use of the term "Nadowek" (also spelled "Nadouek") is an attempt to simplify the terminology concerning the people who are more commonly described as Iroquoian. Both these words are Anishinaabe (Algonquian) in origin and refer to the same group of people, yet "Iroquoian" – the linguistic and cultural category – can easily be confused with the Five Nations Iroquois (Haudenosaunee). Nadowek is therefore a useful alternative to alleviate this misunderstanding. See Sioui, *Huron-Wendat,* 217 fn 22; Hodge, ed., *Handbook of American Indians,* 2:585.

8 Anishinaabe(g) in this context refers to the mid-northeastern Algonquian-speaking nations that created close relationships with the seventeenth-century Wendat including the Ottawa (Odawa), Nipissing, Algonkin, and Ojibwe.

9 See Appendix for an in-depth survey and analysis of the "destruction myth" and its origins.

10 Elizabeth Tooker's *An Ethnography of the Huron Indians* (1964), for example, delivers a concise report on Wendat lifestyle, culture, political and social structures, foreign relations, and material culture. Tooker's detailed compilation set the groundwork for anthropologist Bruce Trigger's *The Huron: Farmers of the North* (1969) and later his seminal two-volume history, *The Children of Aataentsic* (1976). Trigger's books depict a Wendat history centred on the fur trade, though he also touches on Wendat politics, diplomacy, and social conditions. His works constitute the most comprehensive studies

of Wendat society from the prehistoric period to the dispersal. Historical geographer Conrad Heidenreich's *Huronia* (1971) expanded on Trigger's findings, giving more specific information on Wendat territory, villages, demographics, and subsistence economy. In the wake of Tooker, Trigger, and Heidenreich, scholars trained in new methodologies and working in response to the rise of social history and cultural studies created Wendat histories that depart from the more general economic and political studies of the past. Sociologist Karen Anderson's research focuses on Wendat women's experiences. In *Chain Her by One Foot* (1991), Anderson argues that the relationship between Wendat and French missionaries devastated native women and resulted in a loss of social, political, and economic power. Focusing on Wendat cosmology, Georges Sioui also finds dramatic changes in response to the crises of the early seventeenth century. Sioui contends in *Huron-Wendat: The Heritage of the Circle* (1999) that because of European encounters, the Wendat experienced damaging internal power struggles and cultural malaise, as well as disease and warfare. For Sioui, a Huron-Wendat himself, this history is personal; he delivers a revised history of Wendat society from a Wendat perspective. More recently, Roger Carpenter's *The Renewed, The Destroyed, and The Remade* (2004) contextualizes Wendat policy in terms of Nadowekian cultural traditions, rather than economic aspirations or political power. Through this approach, Carpenter explores how the Nadowek compartmentalized their world view into three "thought worlds" based on social renewal, destruction, and remaking. Linguist John Steckley presents an intricate study of Wendat terminology in *Words of the Huron* (2007). Through this linguistic analysis Steckley delivers important information on kinship, material and ceremonial culture, warfare, and disease. Archaeologist Gary Warrick's *A Population History of the Huron-Petun* (2008) is one of the newest contributions to Wendat historical literature. Although covering deceptively similar topics as the works of Trigger and Heidenreich, Warrick's research delivers new insight into Wendat society by engaging with previously undiscovered materials and evidence. Warrick presents updated calculations concerning population size and the effects of disease on the pre-dispersal Wendat. Most recently, Eric R. Seeman's *The Huron-Wendat Feast of the Dead* (2011) delivers a unique analysis of Native and European encounters through the details of Wendat burial rituals, and highlights the collaboration between the Wendat and French missionaries based on common notions of spirituality.

11 It was in the aftermath of the Great Peace of Montreal of 1701 and the beginning of the eighteenth century that most of the Wendat from Michilimackinac migrated to Detroit and began to identify separately from other Wendat by calling themselves the "Wyandot." This division departs from the seventeenth-century notion of a collective Wendat diaspora, and deserves its own unique study.

12 My discussion of "systems of power" is rooted in what Elizabeth Mancke calls "spaces of power." (See Mancke, "Spaces of Power," 32-49.) The definitions are the same, but for the purposes of this particular topic, and especially Native North American alliances, I use "systems" instead of "spaces."

13 Richard White's work on the upper Great Lakes *(pays d'en haut)* is the most well-known and influential study of this nature. White looks at the experience of the Anishinaabeg and French who migrated to the *pays d'en haut* in the seventeenth century. He explores the relationship between these groups, contending that a "middle ground" was created out of these encounters. White states that this represented a new world of accommodation and creative misunderstandings that allowed Anishinaabeg and French to ally and prosper. Many scholars have added to White's work by challenging or supporting his

assertions. Kathleen DuVal and Alan Taylor, for instance, have questioned the framework in geography and chronology, while Brett Rushforth and Heidi Bohaker complicate the notion of "friendly" and universal compromise.

14 The Indian Removals of the nineteenth-century United States often overshadow other forced migrations that took place throughout the continent and during different time periods. The Cherokee Removal is the most well-known and the experience of this relocation has dominated scholarly discussion. See Foreman, *Indian Removal;* Ehle, *Trail of Tears;* Anderson, ed., *Cherokee Removal;* Perdue, *Cherokee Women;* Magliocca, "The Cherokee Removal and the Fourteenth Amendment"; Sturgis, *Trail of Tears and Indian Removal;* Green and Perdue, *The Cherokee Nation and the Trail of Tears.*

15 Mancke, "Spaces of Power," 32-33.

16 See Munck, *Seventeenth-Century Europe.*

17 Mancke, "Spaces of Power," 33.

18 Diasporic polities engaged in a far-flung network of people to whom local authorities granted self-governing privileges. These groups were often associated with trading and financial networks, and many did not have an autonomous territorial base where they were the majority. See Mancke, "Polity Formation," 383-84.

19 Richter, *Facing East from Indian Country,* 69.

20 Steckley, *Words of the Huron,* 24.

Chapter 1: Disease and Diplomacy

Sections of this chapter have been previously published. See Magee, "They Only Spoke in Sighs," 1-33.

1 Thwaites, ed., *Jesuit Relations* [*JR*], 15:41.

2 Warrick, "A Population History," 399.

3 For representative examples of studies on the relationship between disease and North American peoples, see Trigger, "The Jesuits and the Fur Trade," 30-53; Crosby Jr., *The Columbian Exchange* and "Virgin Soil Epidemics," 289-99; Schlesier, "Epidemics and Indian Middlemen," 129-46; Martin, *Keepers of the Game;* Richter, "War and Culture: The Iroquois Experience," 528-59; Kelsey, "European Impact," 494-511; Morrison, "Discourse and the Accommodation of Values," 365-82; Snow and Lanphear, "European Contact and Indian Depopulation," 15-33; Verano and Ubelaker, eds., *Disease and Demography in the Americas;* Starna, "The Biological Encounter," 371-82; Stannard, *American Holocaust;* Salisbury, "Religious Encounters in a Colonial Context," 501-9; MacLeod, "Microbes and Muskets," 42-64; Dobyns, "Disease Transfer at Contact," 273-91; Thornton, "Aboriginal North American Population," 310-15; Sundstrom, "Small Pox Used Them Up," 305-43.

4 Most histories of the Wendat explore the impact of disease on Wendat society. For examples that dedicate a significant focus to this avenue of research, see Warrick, "European Infectious Disease," 258-75; Levasseur, "S'allier pour survivre."

5 Trigger, *Children of Aataentsic,* 601.

6 Heidenreich, *Huronia,* 253; Johnson and Jackson, "Settlement Pattern at the Le Caron Site," 175.

7 Johnson and Jackson, "Settlement Pattern at the Le Caron Site," 500.

8 *JR* 7:221.

9 *JR* 8:87-89.

10 Trigger, *Children of Aataentsic,* 500.

11 *JR* 8:87-89.

12 Letter from Jean de Brébeuf to T.R.P. Mutius Vitelleschi (1636), in Latourelle, ed., *Étude sur les écrits de Saint Jean de Brébeuf,* 1:47-56.
13 Trigger, *Children of Aataentsic,* 527.
14 *JR* 13:213.
15 Ibid.; Warrick, "A Population History," 145.
16 Trigger, *Children of Aataentsic,* 528. To put the numerical loss at Ossossane into context, Warrick estimates that between the years 1634 and 1637 the Confederacy as a whole experienced 20 percent depopulation. See Warrick, "A Population History," 399.
17 Dobyns, *Their Number Become Thinned,* 322.
18 *JR* 13:145.
19 Ibid., 117.
20 Ibid.
21 *JR* 13:121-25.
22 Warrick, "A Population History," 409.
23 Ibid.; Richter, *Ordeal of the Longhouse,* 59.
24 Trigger, *Children of Aataentsic,* 101-2; Anderson, "Huron Women and Huron Men," 66-67.
25 Tooker, "Northern Iroquoian Sociopolitical Organization," 93-95.
26 *JR* 17:161.
27 Trigger, *Children of Aataentsic,* 55-59; Tooker, *An Ethnography,* 42-44; *JR* 38:265-87.
28 Champlain, *Voyages of Samuel de Champlain,* 1:327.
29 Fenton, "The Iroquois in History," 145.
30 *JR* 13:215. The differences between the Northern and Southern Bear seem to be significant enough to merit making a distinction between the two. For more information on the Northern and Southern Bear, see Steckley, *Words of the Huron,* 35-37.
31 *JR* 13:219.
32 Ibid., 215; Toupin, ed., *Les Écrits de Pierre Potier,* 221.
33 *JR* 13:217.
34 Ibid., 217, 219.
35 The Jesuits do not give her a Christian or Wendat name; thus, she is always referred to as the "renegade." Ibid., 219.
36 Ibid.
37 Ibid., 221-23.
38 Ibid., 221.
39 *JR* 10:305; Toupin, *Les Écrits de Pierre Potier,* 228.
40 *JR* 10:309 and *JR* 8:139.
41 *JR* 10:235. In addition to his many public responsibilities, Aenon also faced complex circumstances in his personal life. His son suffered from severe bouts of depression and ultimately committed suicide. According to missionary observers, Aenon's son could not face his family after losing a game of straws. He had gambled a beaver robe and a collar of four hundred porcelain beads. His fear was so great that he hanged himself from a tree. The devastating loss of a child, especially during a time of such critical negotiations, would certainly have influenced Aenon, yet his son's death seems to have had little effect on his ability to excel in the public realm. It was at this same time that a Jesuit missionary asserted that Aenon could still prevail over any other headman in the country. See *JR* 10:237-39.
42 *JR* 10:237-39.
43 *JR* 13:171-73.
44 *JR* 10:241.

45 *JR* 9:237-39.
46 Ibid., 247.
47 This proposed strategy was referred to by the Jesuits as a "Centre Lieu" and roughly translates into "Central Location."
48 *JR* 10:235-37.
49 Ibid., 239.
50 While Aenon was lobbying for the French to join the Centre Lieu, the Wendat villages of Arendaeronnon, Attigneenongnahac, and Ossossane were expressing similar interest in having the French live with them. See *JR* 10:235.
51 Ibid.
52 *JR* 13:233.
53 Ibid., 233-35.
54 Ibid., 217.
55 *JR* 12:89.
56 Ibid.
57 *JR* 11:135.
58 *JR* 12:199.
59 On his deathbed, Aenon asked to be baptized to secure a Christian burial beside the French and other Wendat Christian converts. Ibid.
60 The French refused to support the Centre Lieu unless all the inhabitants converted to Christianity. See *JR* 10:245.
61 See Anderson, *Chain Her by One Foot.*
62 *JR* 13:123.
63 Ibid., 119-25.
64 Ibid., 219-21.
65 Ibid., 121.
66 Anderson, *Chain Her by One Foot,* 201.
67 *JR* 19:233-39.
68 Ibid., 235.
69 Ibid., 233-39.
70 Trigger, *Natives and Newcomers,* 297.

Chapter 2: A Culture of War

Sections of this chapter have been previously published. See Magee, "'They Are the Life of the Nation': 119-38.

1 Thwaites, ed., *Jesuit Relations* [*JR*], 15:43.
2 Andre, "Contagious Disease," 19.
3 Charlevoix, *Journal of a Voyage to North America,* 1:25. This has been observed for the Iroquois, who share a similar cultural heritage (both are Nadowek peoples), so it is likely that Charlevoix's observations hold true to the Wendat as well. Historian Daniel Richter calls this "side-streaming." See Richter, *Ordeal of the Longhouse,* 5.
4 Gendron, *Quelques particularités du pays Hurons en la Nouvelle France,* 19; Lafitau, *Moeurs, coutumes et religions,* 1:90. For more recent scholarship on Nadowekian leadership see Becker, "Linking Arms," 29-41; Fenton, *Great Law,* 195-97, 203, 214, 251; Trigger, *Children of Aataentsic,* 23-24.
5 The name Ondesson is also written as "Ondesonk," meaning 'Hawk,' which suggests that this leader was of the Hawk Clan. See Steckley, *Words of the Huron,* 240.
6 *JR* 15:22.
7 Ibid., 23.

8 Ibid., 27.
9 *JR* 26:273.
10 *JR* 25:27.
11 The Wenro nation joined the Wendat in 1638. The majority of these refugees went to live with the Southern Bear nation. Steckley, *Words of the Huron*, 51.
12 *JR* 26:273.
13 Ibid., 275.
14 Historian Lucien Campeau argues that conversions were the effect of missionary work and a Wendat desire to join the faith, while Bruce Trigger asserts that the reason for conversion was so that Wendat leaders could attain preferential treatment in dealing with French officials and traders. Taking into consideration the need for weapons, conversion by war chiefs was most likely to attain guns. For more on this discussion, see Campeau, *La mission des jésuites;* Trigger, "The French Presence in Huronia," 134.
15 Tooker, *An Ethnography*, 27.
16 *JR* 24:271-73.
17 Tooker, *An Ethnography*, 27.
18 *JR* 10:241.
19 *JR* 25:27.
20 Father Simon Le Moyne to M. le Curé de St. Martin [his cousin], 25 May 1639, Newberry Library, Ayer Collection, MS 507.
21 *JR* 15:43.
22 Ibid.
23 Historian George T. Hunt argues that the Iroquois attacks were out of a desire for control of the fur trade, while Daniel Richter stresses replenishing the population. See Hunt, *Wars of the Iroquois;* Richter, "War and Culture," 528-59.
24 Trigger, *The Huron: Farmers of the North*, 42; Otterbein, "Why The Iroquois Won," 56-63.
25 Havard, *Great Peace of Montreal*, 46; Trigger, *The Huron: Farmers of the North*, 43.
26 Sioui, *Huron-Wendat*, 69.
27 Starkey, *European-Native American Warfare;* Snyderman, "Behind the Tree of Peace"; Snow, *Peoples of America;* Marrin, *Struggle for a Continent;* Horowitz, *First Frontier;* Dolan, *American Indian Wars;* Abler, "Iroquois Cannibalism," 309-16; Blick, "The Iroquois Practice of Genocidal Warfare," 405-29; Schlesier, "Epidemics and Indian Middlemen," 129-45; Keener, "An Ethnohistorical Analysis," 777-807; Otterbein, "Why the Iroquois Won"; Richter, "War and Culture."
28 Trigger, *Children of Aataentsic*, 68.
29 Daniel Richter's article gives an in-depth analysis of the characteristics of the mourning war. See Richter, "War and Culture," 528-59. See also Trigger, *Children of Aataentsic*, 805-6; *JR* 10:225; *JR* 17:11.
30 Sagard, *Long Journey*, 152.
31 René Cuillerier, "Nation Iroquoise," Bibliothèque Mazarin (Paris), Fonds Général (c.1700), Cote: MS 1964, 7.
32 Sagard, *Long Journey*, 152.
33 Tooker, *An Ethnography*, 31.
34 Starna and Watkins, "Northern Iroquoian Slavery," 39.
35 Ibid., 68.
36 Trigger, *Children of Aataentsic*, 69.
37 Ibid., 68.
38 Ibid., 256-58.

39 Sagard, *Long Journey,* 98.
40 Ibid., 154.
41 Ibid.
42 Barbeau, *Huron-Wyandot Traditional Narratives,* 294-95.
43 Tooker, *An Ethnography,* 30.
44 There is no specific title assigned to this ritual (primary observers make reference to an "interesting" and "peculiar" Nadowek ritual); therefore it is henceforth referred to as the "Fort Fight" ritual.
45 Lescarbot, *History of New France,* 3:264.
46 Charlevoix, *History and General Description of New France,* 6:266.
47 *JR* 34:132-33.
48 For more on this topic, see Magee, "'They Are the Life of the Nation,'" 119-38.
49 Lafitau, *Customs of American Indians,* 99.
50 Lescarbot, *History of New France,* 3:264.
51 Lafitau, *Customs of American Indians,* 99.
52 Lescarbot describes the war council, detailing the chronology of events. This account, although seemingly dominated by the male figures of the council, actually supports the importance of women, because it was through the woman's initial communication with the "sire" that the council was called. The proceedings of the council, according to Lescarbot, were as follows: "On the arrival of the other leaders the [sires] would make long orations to explain the situation and to convince them. At each proposal he asks their consent. At any time the others may also speak and give their opinion." Lescarbot, *History of New France,* 3:264.
53 Lafitau, *Customs of American Indians,* 99.
54 Beauchamp, "Iroquois Women," 86.
55 Ibid., 149-50.
56 Brébeuf, *Écrits en Huronie,* 165.
57 *JR* 54:281.
58 Beauchamp, "Iroquois Women," 86.
59 Carpenter, *Renewed,* 17.
60 Fenton, "Northern Iroquoian Culture Patterns," 316.
61 Lafitau, *Customs of American Indians,* 154.
62 Richter, *Ordeal of the Longhouse,* 69.
63 *JR* 13:37.
64 Ibid., 37-49.
65 Ibid., 55.
66 Trigger, *The Huron: Farmers of the North,* 48.
67 Richter, *Ordeal of the Longhouse,* 70.
68 Ibid., 69.
69 Steckley, *Untold Tales,* 19.
70 *JR* 31:21.
71 Ibid., 29.
72 The Iroquois termed this as a "welcoming" for the captives. The French translated the Nadowekian term as *la Saluade.* René Cuillerier, "Nation Iroquoise," Bibliothèque Mazarin (Paris), Cote: MS 1964, Fonds General (c.1700), 9.
73 *JR* 31:33-39.
74 Ibid., 41-49.
75 Ibid., 199.
76 *JR* 33:117-19.

77 Ibid., 95-97.
78 Carpenter, *Renewed,* 22.
79 *JR* 32:161-65.
80 *JR* 23:31.
81 *JR* 26:273.
82 *JR* 23:31.
83 *JR* 14:25, 27.
84 *JR* 13:23, 27.
85 *JR* 23: 25.
86 Ibid., 27.
87 *JR* 32:157.

Chapter 3: Wendat Country

1 Thwaites, ed., *Jesuit Relations* [*JR*] 34:87-99.
2 Ibid., 125, 127.
3 Ibid., 125.
4 Ibid., 137.
5 Carpenter, *Renewed,* 126; *JR* 34:137. It was also during this conflict that the Iroquois captured, tortured, and put to death Jesuit Fathers Jean de Brébeuf and Gabriel Lalemant.
6 Carpenter, *Renewed,* 126; Brandão, *Your Fyre,* 204; Levasseur, "S'allier pour survivre."
7 Otterbein, "Huron vs. Iroquois, 148; Brandão, *Your Fyre,* 204.
8 Carpenter, *Renewed,* 126.
9 *JR* 34:199.
10 The island is now called Christian Island.
11 Bruce Trigger dedicates a small section to the Gahoendoe migration and Roger Carpenter delivers a brief synopsis of this period. See Trigger, *Children of Aataentsic,* 767-82; Carpenter, *Renewed,* 127-29.
12 "Spaces of power" refers to Elizabeth Mancke's conception, which she defines "as a system of social power, whether economic, political, cultural or military, that we can describe functionally and spatially." I have applied the term to Native networks in the case of the Wendat and their allies. See Mancke, "Spaces of Power," 32.
13 Martin, ed., *Autobiographie,* 92-93.
14 Ibid., 94.
15 Translation is my own. The original text is "Fuyons! Fuyons! Sauvons-nous! Voici l'armée ennemie qui vient nous prendre." Martin, ed., *Autobiographie,* 94.
16 *JR* 34:197, 204.
17 Ibid., 203.
18 *JR* 35:173-75.
19 Ibid., 177. The St. Charles villagers struggled with severe bouts of starvation and abandoned their village in less than a year to rejoin the rest of the Wendat.
20 Letter XII (14 May 1721), in Charlevoix, *Journal of a Voyage to North America,* 1:309.
21 *JR* 34:197.
22 Ibid., 205. Today this island is known as Manitoulin Island. According to the Jesuits, it is 225 kilometres (60 leagues) from the mainland.
23 *JR* 34:205.
24 Ibid., 207; Statistics Canada, http://www.statcan.gc.ca/start-debut-eng.html.
25 *JR* 34:203-9; Trigger, *Children of Aataentsic,* 771; Carpenter, *Renewed,* 127.
26 la Potherie, *Histoire,* 2:51; *JR* 21:239.

27 Google maps (https://maps.google.ca/maps?hl=en); *JR* 35:25.
28 William Fenton has calculated that seven thousand acres was needed to sustain a population of twenty thousand Nadowek people. Considering that the Wendat population was at most ten thousand people by 1640, the 13,413 acres of Gahoendoe should have been able to support the entire population. Fenton's analysis is described in Trigger's *The Huron: Farmers of the North,* 28. The Jesuits recorded the good fishing attributed to the island, *JR* 34:199.
29 *JR* 34:197, 203-5; *JR* 35:83.
30 *JR* 35:205; Desrosiers, *Iroquoisie,* 1:xxii.
31 *JR* 34:59-61.
32 Ibid., 209.
33 Ibid., 25.
34 Ibid., 209.
35 Ibid., 203, 211.
36 Historic Sites and Monuments Board of Canada, "Sainte-Marie among the Hurons," located at Highway #12, Township of Tay, Ontario, Canada.
37 "Brief History of Colonial Michilimackinac." http://www.mackinacparks.com.
38 Trigger, *Children of Aataentsic,* 772.
39 *JR* 34:197.
40 *JR* 35:83.
41 *JR* 34:197.
42 *JR* 35:87.
43 The Jesuits who left a few months later took a "few days" to arrive. They travelled by raft and had many able-bodied men (*JR* 35:83). Professional canoeist Steve Magee contends that on average a skilled canoeist, with good weather, can cover 1 km/15 minutes. The paddle to Gahoendoe was approximately 32 km, thus the travel time was at minimum eight hours. Personal correspondence between the author and Steve Magee, 15 February 2010.
44 *JR* 35: 83.
45 Ibid.
46 At the time of Bruce Trigger's publications in the 1970s and '80s, the *Jesuit Relations* provided the most information on population statistics, and it is Trigger's assertion that the Jesuits exaggerated their calculations concerning the Wendat. Trigger, *Children of Aataentsic,* 772.
47 *JR* 35:87.
48 For family size see Trigger, *The Huron: Farmers of the North,* 13.
49 *JR* 35:87.
50 Ontario Association of Professional Archaeologists, The Charity Site, http://www.apaontario.ca/r_charity01.html. Jackson et al., "Winter of Discontent."
51 Ibid.
52 Trigger estimates that the population was at ten thousand after 1640. Trigger, *The Huron: Farmers of the North,* 13.
53 *JR* 34:209.
54 Lettre XCI (1649), in Marie de l'Incarnation, *Lettres,* 1:389. Some historians also contend that the majority of those Wendat on Gahoendoe were Christian. See Trigger, *Children of Aataentsic,* 781.
55 There were roughly three thousand baptisms from 1649 to 1650 on the island. Trigger, *Children of Aataentsic,* 781.
56 Ibid., 772.

57 *JR* 34:217.
58 *JR* 35:23.
59 An analysis of cultures in relation to how they organize and use space on a daily basis is referred to as "practice theory" by archaeologists. See Lightfoot, Martinez, and Schiff, "Daily Practice and Material Culture," 201.
60 *JR* 35:87.
61 Ontario Association of Professional Archaeologists, The Charity Site, http://www.apaontario.ca/r_charity01.html. Jackson et al., "Winter of Discontent."
62 *JR* 35:83.
63 This theory is based on William Fenton's research. It is not clear what type of soil Fenton is referring to, but one can surmise that his theory is focused on tillable land with agricultural potential. Trigger, *The Huron: Farmers of the North,* 28.
64 *JR* 35:87.
65 Trigger, *Children of Aataentsic,* 772; Carpenter, *Renewed,* 128.
66 Google maps (https://maps.google.ca/maps?hl=en); *JR* 35:25.
67 *JR* 35:85.
68 Martin Félix, "Plan of the Remains of Sainte-Marie II on Christian Island (1855)," in Trigger, *Children of Aataentsic,* 773; *JR* 35:85.
69 *JR* 35:85.
70 *JR* 40:47.
71 *JR* 35:27.
72 *JR* 34:225.
73 *JR* 35:85.
74 For the first theory, see Hunt, *Wars of the Iroquois,* 94. For the second theory, see Trigger, *Children of Aataentsic,* 752, 779.
75 Peak fishing season was in the spring (March-May) although a limited amount of fish could be obtained throughout the year. Heidenreich, *Huronia,* 208-12.
76 *JR* 40:49; 35:99-101.
77 US Department of Agriculture Nutrition Database (Standard Reference Release 21) http://www.nutritiondata.com.
78 Tooker, *An Ethnography,* 67-70.
79 For more information on the human consumption of acorns, including methods for preparation and nutritional value, see Gunderson, *American Indian Cooking,* 14; Johnson, Shifley, and Rogers, *Ecology and Silviculture of Oaks,* 73-74; Janick and Paull, eds. *Encyclopedia of Fruit and Nuts,* 407; Müller-Schwarze, *Hands-on Chemical Ecology,* 33.
80 *JR* 35:85. This was most likely a small-scale decadal drought (usually lasting about six years) as opposed to a megadrought that could encompass hundreds of years. For information on the droughts of North America, see Stahle, Fye, Cook, and Griffin, "Tree-ring Reconstructed Megadroughts," 133-49; Herweijer, Seager, Cook, and Emile-Geay, "North American Droughts," 1353-76.
81 *JR* 34:215.
82 *JR* 35:175.
83 Ibid., 93, 95.
84 Ibid., 99.
85 Ibid., 183-85.
86 Ibid., 21. This type of cannibalism was different from the spiritual and ritualized eating of human body parts during torture or prisoner ceremonies, which was why it was forbidden.

87 Ibid., 91-93.
88 Ontario Association of Professional Archaeologists, The Charity Site, http://www.apaontario.ca/r_charity01.html. Jackson et al., "Winter of Discontent."
89 *JR* 34:227; 35:23, 75.
90 *JR* 35:199. Jesuits later equate the number of baptisms (3,000) to the number of deaths.
91 *JR* 40:49.
92 *JR* 35:187.
93 *JR* 36:119.
94 *JR* 35:191.
95 Ibid., 193-97.
96 *JR* 36:179.
97 Ibid., 186-87.
98 *JR* 35:191.
99 Ibid.
100 *JR* 36:180.
101 Ibid., 181.
102 Ibid., 183-85.
103 Ibid., 183.
104 Ibid.
105 Delâge, *Bitter Feast*, 146.
106 *JR* 36:186-87.
107 *JR* 35:201-3.
108 Ibid., 189.

Chapter 4: Anishinaabe Neighbours

1 Historian Léo-Paul Desrosiers introduces the relationship as a "coalition," or, more precisely, "La Coalition Laurentienne," but we are not given any further insight into the nature of the relationship aside from this. Bruce Trigger has outlined the dynamics of the alliance by comparing differences in lifestyle, language, and cosmology, yet he rejects Desrosiers' use of any formal label such as "coalition" in that the relationship was too "ambivalent." Others, such as Denys Delâge, have described the Wendat–Anishinaabe relationship as an unequal partnership, with the Anishinaabeg forced to ally with the Wendat in response to Iroquois attacks. See Desrosiers, *Iroquoisie*, 1:13; Trigger, *Children of Aataentsic*, 65; Delâge, *Bitter Feast*, 96.
2 Michel Sioui (Speech), "François Lantano: texte integral," transcribed by François Lantano, Wendake Archives [WA], Fonds Marguerite Vincent [FMV], Folder 8552-03.
3 Michel Sioui, WA, FMV, 8552-03.
4 Sioui, *Huron-Wendat*, 63.
5 Ibid., 12-16, 63.
6 Hesse, *Algonkin Nation*, 39; Hickerson, "The Feast of the Dead," 84.
7 Hesse, *Algonkin Nation*, 39.
8 Ibid.
9 Thwaites, ed., *Jesuit Relations* [*JR*] 35:179.
10 *JR* 13:191; 14:7; 20:29-41.
11 *JR* 13:21.
12 Sagard, *Long Journey*, 259, 263.
13 *JR* 27:37; 30:87.
14 Trigger, *Children of Aataentsic*, 173.

15 *JR* 13:139.
16 *JR* 33:213-15.
17 Sioui, *Huron-Wendat,* 62
18 Ibid. 63.
19 *JR* 8:115. See also *JR* 13:249; 27:27; 31:209; 33:67.
20 *JR* 21:239.
21 la Potherie, *Histoire,* 2:51.
22 Champlain, *Voyages and Explorations of Samuel de Champlain,* 1:190; Sagard, *Long Journey,* 158.
23 Léo-Paul Desrosiers argues that it may have been the Anishinaabeg along the St. Lawrence that forced the Iroquois south in the sixteenth century. Desrosiers, *Iroquoisie,* 7-8.
24 Champlain, *Voyages and Explorations of Samuel de Champlain,* 190.
25 *JR* 31:287.
26 White, *Middle Ground,* 15.
27 Hickerson, "The Feast of the Dead," 81-107.
28 Hickerson elaborates that the Fox, Sauk, and Potawatomi, for instance, did not have a Feast of Souls. Ibid., 87.
29 Ibid., 81.
30 *JR* 23: 221.
31 Hickerson, "The Feast of the Dead," 81, 88.
32 *JR* 38:199.
33 *JR* 42:57.
34 la Potherie, *Histoire,* 2:91, 94-95.
35 Hickerson, "The Feast of the Dead," 95; Trigger, *Children of Aataentsic,* 837-40.
36 *JR* 38:181. The Anishinaabe nations appear in the text, but the Wendat nations are more elusive because of the spelling employed by the Jesuits. Aenon and Ondaenronk were both names of Bear nation headmen in the 1630s and so these men were probably from the Bear nation. The spelling of the Rock nation description does not match the ethnographic and linguistic information, but its phonetic pronunciation is the closest to the Arendaeronnon's (Rock nation).
37 *JR* 38:181.
38 Radisson, *Voyages,* 232-33.
39 la Potherie, *Histoire,* 4:237.
40 Jean Blanchet, ed., *Collection de manuscrits contenant lettres, mémoires, et autres documents historiques relatifs à la Nouvelle-France recueillis aux Archives de la province de Québec ou copiés à l'étranger; mis en ordre et édités sous les auspices de la Législature de Québec, avec table, etc. Jean Blanchet* (Quebec: s.n., 1884), History of French Canada Collection, University of Ottawa, CIHM 08723, 253.
41 Hennepin, *Voyage curieux,* 116.
42 Charlevoix, *Journal of a Voyage to North America,* 2:6.
43 *JR* 38:199.
44 *JR* 42:57.
45 la Potherie, *Histoire,* 2:353.
46 Ibid., 354.
47 *JR* 35:217-19.
48 Ibid., 219-21.
49 *JR* 30:47.

50 *JR* 35:173, 175, 177.
51 Ibid., 193.
52 *JR* 34:205.
53 *JR* 36:189-91. The calculation is based on six people per canoe and the fact that there were forty canoes that left the island in 1652.
54 Barbeau, *Huron and Wyandot Mythology*, 368-69.
55 *JR* 36:189.
56 Hébert, *Le registre de Sillery*, 38. Charles Tgondatsa was from the Bear village of Ossossane; Paul Atondo and Jean-Baptiste Okhuk8andoron were from the Deer village of Scanonaenrat; Ignace Saoiiaretchi was from the southern Bear village of Taenhatentaron, and Pierre Otarenti was from the Bear village of Arrernte. The village of Thérèse Kinhrcha is unknown. These names are spelled in accordance to the Jesuit records. Missionaries used the 8 as a phonetic indication of the a-u sound before a consonant and an a-w sound before a vowel.
57 Many Native Americans used symbols (or totems) to represent themselves on treaty documents and contracts; Hébert, *Le registre de Sillery*, 38; Governor Charles Huault Montmagny (2 Aout 1646), "Concession des Terres pour les Sauvages Chrétiens à Sillery en aout 1646," WA, FMV, 8552-03, Cote E-1-18.
58 Hébert, *Le registre de Sillery*, 38.
59 On average, most of these unions seem to have been between Wendat fathers and Anishinaabe mothers (80 percent of children in the registry had Wendat fathers). Hébert, *Le registre de Sillery*, 39.
60 Charles Huault Montmagny (2 Aout 1646), WA, FMV, 8552-03.
61 Letter from du Tillet (July 1650, Paris), "Ratification par le roi de la concession de Sillery, par la compagnie de la nouvelle France, en faveur des sauvages, sous la direction des Pères Jésuits," WA, Collection François Vincent [CFV], Folder 1-b.
62 Charles Huault Montmagny (2 Aout 1646), WA, FMV, 8552-03.
63 Hébert, *Le registre de Sillery*, 38.
64 Ibid.
65 *JR* 23:223, 225.
66 Trigger, *Children of Aataentsic*, 789, 823.
67 Hickerson, "The Feast of the Dead," 95.
68 Hesse, *Algonkin Nation*, 2.
69 Hickerson, "The Feast of the Dead," 95.
70 *JR* 34:101.
71 *JR* 35:227-29.
72 Ibid., 223-25.

Chapter 5: The West

1 Thwaites, ed., *Jesuit Relations* [*JR*] 41:79.
2 *JR* 34:203. Some Wendat did move towards southern Nadowek groups, such as the Petun and Susquehannock, while others joined the Iroquois (which is the subject of a subsequent chapter).
3 *JR* 42:221. The region of the "People of the Sea" is synonymous with the upper Great Lakes, Illinois country, and the *pays d'en haut.* Although this area remained a location for several communities of various Native peoples, the Nation of the Sea (the Winnebago) were the most central, which led the French to name the area after this group.

4 Trigger, *Children of Aataentsic,* 821, 818.
5 Steckley, "Wendat Dialects," 23-36. The evidence for the composition of the group is derived from personal names of the Wyandot/Wendat found in a 1740s census. These names come from all four of the Wendat tribes (excluding the Marsh). Names from the Bear Nation included Enons (Aenon) and Taretande. Rock-associated names were Onnonrouten and Atironta. The names that belonged to the Cord were Sondakwa, and Sarenhes. Finally, Tiok8oindoron was the name of a Deer nation member.
6 *JR* 38:235; 34:203-4; Martin, ed., *Autobiographie,* 70.
7 Steckley, "Wendat Dialects," 24.
8 *JR* 35:165-67.
9 Ibid., 167.
10 Ibid.,109.
11 White, *Middle Ground,* 188.
12 Archaeologist William Allen sees the events stemming from this expedition as the pivotal moment that opened up the west for French expansion. William Arthur Allen, "Tchibekanakewin: The 1641 Algonquian Feast of the Dead," presented at the Ontario Archaeological Society Annual Symposium (Orillia, October 2003).
13 Trigger, *Children of Aataentsic,* 821.
14 Steckley, "Wendat Dialects."
15 Trigger, *Children of Aataentsic,* 821.
16 *JR* 45:234; 50:306; 56:114.
17 Michilimackinac is an Ottawa/Anishinaabe term for "turtle," because the island was said to resemble the shape of a turtle. Vogel, *Indian Names in Michigan,* 110-11.
18 *JR* 55:157.
19 Ibid., 173.
20 Ibid., 157-59.
21 *JR* 56:115-17.
22 Trigger, *Children of Aataentsic,* 820.
23 *JR* 45:235.
24 Radisson, *Voyages,* 167-68.
25 *JR* 56:117-19.
26 *JR* 55:169.
27 Bohaker, *"Nindoodemag,"* 43, 48.
28 *JR* 55:171.
29 Ibid., 161.
30 Ibid., 171-73.
31 Ibid., 137-39; Hickerson, "The Feast of the Dead," 89.
32 *JR* 41:77.
33 Jesuits describe it as a "parhelion." Modern science would call the phenomenon a "sundog." In brief, parhelia are formed by plate crystals high in the cirrus clouds that occur worldwide. In cold climates the plates can also be at ground level as diamond dust. See *JR* 55:177 and Les Cowley, "Atmospheric Optics," http://www.atoptics.co.uk.
34 *JR* 55:173-77.
35 Ibid., 177-79.
36 White, *Middle Ground,* 188.
37 *JR* 55:251.
38 *JR* 66:103; Peyser and Brandão, *Edge of Empire,* xxviii fn 30. There is some contention over these numbers; Antoine Laumet de la Mothe, sieur de Cadillac, the French commander at Michilimackinac in 1695, reported that there were six or seven thousand

Natives within gunshot of the fort. His estimation sounds high, and most scholars believe he was reporting on the entire Native population of the region, not the population at Michilimackinac.

39 *JR* 66:105. Given that Wendat men left the village during the hunting season and that the Jesuits recorded that the Wendat population at Michilimackinac dwindled from five hundred to three hundred during the hunting season, one can surmise that the population of women, children, and elders was 60 percent.

40 *JR* 66:107; 57:251.

41 *JR* 42:225.

42 Ibid., 225.

43 Steele, *Warpaths,* 75.

44 La Barre au ministre (4 November 1684), Archives nationales d'outre-mer [ANOM], Archives des colonies [AC], series C11A, 6:134-44v.

45 Peyser and Brandão, *Edge of Empire,* xxix.

46 *JR* 65:237-39.

47 Ibid., 237.

48 Ibid., 193. Matrilocal custom requires the husband to live with his wife's family.

49 *JR* 66:107.

50 *JR* 60:210.

51 Hennepin, *Voyage curieux,* 311.

52 Michigan State University, Anthropology Department, "The Marquette Mission," http://anthropology.msu.edu/marquettemission/Photo_Gallery.html.

53 *JR* 66:113.

54 Ibid., 105; "Dispatch from Colonel Francis Nicholson, accompanied by a trade proposition about trade" (1 July 1699), National Archives (UK), CO5/1310.

55 *JR* 56:115-19.

56 *JR* 60:211.

57 *JR* 57:253.

58 Ibid.

59 *JR* 66:105-7.

60 Ibid., 105.

61 Ibid., 107.

62 Ibid., 113.

63 Ibid., 113-17.

64 Elizabeth Tooker explains that the Wendat typically had four reasons to dance: "1) to propitiate the spirits who they thought conferred benefits on them, 2) to welcome someone, 3) to rejoice for some victory, 4) to prevent or cure disease." See Tooker, *An Ethnography,* 76.

65 *JR* 66:121.

66 *JR* 57:253; Tooker, *An Ethnography,* 76.

67 *JR* 17:81, 193.

68 Gabriel Sagard witnessed this dance in the 1620s in Wendake. Sagard, *Long Journey,* 118.

69 *JR* 57:255.

70 Ibid., 257.

71 *JR* 66:113.

72 *JR* 57:251.

73 Ibid., 259.

74 *JR* 66:115, 121.

75 Ibid., 107, 109.
76 *JR* 57:251.
77 Ibid.; 66:107; 66:113.
78 Hennepin, *Voyage curieux,* 311.
79 *JR* 61:119.
80 Ibid., 121.
81 Ibid., 147.
82 Trigger, *Children of Aataentsic,* 824.

Chapter 6: The East

1 Thwaites, ed., *Jesuit Relations* [*JR*] 66:147-49.
2 Trigger, *Children of Aataentsic,* 801-2; Delâge, *Bitter Feast,* 147-49; Dêlage, "Hurons de Lorette," 109-10; Calloway, *After King Philip's War,* 56; Havard, *Great Peace of Montreal,* 35.
3 While historian Susan Sleeper-Smith speaks more specifically about Native women, this chapter demonstrates that the same argument can be said of Native North Americans in general. Sleeper-Smith, *Indian Women and French Men.*
4 *JR* 66:159. The Jesuits referred to the Eastern Wendat who eventually settled at Lorette as the "lorettains."
5 *JR* 41:77.
6 *JR* 35:209; Jean Blanchet, ed., *Collection de manuscrits contenant lettres, mémoires, et autres documents historiques relatifs à la Nouvelle-France recueillis aux Archives de la province de Québec ou copiés à l'étranger; mis en ordre et édités sous les auspices de la Législature de Québec, avec table, etc. Jean Blanchet* (Quebec: s.n., 1884), History of French Canada Collection, University of Ottawa, CIHM 08723, 253.
7 *JR* 34:39, 229.
8 Delâge, *Bitter Feast,* 119, 166.
9 Ibid., 118-19.
10 Eccles, *France in America,* 42-43.
11 Delâge, *Bitter Feast,* 167.
12 Ibid., 119.
13 Eccles, *France in America,* 52.
14 Magnuson, *Education in New France,* 60.
15 Trigger, *Children of Aataentsic,* 801-2.
16 Parmenter, *Edge of the Woods,* 82.
17 The original funds allocated for the Wendat settlement were recorded as 500 *écus,* but Bruce Trigger has converted that number to 3,000 livres. *JR* 34:39; Trigger, *Children of Aataentsic,* 801.
18 *JR* 35:191-3.
19 Ibid., 209. This was the case with the Wenro refugees, for instance, in the 1630s.
20 Ibid., 237.
21 Translation is my own, from "aie en pitie, sois leur pere et leur protecteur." See "Discours des Sauvages Hurons qui demandent des terres aux Seigneurs du Montreal dedans leur ville," Wendake Archives [WA], Fonds Marguerite Vincent [FMV], Cote: G-1-94.
22 "Discours des Sauvages Hurons," WA, FMV, Cote G-1-94.
23 *JR* 35:197.
24 Ibid., 39.
25 Ibid., 215; Trigger, *Children of Aataentsic,* 802.
26 *JR* 35:199, 209.

27 Ibid., 199.
28 Ibid., 201.
29 Ibid.
30 *JR* 36:188.
31 Marie de l'Incarnation, *Lettres,* 1:389.
32 *JR* 35:209-11.
33 *JR* 36:117. The original measurements are given in French arpents, but there is marginal difference (1 arpent = .99 acres).
34 Léonard Garreau to sieur Beauregard (27 January 1652), Bibliothèque et Archives nationales du Québec [BAnQ], Collection Centre d'archives de Québec [CCAQ], fonds cour supérieure, district judicaire de Québec, Grèffes d'arpenteurs, Cote: P1000, S3, D814.
35 Trigger, *Children of Aataentsic,* 804; *JR* 44:189.
36 The details of these negotiations are the basis of Chapter 7, but for the purposes of this section what is important to know is that the Wendat continued to be the focus of Iroquois assaults.
37 Trigger, *Children of Aataentsic,* 806.
38 *JR* 42:49.
39 *JR* 43:107-13.
40 Ibid., 115-19. The fact that the Wendat sought refuge in the mission indicates that the governor had not built the fort he had originally promised.
41 This was two years before their tenure of eight years was due to expire, so the reason for the move was most likely due to the Iroquois attacks and lack of security on the island. *JR* 70:207.
42 "Veritable plan de Québec comme il est en l'an 1664 et la fortification que l'on y puisse faire." WA, Fonds Paul Picard [FPP], Cote: P2-S3-D37.
43 Trigger, *Children of Aataentsic,* 815; *JR* 44:191-3.
44 *JR* 47:261.
45 *JR* 45:245-61; Trigger, *Children of Aataentsic,* 816-17. For more on the Battle of Long Sault, see Lanctôt, "Dollard des Ormeaux," 137-46, and Keener, "An Ethnohistorical Analysis," 777-807.
46 *JR* 52:229.
47 *JR* 57:47-49.
48 *JR* 60:83.
49 Ibid., 71.
50 The Eastern Wendat made one more move in 1697 to "Jeune Lorette," which was in very close proximity to Ancienne Lorette. They have remained there ever since. Trigger, *Children of Aataentsic,* 819.
51 *JR* 60:69.
52 René Cloutier, "Souvenirs lorettains," *La Vie Journal* (14 avril 1965) WA, FMV, Boîte 8552.
53 *JR* 60:77.
54 Ibid., 75-81; 58:147.
55 *JR* 60:77.
56 Trigger, *Children of Aataentsic,* 813.
57 To date, there has been very little done on the demographics of the seventeenth-century Eastern Wendat. Although Jesuit records are fairly clear that roughly three hundred Wendat made their way from Wendake, scholars tend to take this at face value or use ambiguous terms such as "group" or "the hurons" with no detail about who these three

hundred people were or how the population changed over the years. For examples, see Delâge, *Bitter Feast,* 147; Havard, *Great Peace of Montreal,* 35. Complicating this narrative even further is Ian Steele's assertion that there were six hundred Eastern Wendat, and Roger Carpenter's oversight by not including the Wendat migration to Quebec in his otherwise informative description of the Wendat dispersal. See Steele, *Warpaths,* 71 and Roger Carpenter, *Renewed,* 129-31. The exception to this is Bruce Trigger, who affirms the three hundred and traces some of the population fluxes that transpired in the post-dispersal Eastern Wendat population. See Trigger, *Children of Aataentsic,* 802-4.

58 *JR* 36:143, 189. The count of 240 Wendat from Ekaentoton is my estimate based on the number of canoes in the party; I assume that there were approximately six adults per canoe.

59 "Ratification par le roi de la concession de Sillery, par la compagnie de la nouvelle France, en faveur des sauvages, sous la direction des Pères Jesuits" (July 1651), WA, CFV, cartable: 1-b; "Village Huron, Jeune Lorette," WA, CFV, cartable: 1-f; *JR* 70:207.

60 In 1650 there were "30 families" waiting at Sillery and Quebec to move to Île d'Orléans. Léo-Paul Hébert indicates it was approximately 120 people. See Hébert, *Le registre de Sillery,* 38.

61 *JR* 36:179.

62 *JR* 70:205-7.

63 Léonard Garreau to sieur Beauregard (27 January 1652), BAnQ, CCAQ, Cote: P1000, S3, D814.

64 Trigger, *Children of Aataentsic,* 802.

65 *JR* 54:285.

66 José António Brandão has done a meticulous job of recording all Iroquois battles from 1603-1701. See Brandão, *Your Fyre,* Appendix D.

67 Ibid. In this case "lost" may indicate "runaway."

68 *JR* 43:117-19; 187-89; Library and Archives Canada [LAC], Colonial Records [Col], C11A, 583-584.

69 *JR* 43:191.The Deer had already gone to live with the Seneca by this time.

70 Ibid.

71 *JR* 60:27.

72 Ibid.

73 la Potherie, *Documents,* 291.

74 Eccles, *France in America,* 77.

75 Ministre Colbert à Talon, LAC, Col, C11A 3/fol.11-18; Magnuson, *Education,* 60.

76 *JR* 47:287.

77 Ibid.; 311 fn 20.

78 "Contrat de marriage entre Louis Durand et Elizabeth A. Michel – 1698" WA, FMV, Boîte 8552, Cote E-3-67.

79 *JR* 47:311 fn 20.

80 *JR* 60:27.

81 *JR* 57:67-69.

82 Ibid., 67.

83 *JR* 66:157-59.

84 Ibid., 149.

85 Ibid., 157.

86 Ibid., 159.

87 Richter, *Ordeal of the Longhouse,* 120; *JR* 60:29.

88 *JR* 60:27.
89 *JR* 57:3.
90 *JR* 60:29-31. The Jesuits make particular reference to the Iroquois Jacques and Cécile Sogarese, as well as Marie Tsaoueate. The latter becomes so well known for her piety that she is deemed "La Précieuse."
91 *JR* 57:55.
92 Samuel de Champlain, *Voyages of Samuel de Champlain,* 1:231.
93 Sagard, *Long Journey,* 130-31.
94 Sioui, *Huron-Wendat,* 36.
95 Trigger, *Children of Aataentsic,* 47.
96 *JR* 57:61.
97 Ibid. It is unclear what "punishments" the children received, but corporal punishment cannot be ruled out.
98 *JR* 57:61.
99 Ibid., 69.
100 *JR* 52:237.
101 *JR* 57:55-57.
102 Ibid., 57.
103 Ibid., 61.
104 Ibid., 55. The children were encouraged to burn down the cabin of the guilty alcoholics, for instance.
105 *JR* 28:49; Tooker, *An Ethnography,* 57. Traditionally, Wendat who did not comply with the various social expectations lost respect within the community, isolating them from the rest of the village.
106 *JR* 53:129.
107 Ibid., 113.
108 Ibid., 121.
109 *JR* 54:295, 297.
110 *JR* 57:47, 49.
111 *JR* 60:37.
112 *JR* 66:147; Trigger, *Children of Aataentsic,* 818.
113 *JR* 66:147-49.
114 Ibid., 66:173.
115 Ibid., 163.
116 Ibid., 161.
117 Ibid., 163.

Chapter 7: Iroquois Country

1 Brandão, *Your Fyre,* 77.
2 Fenton, *Great Law,* 283-84; Richter, "Ordeals of the Longhouse: The Five Nations in Early American History," in Richter and Merrell, ed., *Beyond the Covenant Chain,* 21; Anthony, *Cardinal Richelieu,* 433.
3 Parmenter, *Edge of the Woods,* 80.
4 Ibid., 81.
5 Dennis, *Cultivating a Landscape of Peace.*
6 Parmenter, *Edge of the Woods,* 86-87.
7 Thwaites, ed., *Jesuit Relations* [*JR*] 40:165.
8 Parmenter, *Edge of the Woods,* 84.
9 *JR* 36:183.

10 *JR* 42:53; 43:187.
11 *JR* 42:253.
12 Steele, *Warpaths,* 71. The following also give insight into the Wendat removal to Iroquois country post-dispersal: Richter, *Ordeal of the Longhouse,* 108; Trigger, *Children of Aataentsic,* 767, 809, 828, 840; Tooker, ed. *An Iroquois Source Book,* 227; Jennings, *Ambiguous Iroquois Empire,* 104; Hunt, *Wars of the Iroquois,* 94-95; Brandão, *Your Fyre,* 77.
13 As discussed in Chapter 2, adoption of individual war captives of varying ethnicities by Nadowek captors often resulted in full assimilation into the community.
14 Richter, *Ordeal of the Longhouse,* 108.
15 Fenton, *Great Law,* 283.
16 *JR* 56:115.
17 *JR* 43:115-19.
18 *JR* 43:189.
19 Ibid.
20 *JR* 42:253-55.
21 *JR* 40:165.
22 Ibid. 165-67.
23 Ibid., 55. The Wendat at Gahoendoe stated explicitly that many Wendat thought about joining the Iroquois in the hopes of reconnecting with family.
24 *JR* 40:179.
25 *JR* 43:193.
26 *JR* 42:207.
27 *JR* 41:57.
28 Ibid., 57, 59.
29 *JR* 43:193.
30 Ibid., 191.
31 *JR* 56:115.
32 Brandão, *Your Fyre,* 327. Brandão uses this term to describe those Wendat who agreed to live with the Iroquois, as opposed to "involuntary" cases such as Wendat prisoners of war.
33 *JR* 36:141-43.
34 Ibid., 143.
35 *JR* 43:189, 191, 193.
36 *JR* 42:205.
37 *JR* 43:191.
38 Lettre de Talon au ministre, October 27, 1667, Archives nationales d'outre-mer [ANOM], Archives des colonies [AC], series C11A 2/fol. 306-320v.
39 Parmenter, *Edge of the Woods,* 95.
40 Greer, *Mohawk Saint,* 98.
41 Parmenter, *Edge of the Woods,* 154.
42 *JR* 43:193.
43 Ibid., 195. The Jesuits recorded this speech as given by the "Captain of the Bear Nation." Because there was no single "captain" of any Wendat nation, it may be surmised that Atsena was the captain in question, given that he was highly respected and well known by the Jesuits.
44 Ibid., 193.
45 Brandão, *Your Fyre,* 78; Trigger, *Children of Aataentsic,* 826.
46 Parker, *History of the Seneca Indians,* 36-52; Merrell, *Indians' New World,* 78-83.

47 *JR* 54:83.
48 Brandão, *Your Fyre*, 78. Brandão suggests that the calculation of ten people per family was still valid during this period. See also *JR* 56:69.
49 The Onnontioga may have been a tribe dwelling on the river called Onnondokoui (now known as Gananoque), which flowed into the St. Lawrence twenty-four kilometres northeast of what is now Kingston, Ontario. *JR* 54:305 fn ii.
50 *JR* 54:81, 83.
51 *JR* 57:195.
52 *JR* 41:243.
53 Trigger, *Children of Aataentsic*, 767.
54 The Gandougare Wendat continued to practise curing rituals after relocation; a custom that the People of the Deer were well known for before the dispersal. *JR* 58:229.
55 *JR* 54:87.
56 Ibid., 85. The Jesuits recorded that the other two towns at Gandougare were not Christian and had very little knowledge of the faith.
57 *JR* 54:87.
58 *JR* 56: 7.
59 *JR* 54:87.
60 *JR* 44:25.
61 *JR* 57:193.
62 *JR* 54:91.
63 Ibid., 89.
64 Ibid., 87.
65 *JR* 56:69.
66 *JR* 54: 91, 93.
67 Ibid., 87.
68 *JR* 56:69.
69 *JR* 44:25.
70 *JR* 57:89.
71 *JR* 51:189.
72 Brandão, *Your Fyre*, 78.
73 Greer, *Mohawk Saint*, 96.
74 Ibid., 97; Devine, *Historic Caughnawaga*, 22.
75 *JR* 51:193.
76 Ibid., 193-97.
77 Devine, *Historic Caughnawaga*, 42 fn 2. The belt is still in the possession of the present-day Kahnawake community.
78 Greer, *Mohawk Saint*, 90.
79 Alfred, *Heeding the Voices*, 25, 44.
80 Parmenter, *Edge of the Woods*, 154; Greer, *Mohawk Saint*, 99.
81 Alfred, *Heeding the Voices*, 46.
82 René Cuillerier, "Nation Iroquoise," Bibliothèque Mazarin (Paris), Cote: MS 1964, Fonds General (c.1700), 3-4.
83 *JR* 51:133.
84 *JR* 57:195; 51:133. Father Jacques Bruyas recorded sixty baptisms in four months at Ganowarohare.
85 *JR* 51:133.
86 Ibid., 129.

87 Trigger, *Children of Aataentsic,* 49.
88 *JR* 51: 127.
89 Ibid.
90 Ibid., 135.
91 *JR* 43:127-33; Jennings, *Ambiguous Iroquois Empire,* 107.
92 *JR* 44:71.
93 *JR* 42:53.
94 René Cuillerier, "Nation Iroquoise," Bibliothèque Mazarin (Paris), Cote: MS 1964, Fonds General (c.1700), 10. Translation is my own. The original reads: "De toutes les nations que nous avons en ce pays, il n'y à que le huron qui les surpasse pour l'ésprit."
95 *JR* 57:195.
96 *JR* 40:165.
97 *JR* 55:275.
98 Ibid.
99 Ibid.

Chapter 8: Leadership

1 Eastman, *Indian Heroes,* 1.
2 This is based on the information given in the sources gathered predominantly by French Catholic men. There may have been leaders who were traditionalists, but if there were they do not surface in the records.
3 Bruce Trigger, *Children of Aataentsic,* 799.
4 See the Dictionary of Canadian Biography Online [DCB], http://www.biographi.ca: Elsie McLeod Jury, "Pierre Atironta," "Étienne Annaotaha," DCB 1; André Vachon, "Louis Taondechoren," DCB 1; William Fenton, "Kondiaronk," DCB 2; Harry Kelsie, "Michipichy," DCB 3.
5 Havard, *Great Peace of Montreal,* 199-202, 203, 207-8.
6 Kondiaronk is the Wendat leader most frequently discussed in these works. For representative examples, see White, *Middle Ground,* 142-56; Skinner, *Upper Country,* 71-73; Schmitz, *White Robe's Dilemma,* 162-66; Sayre, *Les sauvages américains,* 127-28; Mann, *1491,* 123; Fenton, *Great Law,* 287-94. For the most part, the other leaders receive little to no mention in the literature.
7 Havard, *Great Peace of Montreal,* 199-201; Charlevoix, *Histoire,* 2:214; la Potherie, *Histoire,* 3:299, 4:201.
8 Charlevoix, *Histoire,* 1:277. The English translation is taken from Havard, *Great Peace of Montreal,* 200.
9 la Potherie, *Histoire,* 4:228. The English translation is taken from Havard, *Great Peace of Montreal,* 199.
10 Lettre de Champigny au ministre (18 August 1696). Archives nationales d'outre-mer [ANOM], Archives des colonies [AC], series C11A 14/fol. 182-92.
11 la Potherie calls Le Baron "Sastaretsi," but it is unclear whether this was a misunderstanding (la Potherie also explains that this is the name used to describe the Wendat of Michilimackinac) or if Le Baron also used this name. La Potherie, *Histoire,* 3:233.
12 Relation par Charles de Monseignat (November 1690) ANOM, AC, series C11A 11/fol.5040; "Relation de ce qui s'est passé de plus remarquable au Canada" (1697) ANOM, AC, series C11A 15/fol. 3-21.
13 Translation is my own. La Potherie, *Histoire,* 4:24-25.
14 Charlevoix, *Histoire,* 2:156.

15 la Potherie, *Histoire,* 4:24; "Traité de la grande paix de Montréal de 1701," Library and Archives Canada [LAC], Colonial Records [Col] C11A 19.

16 *Mishi* translates to "large" in several Anishinaabe languages. Further, seventeenth-century Nadowekian languages did not have the phonemes "m" or "p." The author is grateful for the manuscript reader's insight regarding this theory.

17 This section does not include information on the aforementioned Eastern leaders Étienne Annaotaha and Louis Taondechoren. This does not mean that they were not important Wendat headmen, but the information we have on them is relegated almost entirely to their involvement in a military expedition against the Iroquois at Long Sault, and gives few details of their influence on the Wendat community at large. For more information on them, see Thwaites, ed., *Jesuit Relations* [*JR*] 19:148-50; 20:210-12; 22:236; 25:266-68, 276, 300; 28:134, 148, 150, 196-98; 30:78, 306; Vachon, "L'affaire du Long-Sault, 495-515.

18 *JR* 43:191.

19 Ibid., 195.

20 *JR* 55:25; *JR* 53:115; *JR* 53:121.

21 *JR* 53:121-23.

22 Ibid., 115.

23 Ibid., 103.

24 Ibid., 111.

25 *JR* 66:167.

26 Ibid., 161-63.

27 Ibid., 169.

28 *JR* 57:37-43.

29 The Holy Family was established by the Jesuits in 1653. It was selective in its members, and included both Wendat men and women. See Griffiths and Cervantes, eds., *Spiritual Encounters,* 75.

30 *JR* 57:43-45.

31 Ibid., 67.

32 *JR* 45:109. The Jesuits use this term to describe captive Wendat who became incorporated into Iroquois society.

33 de Quen, *Relation,* 23.

34 Translation is my own. De Quen, *Relation,* 23.

35 Bruce Trigger argues this last point explicitly. Trigger, *Children of Aataentsic,* 837.

36 *JR* 43:117. The Jesuits testified that they could hear his song for over half a league, even though they were not present for the actual event.

37 Ibid., 119.

38 Ibid., 191.

39 la Potherie, *Histoire,* 3:94; Lettre de Cadillac au ministre (Phelyeaux) (27 October 1695), LAC, Col, C-2379, XIII: 449-79.

40 la Potherie, *Histoire,* 4:201, 213. The French fort at St. Joseph River was built in 1691. Le Baron, along with Michipichy and a group of Western Wendat, relocated to this area in the 1690s. Significantly, Michipichy told the French that the Wendat of Michilimackinac and those of St. Joseph were "one body." For information on Fort St. Joseph, see Peyser and Brandão, *Edge of Empire,* xxvii.

41 la Potherie, *Histoire,* 4:258.

42 "Paroles échangées entre Frontenac et les allies hurons," (August 1682) ANOM, C11A 6/fol. 5-13v.

43 *JR* 35:47-49.
44 *JR* 57:63-65.
45 Ibid., 253.
46 Letter XIV (26 May 1688), in Lahontan, *Nouveaux Voyages,* 1:141.
47 *JR* 49:227-29.
48 "Mémoire de Denonville," (1688) ANOM, AC, series C11A 10/fol. 100-11; "Memoire de l'état des affaires" (6 November 1688) LAC, MG1 C11A Correspondance Générale [CG], R12297-2-8-F; microfilm C-13995, vol. 5, 174-96.
49 Lettre XVII (28 September 1689), in Lahontan, *Nouveaux Voyages,* 1:266.
50 la Potherie, *Histoire,* 3:94-100.
51 Translation is my own. "Relation d'événements survenus en 1694 et 1695," (1695), ANOM, AC, series C11A 14/fol. 98v.
52 Letter XIV (26 May 1688), in Lahontan, *Nouveaux Voyages,* 1:136.
53 *JR* 66:165.
54 Toupin, ed., *Les Écrits de Pierre Potier,* 221, 236.
55 Steckley, "The 1747 Wyandot Elders Council," 14.
56 Ibid., 6.
57 There is some ambiguity here because the name recorded is "P. Shataresti." See "La Mosaïque de Grands Chefs Hurons," Wendake Archives [WA] (1972) cartable: 6-c.
58 Steckley, "The 1747 Wyandot Elders Council," 6.
59 Lahontan, *Nouveaux Voyages,* 2:142-43.
60 Hale, "Huron Historical Legend," 475-83.
61 Ibid., 479.
62 Ibid. 480.
63 *JR* 53:119.
64 Barbeau, *Huron and Wyandot Mythology,* 250.
65 Ibid.
66 Eastman, *Indian Heroes,* 1.

Chapter 9: Women

1 Trigger, *The Huron: Farmers of the North,* 26, 29; O'Brien, "'Divorced,'" 335, 337, 341; Bales, "Native American Women," http://www.oah.org/pubs/magazine/women/bales.htm.
2 Quoted in Perdue, "Cherokee Women," 283-84. Also found in Presidential Papers Microfilm: Andrew Jackson (Washington, 1961), Series 1, Reel 22.
3 Thwaites, ed., *Jesuit Relations* [*JR*] 57:47-49.
4 In particular, Bruce Trigger argues Wendat women of the east became more dependent on the Jesuits because of the loss of Wendat men during the Iroquois attacks at Île d'Orléans. Jacki Andre expands on this and contends that no matter what the destination of resettlement, Wendat women lost their pre-dispersal status and influence within their new community. Andre argues specifically that women lost political sway among the Iroquois, lost social status in the west because of the influence of Anishinaabe systems of patrilineality, and lost status in the east because of the patriarchal nature of Christianity. See Andre, "Contagious Disease," 129, 134, 136; Trigger, *Children of Aataentsic,* 817.
5 Anderson, *Chain Her by One Foot;* Devens, *Countering Colonizing.*
6 Bales, "Native American Women."

7 *JR* 34:209. Although the production of wampum belts was not necessarily a gendered task, there is some evidence to suggest that women may have had a principal role in creating the belts within some Native societies. In this case, however, the Jesuits explicitly stated that these ten belts were made by the women "who made us a present of the little which was left to them in their misery." For more on gender roles and the production of wampum belts, see Jonathan C. Lainey, *La "Monnaie des sauvages,"* 30-31.

8 *JR* 34:209.

9 Ibid., 209-11.

10 Ibid., 211.

11 The seigneurial system was introduced in New France in 1627. Land was arranged in long strips called seigneuries along the bank of the St. Lawrence River. Although each property was owned by the French king, it was maintained by the landlord or seigneur. In this case, the "seigneur" happened to be a woman, hence, "seigneuresse."

12 Jean-Jacques Lefebvre, "Éléonore de Grandmaison," Dictionary of Canadian Biography, http://www.biographi.ca/; *JR* 11:68, 278; 28:225; 37:92.

13 Léonard Garreau to sieur Beauregard (27 January 1652), Bibliothèque et Archives nationales du Québec [BAnQ], Collection Centre d'archives de Québec [CCAQ], fonds cour supérieure, district judicaire de Québec, Grèffes d'arpenteurs, Cote: P1000, S3, D814.

14 Ibid.

15 *JR* 57:63.

16 Ibid., 65.

17 Nicholas Griffiths and Fernando Cervantes, eds. *Spiritual Encounters,* 75-76.

18 *JR* 54:297.

19 Letter from Father Simon Le Moyne to M. le Curé de St. Martin [his cousin], 25 May 1639, Newberry Library, Ayer Collection, MS 507.

20 *JR* 44:61-63.

21 *JR* 35:233-35.

22 *JR* 55:179.

23 *JR* 57:259.

24 *JR* 41:155.

25 *JR* 8:145-47.

26 *JR* 52:247.

27 *JR* 60:299.

28 *JR* 41:153-59.

29 *JR* 42:41.

30 *JR* 44:229-31.

31 *JR* 44:263.

32 Sister Mary of Jesus, "Ursulines," in Wallace, ed., *Encyclopedia of Canada,* 6:221-24.

33 *JR* 44:229.

34 Mère Saint-Thomas, *Les Ursulines de Québec, depuis leur établissement jusqu'à nos jours* (Quebec, 1863), University of Ottawa Collection: Women's History, microfilm CIHM 34242, vol. 1-4.

35 *JR* 35:209-11.

36 Translation is my own. Richaudeau, ed. *Lettres,* 1:422-23.

37 Ibid., 423.

38 *JR* 44:229-231.

39 Ibid., 259.
40 Ibid., 261-65.
41 Ibid., 265.
42 *JR* 43:67-69.
43 *JR* 44:275.
44 *JR* 40:225.
45 *JR* 36:213.
46 Ibid., 213-15.
47 *JR* 42:187.
48 Ibid., 187-89.
49 *JR* 30: 55-57.
50 *JR* 43:299.
51 *JR* 42:189.
52 *JR* 43:253.
53 *JR* 49:107.
54 *JR* 40:229.
55 *JR* 41:119.
56 Ibid.
57 *JR* 52: 247.
58 Ibid., 251.
59 Ibid., 249.
60 Ibid.
61 *JR* 52:253.
62 Ibid., 257.
63 Ibid., 251. Her success rate was so high that many assumed she could ready a student for baptism with only three days of training.
64 Ibid., 255.
65 Ibid.
66 Ibid., 257.

Chapter 10: Power

1 See Brah, *Cartographies.*
2 Thwaites, ed., *Jesuit Relations* [*JR*] 49:227-29.
3 Ibid., 229.
4 For more on the relationship between social power and diasporic communities, see Brah, *Cartographies;* Mann, *Sources of Social Power;* Shuval, "Diaspora Migration," 41-56; Kokot, Tölölyan, and Alfonso, *Diaspora.*
5 For the continuation of these traditions in the west, see *JR* 57:251; 66:113-17; 57:255. For customs in the east, see *JR* 53:113; 54:296; 53:121; 66:147.
6 Sulte, *Pierre Boucher,* 146.
7 *JR* 49:227.
8 "Traité fait avec les Iroquois le 22 mai 1666" (25 mai 1666) Archives nationales d'outre-mer [ANOM], Archives des colonies [AC], series C11A 2/ fol. 232-233v. The Wendat did not use a written form of their language, but the Jesuits had created a written dictionary that spelled the words phonetically. For more on these dictionaries, see Steckley, ed., *First French-Huron Dictionary.*
9 *JR* 8:114-16
10 Linguist Marianne Mithun speculates that Wendat captives among the Iroquois not only made the Iroquois more familiar with their language but also inadvertently began

a process of Wendat linguistic innovation among Iroquois speakers. See Mithun, "Untangling the Huron and the Iroquois," 504-7.

11 This is because the Jesuits started working on an Iroquois dictionary decades after they began to learn the Wendat and Anishinaabe languages.

12 *JR* 60:51-53.

13 "Testimony of Simone Coté and others on alleged embezzlement at Michilimackinac in the case of Couagne vs. Louis Ouakouts, Marie Félix, et al." Bibliothèque et Archives nationales du Québec à Montréal [BAnQM], Documents judicaires de la jurisdictions seigneuriale de Montréal (1651-1695) [DJ], Cote TL 2, feuilles détachées, 1681-1692. See also Peyser and Brandão, *Edge of Empire,* 12-17.

14 See fn 13.

15 Eccles, *France in America,* 77.

16 *JR* 65:237-39.

17 *JR* 47:287.

18 Kondiaronk states this explicitly. See la Potherie, *Histoire,* 4:23.

19 Griffiths and Cervantes, eds., *Spiritual Encounters,* 75.

20 Pomedli, *Ethnophilosophical and Ethnolinguistic Perspectives,* 55.

21 This is a common phenomenon with any diaspora. Baker, *Cultural Studies.*

22 *JR* 38:177.

23 Ibid., 189.

24 Zedeno and Stoffle, "Tracking," 68.

25 For examples of the east, see *JR* 60:20, 101; la Potherie, *Histoire,* 3:143, 4:7; "Revue des Indiens qui ont suivi les Français" (17 August 1684) ANOM, C11A 6/fol. 267. For examples of the west, see la Potherie, *Histoire,* 3:143; Letter XIV (26 May 1688), in Lahontan, *Nouveaux voyages* 1:143; "Relation d'événement survenues en 1694-1695" Library and Archives Canada [LAC], Col, vol. 14; 92.

26 "Map of Louisiana Pass" (1698), National Archives (UK), MPG1/1221.

27 *Wendake* (meaning Wendat territory before 1649) and *ronon* (meaning nation or people).

28 This departs from Bruce Trigger's assertion that the past "had no meaning" for the post-dispersal seventeenth-century Wendat. Trigger bases this interpretation on the lack of information retained by the nineteenth-century Wendat concerning their society before the exodus from Wendake. The circumstances of the nineteenth-century Wendat, however, do not necessarily reflect the attitudes of seventeenth-century Wendat. Still, Roger Carpenter supports Trigger's interpretation, arguing that Wendat identity had "no value" after 1650 because the Wendat thought that others, such as the French, viewed them as economically and politically "disposable." Carpenter points to French decisions to remain neutral in certain Wendat/Iroquois conflicts in the 1650s, which he reads as a French betrayal of their former Wendat allies. While this may highlight moments of neglect by the French, it should not overshadow the more frequent accounts of the French privileging the Wendat because of their strong historic identity. Trigger, *Children of Aataentsic,* 825; Carpenter, *Renewed,* 134.

29 *JR* 57:259.

30 *JR* 56:119.

31 la Potherie, *Histoire,* 2:51; la Potherie, *Documents,* 290.

32 la Potherie, *Documents,* 291.

33 Translations are my own. Lahontan, *Nouveaux voyages,* 2:95.

34 *JR* 43:291.

35 Ibid.

36 Hodge, ed., *Handbook of American Indians,* 2:337-38.
37 Mancke, "Polity Formation."
38 Mancke, "Spaces of Power, 32-49.
39 Ibid., 32-33.
40 Lettre de Denonville au ministre, LAC, Col, C-2377; 9, 31-50.
41 This was one of the main topics of discussion at the American Society of Ethnohistory's annual conference in Ottawa 2010. Thanks to John Steckley, Thomas Peace, Megan McCullen, and Andrew Sturtevant for fleshing out some of these ideas. In addition, see Hickerson, "The Feast of the Dead," 96.
42 la Potherie, *Histoire,* 2:353.
43 Nicholas Perrot, *Mémoire sur les mœurs,* 143, 145.
44 Translation is my own. La Potherie, *Histoire,* 4:23-25.
45 White, *Middle Ground,* 192-94.
46 *JR* 57:69.
47 This tradition continued after 1701 when the Western Wendat moved with the French to Detroit, but dissipated with subsequent Wendat migrations to Ohio, Kansas, and Oklahoma.
48 *JR* 53:105-7.
49 *JR* 57:195.
50 See references in Appendix for numerous accounts of the "destruction" of the Confederacy.
51 Hodge, ed., *Handbook of American Indians,* 337-38.
52 Mancke, "Polity Formation," 383.
53 Ibid. This is the closest description of the Wendat system of power, although Mancke defines diasporic polities as being a union of culturally alien people, which the seventeenth-century Wendat were not.
54 Ibid., 3.
55 Radisson, *Voyages of Peter Radisson,* 152.
56 Most likely the Sioux.
57 *JR* 54: 283-85.
58 *JR* 57:253.
59 "Statement of trade goods belonging to Marie Félix du Bocq left with Fathers at Missilimakina 1683," BAnQM, DJ, Cote TL2, feuilles detachées.
60 "Testimony of Simone Coté and others on alleged embezzlement at Michilimackinac in the case of Couagne vs. Louis Ouakouts, Marie Félix, et al." BAnQM, DJ, Cote TL2.
61 *JR* 60:53. Jacques Otratenkoui had at least one daughter with his second wife.
62 "Traité de la grande paix de Montréal de 1701," LAC, C11A 19; Havard, *Great Peace of Montreal,* 94 fn 4; Lainey, *La "Monnaie des sauvages,"* 193 fn 7; "Indian Peace Pact Belt May Be 250 Years Old," Wendake Archives [WA], Collection François Vincent [CFV], cartable: 2-b.
63 la Potherie, *Documents,* 290.
64 *JR* 49:229.

Epilogue

1 The descendants of the Wendat Confederacy are identified presently within four branches spanning the States and Canada. The communities are La Nation huronne-wendat (Québec), the Wyandot of Anderdon Nation (Ontario/Michigan), the

Wyandotte Nation of Oklahoma, and the Wyandot Nation of Kansas. For more information on the Wendat migrations taking place after 1701, see Larry Hancks, "The Emigrant Tribes: Wyandot, Delaware, and Shawnee – A Chronology" (2007) Wyandot Nation of Kansas, http://www.wyandot.org.

2 Brian Baker, "Ceremony Marks Return of Huron Bones to Final Resting Place," *Barrie Examiner,* 4 September 1999.

3 Despite these group's varied use of the term "Wendat" (Wyandotte, Wyandot, Huron-Wendat, and Huron), they all self-identify with being Wendakeronon.

4 Carey Moran, "Hurons Headed Home after 350 Years: Return of Remains to Proper Place Fulfils Man's Dream," *Barrie Examiner,* 13 August 1999.

5 Ibid.

6 Brian Baker, "Solemn Ceremony Rights a Wrong," *Free Press,* 31 August 1999.

7 Chief Janith English, written correspondence to the author, 6 May 2007.

8 The Wendat Nation of Kansas, "The Wendat Confederacy," http://www.wyandot.org/confederacy.html.

9 Emphasis is my own. Chief Janith English, written correspondence to author, 6 May 2007.

10 Ibid.

11 Moran, "Hurons Headed Home."

12 Michel Gros-Louis, Michel Savard, and Annette Vincent, "Letter to the editor," *Free Press,* 30 August 1999

13 Chief Janith English, to the author, 7 May 2007.

14 The story that follows of this event is taken from Roberta Avery, "Reunion Brings Tears of Joy, Sense of Belonging," *Toronto Star,* 30 August 1999; Moran, "Hurons Headed Home"; and Baker, "Ceremony Marks Return."

15 Chief Janith English, to the author, 7 May 2007.

16 Avery, "Reunion Brings Tears of Joy."

17 *Agondachia* is the Wendat word for "the Elder's House." The mandate of the Agondachia Association is published on their website, http://www.agondachia.com.

18 Chief Janith English, to the author, 7 May 2007.

Appendix

1 Steckley, *Words of the Huron,* ix-x.

2 Emphasis and translation are my own. Cornelius Jaenen quoted in Vaugeois, ed. *Les Hurons de Lorette,* 171.

3 White, *Middle Ground,* 1.

4 Wilson, *Lost Atlantis,* 254.

5 Hathaway, *Story of the Hurons,* 25.

6 Jones, *"8endake Ehen,"* v.

7 John Sloan (Director of Huronia Historical Parks) to D. Brown (Travel Research Branch of Department of Tourism and Information), 4 December 1968, Archives of Ontario [AO], RG 5-46, box MB139.

8 Ontario Department of Tourism and Information, "Attitude of Metro Toronto to Sainte Marie among the Hurons," January 1969, AO, RG 5-46, box MB135.

9 Connelly, *Kansas City,* 5.

10 For many scholars, and particularly Native intellectuals, the general writing of Native history by non-Natives is seen as a continuation of the process of colonization, often damaging the veracity of Indigenous cultures and communities. For more on this

discussion, see Kidwell and Velie, "Historical Contact and Conflict," in *Native American Studies,* 41-59. Also useful is Mihesuah, ed., *Natives and Academics.*

11 Officially, these descendants are members of La Nation huronne-wendat (Quebec), the Wyandot of Anderdon Nation (Ontario/Michigan), the Wyandotte Nation of Oklahoma, and the Wyandot Nation of Kansas. They may, however, live in various additional locations as well.

12 The term "contact zone" is defined by Mary Louise Pratt as "social spaces where disparate cultures meet, clash, and grapple with each other, often in highly asymmetrical relations of domination and subordination – such as colonialism." In the context of this appendix, the term describes less conventional encounters, focusing on the interaction between the North American public and Wendat history. See Pratt, *Imperial Eyes,* 7.

13 Until recently, historians seeking to draw from Jesuit sources used these original published reports or reprinted edited volumes. Since 1967, however, Jesuit historian Lucien Campeau has gained access to the Jesuit archives in Rome and compiled several volumes of unpublished Jesuit documents. These include letters as well as *Relations* in their original languages of French, Latin, and Italian. See Campeau, ed., *Monumenta Novae Franciae.*

14 The theme of destruction is used throughout the *Relations,* such as the entry for 20 July 1649, which describes the "destruction of the Hurons." See Thwaites, ed., *Jesuit Relations* [*JR*], 34:57. For similar examples, see *JR* 35:15, 83, 105, 211.

15 For representative examples of the "early scholars," see Connelly, *Kansas City* (1918); Jones, *"8endake Ehen"* (1908); Hathaway, *Story of the Hurons* (1915); Wilson, *Lost Atlantis* (1892); Cass, *Remarks* (1827); Parkman, *Jesuits in North America* (1867); Hale, "Four Huron Wampum Records (1897); Hunter, *Notes* (1901); Barbeau, *Huron and Wyandot Mythology* (1915).

16 Hathaway's work was funded by the Ontario Historical Society, and Arthur Jones's publication by the Bureau of Archives.

17 Parkman, *Jesuits in North America,* 668. The section titled the "The Doomed Nation" begins on page 634. Parkman also includes a section titled "The Ruin of the Hurons," 664.

18 Ibid., 675.

19 Hathaway, *Story of the Hurons,* 22.

20 Cass, *Remarks,* 59.

21 Emphasis is my own. Hodge, ed., *Handbook of Indians of Canada,* 207.

22 Tooker, *An Ethnography;* Trigger, *The Huron: Farmers of the North;* Trigger, *Children of Aataentsic;* Heidenreich, *Huronia;* Anderson, *Chain Her by One Foot;* Sioui, *Huron-Wendat;* Carpenter, *Renewed;* Warrick, *A Population History;* Seeman, *The Huron-Wendat Feast of the Dead.*

23 This line is taken from Bruce Trigger's *The Huron: Farmers of the North,* 1.

24 "Destruction of Huronia" is a chapter from Georges Sioui's *For an Amerindian Autohistory,* 39-60. "The End of the Confederacy" is a chapter from Trigger's *Children of Aataentsic,* 725-88.

25 For representative examples, see: McMullen, *History of Canada,* 28-30; Weaver, *A Canadian History for Boys and Girls;* Choquette, *L'Ontario français,* 25-26; Roderick and McLean, *L'histoire du Canada,* 97; White, *Ontario 1610-1985,* 37; Bumsted, *Peoples of Canada,* 75; Francis, Jones, and Smith, *Origins,* 45-46; Davidson, DeLay, Heyrman, Lytle, and Stoff, *U.S.,* 1:62-64.

26 Emphasis is my own. McMullen, *History of Canada,* 30.

27 Bumsted, *Peoples of Canada,* 75.
28 Francis et al., *Origins,* 45-46.
29 Translation is my own. See Choquette, *L'Ontario français,* 25-26.
30 Davidson et al., *U.S.,* 64.
31 The Ontario Ministry of Education has a mandatory lesson plan for the Ontario Social Studies unit "Aboriginal Peoples and Early Explorers Expectations" – for grade 6 it includes Wendat history (http://www.linktolearning.com/grade6ss.htm). Similarly, the Quebec Ministry of Education includes a discussion on the "similarities and differences between the traditional ways of life of the Algonquian, Huron-Iroquois and Inuit" in their social studies program for ages six to eleven (http://www.mels.gouv.qc.ca/publications/). In the United States, the American National and Records Administration has created a lesson plan for grades 4 to 6 on the "Ohio Frontier" that includes accounts of migrating Wendat (http://www.archives.gov/education/lessons).
32 Emphasis is my own. Canadian Broadcasting Corporation, "Elementary School Resources," http://www.cbc.ca/history/.
33 Peers, *Playing Ourselves,* 39, 43.
34 Ontario Heritage Foundation, Plaque: "Crawford Lake Indian Village Site," located at Crawford Lake Indian Village, Guelph Line, Campbellville, Ontario, Canada.
35 "Speech of the Honourable Fern Guidon, Minister of Tourism and Information – Sainte-Marie among the Hurons – May 15, 1971," AO, RG 5-7, box MB31.
36 John Sloan (Director of Huronia Historical Parks) to D. Brown (Travel Research Branch of Department of Tourism and Information), 4 December 1968, AO, RG 5-46, box MB139.
37 Jury and Jury, *Sainte-Marie among the Hurons,* xi-xii.
38 See fn 35.
39 Mackinac State Historic Parks website, http://www.mackinacparks.com.
40 Historic Sites and Monuments Board of Canada, Plaque: "Sainte-Marie Among The Hurons" located at Highway #12, Township of Tay, Ontario, Canada.
41 Ontario Archaeological and Historic Sites Board, Plaque: "Manitoulin Mission," located in the District of Manitoulin, the Town of Northeastern Manitoulin and the Islands, Ontario, Canada.
42 Ontario Archaeological and Historic Sites Board, Plaque: "Champlain's War Party, 1615," Quinte Street, Trenton, Ontario, Canada.
43 Mackinac State Historic Parks website: "Brief History of Colonial Michilimackinac," http://www.mackinacparks.com.
44 "Wampum Belt," National Museum of the American Indian, catalogue number: 1/2132.
45 "Jesuit Mortar, 1636," Canadian Museum of Civilization, Canada Hall Exhibit.
46 "The History of the Huron or Ouendat People," Huronia Museum, http://www.huroniamuseum.com/public/.
47 Laura Peers argues this point explicitly. Peers, *Playing Ourselves,* 151.
48 See Brébeuf, *A Huron Carol.*
49 Adam Kidd, *Huron Chief,* xii.
50 François-Xavier Garneau, "Le dernier huron," in *Traverse Les Vents* (1840), Wendake Archives [WA], Collection François Vincent [CFV], cartable C-J.
51 English translation is my own. The original poem in its entirety is "Triomphe, destinée! Enfin, ton heure arrive. / O peuple, tu ne seras plus. / Il n'errera bientôt de toi sur cette rive / Que des mânes inconnus / En vain le soir, du haut de la montagne /

J'appelle un nom : tout est silencieux / O guerriers, levez-vous; couvrez cette campagne / Ombres des mes aïeux!"

52 Moore, *Black Robe.* Also published this same year was Duff, *In the Land of the People Apart.*

53 Moore, *Black Robe,* ix.

54 *Black Robe* (Montreal: Alliance Releasing Corporation, 1992).

55 Churchill, "And They Did It Like Dogs in the Dirt ... An Indigenist Analysis of *Black Robe,*" in *From a Native Son,* 423-37.

56 See fn 54.

57 Nichol, *Sainte-Marie Among the Hurons.*

58 Ibid., 79.

59 *Wikipedia,* http://en.wikipedia.org/wiki/Wyandot.

60 Ontario Association of Professional Archaeologists, The Charity Site, http://www.apaontario.ca/r_charity05.html (link now expired; copy of document in possession of the author).

61 Emphasis is my own. Ontario Association of Professional Archaeologists, with support from the Ministry of Citizenship, Culture and Recreation, and Human Resources Development Canada, "Christian Island," http://www.apaontario.ca/r_archhistory.html (link now expired; copy of document in possession of the author).

62 Barbeau, *Huron and Wyandot Mythology,* xi, 5.

63 Anne-Marie Sioui, interview by Catherine Gros-Louis Dubé, 1979, WA, Fonds Marguerite Vincent [FMV], cartable G-2-40.

64 Baker, *Cultural Studies,* 256.

65 "Memory," Huron Museum, main exhibit (1 October 2009).

66 Dower, *Embracing Defeat,* 28.

67 Said, "The Mind of Winter," 269.

68 Schivelbusch, *Culture of Defeat,* 5.

69 Gros-Louis, *Gros-Louis,* 10.

70 Ibid., 24-25.

71 Sioui, *Huron-Wendat,* xvi.

72 This is not true. The Iroquois captured, tortured, and killed the Jesuit martyrs.

73 Sioui, *Huron-Wendat,* xvi.

74 Peers, *Playing Ourselves,* 122.

75 Ibid.

76 Roberta Avery, "Reunion Brings Tears of Joy, Sense of Belonging," *Toronto Star,* 30 August 1999.

77 Sioui, *Huron-Wendat,* xx.

78 Sioui defines this as an Amerindian autohistorical approach. For more information on the subject, see his methodological guide, *For An Amerindian Autohistory.*

79 Sioui, *Huron-Wendat,* 176.

80 Conseil de la nation huronne-wendat, *Anontaché,* 9-11. Translation is my own.

81 *Traditional Huron Site, Onhoüa Chetek8e* (Wendake: Huron Village, 2007), 5.

82 Mario Gros-Louis quoted in ibid.

83 *Traditional Huron Site,* 9.

84 See Conseil de la nation huronne-wendat, *Territoires, Mémoires, Savoirs,* 5.

85 Huron Museum, main exhibit (1 October 2009).

86 The Wyandot of Anderdon Nation (Ontario and Michigan), http://www.wyandotofanderdon.com; Wyandot Nation of Kansas, http://www.wyandot.org;

Wyandotte Nation of Oklahoma, http://www.wyandotte-nation.org; Huron-Wendat of Wendake, http://www.wendake.ca.

87 Wyandot of Anderdon Nation, http://www.wyandotofanderdon.com.

88 Larry Hancks, "The Emigrant Tribes: Wyandot, Delaware and Shawnee – A Chronology" (2007), 13, http://www.wyandot.org.

89 Wydandotte Nation of Oklahoma, http://www.wyandotte-nation.org.

Bibliography

Archival Materials

Bibliothèque et Archives nationales du Québec, Canada
  Collection Centre d'archives de Québec
  Fonds cour supérieure
Archives nationales d'outre-mer, France
  Archives des Colonies, series B, Lettres Envoyées
  Archives des Colonies, series C11A, Correspondance Générale, Canada
  Archives des Colonies, series C11E, Des Limites des Postes
Bibliothèque Mazarin, France
  Fonds Général, Cote MS 1964
Library and Archives Canada, Canada
  Colonial Records, C11A
National Archives, United Kingdom
  Colonial Office and Predecessors: Canada, formerly British North America, CO5
Ontario Provincial Archives, Canada
  RG 5-46
  RG 5-7
  RG 1-524-2
  RG 1-61-0-33
Newberry Library, United States
  Ayer Collection, MS 507
University of Ottawa, Canada
  Collection History of French Canada
  Women's History Collection
Wendake Archives, Canada
  Collection François Vincent
  Fonds Marguerite Vincent
  Fonds Paul Picard

Museums and Material Culture

Canadian Museum of Civilization
  "Jesuit Mortar," Canada Hall Exhibit
Huron Museum
  "Memory," Main Exhibit
National Museum of the American Indian
  "Wampum Belt," Lobby

Other Sources

Abler, Thomas S. "Iroquois Cannibalism: Fact not Fiction." *Ethnology* 27, 4 (Autumn 1980): 309-16.

Alfred, Gerald. *Heeding the Voices of Our Ancestors: Kahnawake Mohawk Politics and the Rise of Native Nationalism.* Toronto: Oxford University Press, 1995.

Anderson, Karen Lee. *Chain Her by One Foot: The Subjugation of Native Women in Seventeenth-Century New France.* New York and London: Routledge, 1991.

–. "Huron Women and Huron Men: The Effects of Demography, Kinship, and the Social Division of Labour on Male/Female Relations among the Seventeenth-Century Huron." PhD diss., Department of Sociology, University of Toronto, 1983.

Anderson, William L., ed. *Cherokee Removal: Before and After.* Athens: University of Georgia Press, 1991.

Andre, Jacki. "Contagious Disease and Huron Women 1630-1650." MA thesis, Department of History, University of Saskatchewan, 1996.

Anthony, Levi. *Cardinal Richelieu and the Making of France.* New York: Carroll and Graf, 2000.

Baker, Chris. *Cultural Studies: Theory and Practice.* Thousand Oaks, CA: Sage Publications, 2008.

Bales, Rebecca. "Native American Women: Living with Landscape." *OAH Magazine of History* 12, 1 (Fall 1997): 13-16.

Barbeau, Charles Marius. *Huron and Wyandot Mythology.* Ottawa: Department of Mines, Geology Survey, 1915.

–. *Huron-Wyandot Traditional Narratives.* Ottawa: National Museum of Canada, 1960.

Barr, Daniel P. *Unconquered: The Iroquois League at War in Colonial America.* Westport, CT: Praeger, 2006.

Beauchamp, W.M. "Iroquois Women." *Journal of American Folklore* 13, 49 (April-June 1900): 81-91.

Beaulieu, Alain. "Les Hurons et la Conquête: Un nouvel éclairage sur le 'traité de Murray.'" *Recherches amérindiennes au Québec* 30, 4 (2000): 53-63.

–. "L'on n'a point d'ennemis plus grands que ces sauvages: L'alliance franco-innue revisitée (1603-1653)." *Revue d'histoire de l'Amérique française* 61, 3-4 (Winter-Spring 2008): 365-95.

Becker, Mary Druke. "Linking Arms: The Structure of Iroquois Intertribal Diplomacy." In Richter and Merrell, 29-41.

Birx, James H. *Encyclopedia of Anthropology.* Thousand Oaks, CA: Sage Publications, 2005.

Blick, Jeffrey P. "The Iroquois Practice of Genocidal Warfare (1534-1787)." *Journal of Genocide Research* 3 (2001): 405-29.

Bogaert, Harmen Meyndertsz van den. *A Journey into Mohawk and Oneida Country, 1634-1635: The Journal of Harmen Meyndertsz van den Bogaert.* Translated and edited by Charles T. Gehring and William Starna. Syracuse, NY: Syracuse University Press, 1988.

Bohaker, Heidi. "*Nindoodemag*: The Significance of Algonquian Kinship Networks in the Eastern Great Lakes Region, 1600-1701." *William and Mary Quarterly* 63, 1 (January 2006): 23-52.

Brah, Avtah. *Cartographies of Diaspora: Contesting Identities.* London and New York: Routledge, 1996.

Brandão, José António. *Your Fyre Shall Burn No More: Iroquois Policy toward New France and Its Native Allies to 1701.* Lincoln: University of Nebraska Press, 1997.

Brébeuf, Jean de. *Écrits en Huronie.* Edited by Gilles Thérien. Montreal: Bibliothèque Nationale du Québec, 1996.

–. *A Huron Carol.* Illustrated by Francis Tyrrell. Grand Rapids, MI: Eerdmans Books For Young Readers, 2003.

Bumsted, James M. *The Peoples of Canada: A Pre-Confederation History.* Toronto: Oxford University Press, 1992.

Calloway, Colin. *After King Philip's War: Presence and Persistence in Indian New England.* Hanover: University Press of New England, 1997.

Campeau, Lucien. *La mission des jésuites chez les Hurons, 1634-1650.* Montreal: Éditions Bellarmin, 1987.

–, ed. *Monumenta Novae Franciae.* 7 vols. Montreal: Éditions Bellarmin, 2003.

Carmack, R.M., ed. *Harvest of Violence: The Maya Indians and the Guatemalan Crisis.* Norman: University of Oklahoma, 1988.

Carpenter, Roger. *The Renewed, the Destroyed, and the Remade: The Three Thought Worlds of the Iroquois and the Huron, 1609-1650.* East Lansing: Michigan State University Press, 2004.

Cass, Lewis. *Remarks on the Policy and Practice of the United States and Great Britain in Their Treatment of Indians.* Boston: F.T. Gray, 1827.

Champlain, Samuel de. *The Voyages and Explorations of Samuel de Champlain:1604-1616.* Edited by Edward Gaylord Bourne. 3 vols. New York: A.S. Barnes and Company, 1906.

–. *The Voyages of Samuel de Champlain, 1604-1618.* Edited by J. Franklin Jameson. 3 vols. New York: Charles Scribner's Sons, 1907.

–. *The Works of Samuel de Champlain.* 6 vols. Toronto: University of Toronto Press, 1922-36.

Charlevoix, Pierre François Xavier de. *Histoire et description générale de la Nouvelle-France, avec le journal historique d'un voyage fait par ordre du roi dans l'Amérique septentrionale.* [1744] 6 vols. Montreal: Éditions Élysée, 1976.

–. *History and General Description of New France.* Translated by John G. Shea. 6 vols. Chicago: Loyola University Press, 1962.

–. *Journal of a Voyage to North America.* 2 vols. London: R. and J. Dodsley, 1761.

Choquette, Robert. *L'Ontario français, historique.* Montreal: Éditions Études Vivantes, 1980.

Churchill, Ward. *From a Native Son: Selected Essays in Indigenism, 1985-1995.* Cambridge: South End Press, 1996.

Connelly, William. *Kansas City, Kansas: Its Place in the History of the State.* Kansas City: John Brown Press, 1918.

Conseil de la nation huronne-wendat. *Anontaché: Pérégrinations des Hurons Wendat.* Wendake: Conseil de la nation huronne-wendat in collaboration with the Ministère de l'éducation du Québec, 1992.

–. *Territoires, Mémoires, Savoirs: Au Coeur du peuple Wendat.* Edited by Louis-Karl Picard-Sioui. Wendake: Éditions du CDFM, 2009.

Crosby, Alfred W. Jr. *The Columbian Exchange.* Connecticut: Greenwood Press, 1972.

–. "Virgin Soil Epidemics as a Factor in the Aboriginal Depopulation in America." *William and Mary Quarterly* 33 (1976): 289-99.

Davidson, James West, Brian DeLay, Christine Leigh Heyrman, Mark H. Lytle, and Michael B. Stoff. *U.S.: A Narrative History.* Vol. 1, *To 1877.* New York: McGraw-Hill, 2009.

Delâge, Denys. *Bitter Feast: Amerindians and Europeans in Northeastern North America, 1600-64.* Vancouver: UBC Press, 1993.

–. "Hurons de Lorette." In Vaugeois, 109-10.

Dennis, Matthew. *Cultivating a Landscape of Peace: Iroquois-European Encounters in Seventeenth-Century America.* Ithaca, NY: Cornell University Press, 1993.

Desrosiers, Léo-Paul. *Iroquoisie.* 4 vols. Sillery, QC: Septentrion, 1999.

Devens, Carol. *Countering Colonizing: Native American Women and Great Lakes Missions, 1630-1900.* Berkeley: University of California Press, 1992.

Devine, Edward James. *Historic Caughnawaga.* Montreal: Messenger Press, 1922.

Dobyns, Henry F. "Disease Transfer at Contact." *Annual Review of Anthropology* 22 (1993): 273-91.

–. *Their Number Become Thinned: Native American Population Dynamics in Eastern North America.* Knoxville: University of Tennessee Press, 1983.

Dolan, Edward F. *The American Indian Wars.* Brookfield, CT: Millbrook Press, 2003.

Dower, John W. *Embracing Defeat: Japan in the Wake of World War II.* NY: W.W. Norton and Company, 2000.

Duff, Steven. *In the Land of the People Apart: Being the Journal of Jean-Paul Dufour among the Huron Indians, 1634-1650.* Belleville, ON: Mika Publishing, 1985.

DuVal, Kathleen. *The Native Ground: Indians and Colonists in the Heart of the Continent.* Philadelphia: University of Pennsylvania Press, 2006.

Eastman, Charles. *Indian Heroes and Great Chieftains.* Boston: Little, Brown and Company, 1918.

Eccles, William. *France in America.* New York: Harper and Row, 1972.

Ehle, John. *Trail of Tears: The Rise and Fall of the Cherokee Nation.* New York: Doubleday, 1988.

Fenton, William Nelson. *The Great Law and the Longhouse: A Political History of the Iroquois Confederacy.* Norman: University of Oklahoma, 1998.

–. "The Iroquois in History." In Leacock and Lurie, 129-68.

–. "Northern Iroquoian Culture Patterns." In Trigger, *Handbook,* Vol. 15, 296-321.

Foreman, Grant. *Indian Removal: The Emigration of the Five Civilized Tribes of Indians.* Norman: University of Oklahoma Press, 1932.

Francis, Douglas R., Richard Jones, and Donald B. Smith, eds. *Origins: Canadian History to Confederation.* Toronto: Harcourt Canada, 2000.

Gendron, François. *Quelques particularités du pays Hurons en la Nouvelle France: remarquées par Sieur Gendron, docteur en médecine, qui a demeuré dans ce pays-là fort long-temps.* Albany, NY: J. Mansell, 1868.

Green, Michael D., and Theda Perdue. *The Cherokee Nation and the Trail of Tears.* New York: Viking, 2008.

Greer, Allan, ed. *The Jesuit Relations: Natives and Missionaries in Seventeenth Century North America.* New York: Bedford, 2000.

–. *Mohawk Saint: Catherine Tekakwitha and the Jesuits.* New York: Oxford University Press, 2005.

Griffiths, Nicholas, and Fernando Cervantes, eds. *Spiritual Encounters: Interactions between Christianity and Native Religion in Colonial America.* Lincoln: University of Nebraska Press, 1999.

Gros-Louis, Max. *Gros-Louis: First among the Hurons.* Montreal: Harvest House Press, 1973.

Gunderson, Mary. *American Indian Cooking before 1500.* North Mankato, MN: Capstone Press, 2001.

Hale, Horatio. "A Huron Historical Legend." *Magazine of American History* (December 1883): 475-83.

–. "Four Huron Wampum Records: A Study of Aboriginal American History and Mnemonic Symbols." *Journal of Anthropological Institute* (February 1897): 254-97.

Harris, Cole, ed. *Historical Atlas of Canada.* Vol. 1, *From the Beginning to 1800.* Toronto: University of Toronto Press, 1987.

Hathaway, Ernest Jackson. *The Story of the Hurons.* Toronto: Ontario Historical Society, 1915.

Havard, Gilles. *The Great Peace of Montreal of 1701: French-Native Diplomacy in the Seventeenth Century.* Translated by Phyllis Arnoff and Howard Scott. Montreal and Kingston: McGill-Queen's University Press, 2001.

Hébert, Léo-Paul. *Le registre de Sillery (1638-1690): Introduction, présentation et notes.* Quebec: Presses de l'Université du Québec, 1994.

Heidenreich, Conrad. *Huronia: A History and Geography of the Huron Indians 1600-1650.* Toronto: McClelland and Stewart, 1971.

Hennepin, Louis. *Voyage curieux du R.P. Louis Hennepin.* Leide: P. Van Der A.A., 1704.

Herweijer, Celine, Richard Seager, Edward R. Cook, and Julien Emile-Geay. "North American Droughts of the Last Millennium from a Gridded Network of Tree-Ring Data." *Journal of Climate* 20 (April 2007): 1353-76.

Hesse, Peter. *The Algonkin Nation – The Algonkins of the Ottawa Valley: An Historical Outline.* Arnprior, ON: Kichesippi Books, 1993.

Hickerson, Harold. "The Feast of the Dead among the Seventeenth Century Algonkians of the Upper Great Lakes." *American Anthropology* 62, 1 (February 1960): 81-107.

Hodge, Frederick Webb, ed. *Handbook of Indians of Canada: Tenth Report of the Geographic Board of Canada.* Ottawa: C.H. Parmelee, 1913.

–, ed. *Handbook of American Indians North of Mexico.* 15 vols. New York: Pageant, 1959.

Hornsby, Stephen, and John G. Reid, eds. *New England and the Maritime Provinces: Connections and Comparisons.* Montreal: McGill-Queen's University Press, 2005.

Horowitz, David. *The First Frontier: The Indian Wars and America's Origins: 1607-1776.* New York: Simon and Schuster, 1978.

Hunt, George T. *The Wars of the Iroquois: A Study in Intertribal Trade Relations.* Madison: University of Wisconsin Press, 1940.

Hunter, Andrew F. *Notes of Sites of Huron Villages in the Township of Medonte (Simcoe County).*, Reprinted from the Ontario Archaeological Report for the *Report of the Minister of Education for Ontario.* Toronto: OAR, 1901.

Jackson, J.H. "The Dynamic of Indian Demographic Collapse in the San Francisco Bay Missions, Alta, California, 1776-1840." *American Indian Quarterly* 15 (1992): 141-56.

Jackson, L.J., R. Rose, A. Ariss, and C. Theriault. "A Winter of Discontent: The Charity Site, 1991." *Arch Notes* 92, 6 (Nov-Dec 1992): 5-9.

Janick, Jules, and Robert E. Paull, eds. *Encyclopedia of Fruit and Nuts.* Cambridge: CAB International, 2008.

Jennings, Francis. *The Ambiguous Iroquois Empire: The Covenant Chain Confederation of Indian Tribes with English Colonies from Its Beginning to the Lancaster Treaty of 1744.* New York: W.W. Norton and Company, 1984.

Johnson, Paul, Stephen R. Shifley, and Robert Rogers. *The Ecology and Silviculture of Oaks.* Cambridge: CAB International, 2009.

Johnson, Richard B., and L.J. Jackson, "Settlement Pattern at the Le Caron Site, a 17th Century Huron Village." *Journal of Field Archaeology* 7, 2 (Summer 1980): 175.

Jones, Arthur Edwards. *"8endake Ehen" or Old Huronia.* Toronto: 5th Report of the Bureau of Archives for the Province of Ontario, 1908.

Jury, Wilfred, and Elsie McLeod Jury. *Sainte-Marie among the Hurons.* Toronto: Oxford University Press, 1954.

Keener, Craig S. "An Ethnohistorical Analysis of Iroquois Assault Tactics Used against Fortified Settlements of the Northeast in the Seventeenth Century." *Ethnohistory* 46, 4 (Autumn 1999): 777-807.

Kelsey, H. "European Impact on the California Indians, 1530-1830." *Americas* 41 (1985): 494-511.

Kennedy, J.H. *Jesuit and Savage in New France.* New Haven, CT: Yale University Press, 1950.

Kidd, Adam. *The Huron Chief and Other Poems.* Montreal: n.p., 1830.

Kidwell, Clara Sue, and Alan R. Velie. *Native American Studies.* Edinburgh: Edinburgh University Press, 2005.

Kokot, Waltraud, Khachig Tölölyan, and Carolin Alfonso. *Disapora, Identity, and Religion: New Directions in Theory and Research.* New York: Routledge, 2006.

la Potherie, Claude-Charles Bacqueville de. *Documents Relating to the Early History of Hudson Bay.* Edited by Joseph Burr Tyrrell. Toronto: Champlain Society, 1931.

Lafitau, Joseph-François. *Customs of American Indians Compared with the Customs of Primitive Times.* Edited and translated by William N. Fenton and Elizabeth L. Moore. Toronto: Champlain Society, 1977.

–. *Mœurs, coutumes et religions des sauvages Américains.* 2 vols. Lyon: Périsse, 1839.

Lahontan, Louis Armand de Lom d'Arce, Baron de. *Histoire de L'Amérique septentrionale.* 3 vols. Paris: Brocas, 1753.

–. *Nouveaux voyages de M. Le baron de Lahontan dans l'Amérique septentrionale.* 2 vols. La Haye: Frères l'Honoré, 1703.

Lainey, Jonathan C. *La "Monnaie des sauvages:" Les colliers de Wampum d'hier à aujourd'hui.* Sillery, QC: Septentrion, 2004.

–. "Les colliers de porcelaine de l'époque coloniale à aujourd'hui." *Recherches Amérindiennes au Québec* 35, 2 (2005): 61-73.

Lanctôt, Gustave. "Dollard des Ormeaux and the Fight at the Long Sault: Was Dollard the Saviour of New France?" *Canadian Historical Review* 13, 1 (1932): 137-46.

Latourelle, René, ed. *Étude sur les écrits de Saint Jean de Brébeuf.* 2 vols. Montreal: Éditions de l'Immaculée-Conception, 1952.

Leacock, Eleanor Burke, and Nancy Oestreich Lurie, eds. *North American Indians in Historical Perspective.* New York: Random House, 1971.

Lescarbot, Marc. *The History of New France.* Translated by W.L. Grant. 3 vols. Toronto: Champlain Society, 1914.

Levasseur, Gisèle. "S'allier pour survivre: Les épidémies chez les Hurons et les Iroquois entre 1634 et 1700: Une étude ethnohistorique comparative." PhD diss., Department of History, Université Laval, 2009.

Lightfoot, Kent G., Antoinette Martinez, and Ann M. Schiff. "Daily Practice and Material Culture in Pluralistic Social Settings: An Archaeological Study of Culture Change and Persistence from Fort Ross, California." *American Antiquity* 63, 2 (April 1998): 199-222.

MacLeod, D.P. "Microbes and Muskets." *Ethnohistory* 39 (1992): 42-64.

Magee, Kathryn. "History Repeats Itself: Huron Childrearing Attitudes, Eurocentricity, and the Importance of Indigenous Worldview." *Canadian Journal for Native Education* 31, 2 (2008): 4-14.

–. "'They Are the Life of the Nation': Women and War in Traditional Nadowek Society." *Canadian Journal of Native Studies* 28, 1 (2008): 119-38.

Magee Labelle, Kathryn. "'They Only Spoke in Sighs': The Loss of Leaders and Life in Wendake, 1633-1639." *Journal of Historical Biography* 6 (Autumn 2009): 1-33.

Magliocca, Gerard N. "The Cherokee Removal and the Fourteenth Amendment." *Duke Law Journal* 53, 3 (December 2003): 875-965.

Magnuson, Roger. *Education in New France.* Montreal: McGill-Queen's University Press, 1992.

Mancall, Peter C., and James Hart Merrell, eds. *American Encounters: Natives and Newcomers from European Contact to Indian Removal.* New York: Routledge, 2000.

Mancke, Elizabeth. "Polity Formation and Atlantic Political Narratives." In Morgan and Canny, 382-99.

–. "Spaces of Power in the Early Modern Northeast." In Hornsby and Reid, 32-49.

Mann, Charles C. *1491: New Revelations of the Americas before Columbus.* New York: Knopf, 2005.

Mann, Michael. *The Sources of Social Power: A History of Power from the Beginning.* Cambridge: Cambridge University Press, 1986.

Margry, Pierre, ed. *Découvertes et établissements des Français dans l'ouest et dans le sud de l'Amérique septentrionale (1683-1724).* 5 vols. Paris: Maisonneuve frères et C.H. Leclerc éditeurs, 1887.

Marie de l'Incarnation, Mère. *Lettres de la Révérende Mère Marie de l'Incarnation.* Edited by Abbé Richaudeau. 2 vols. Tournai, 1876.

Marrin, Albert. *Struggle for a Continent: The French and Indian Wars, 1690-1760.* New York: Atheneum, 1987.

Martin, Calvin. *Keepers of the Game.* Los Angeles: University of California Press, 1978.

Martin, Felix, ed. *Autobiographie du Père Chaumonot de la Compagnie de Jésus et son complément par Rev. P. Felix Martin de la même compagnie.* Paris: Oudin, 1885.

McMullen, John Mercier. *The History of Canada: From Its First Discovery to the Present Time.* Brockville, ON: 1891.

Meighan, C.W. "Indians and California Missions." *Southern California Quarterly* 69 (1987): 187-201.

Merrell, James H. *The Indians' New World: Catawbas and Their Neighbours from European Contact through the Era of Removal.* Chapel Hill: University of North Carolina Press, 1989.

Michaelsen, Robertson S. "Red Man's Religion / White Man's Religious History." *Journal of the American Academy of Religion* 51 (December 1983): 667-84.

Mihesuah, Devon, ed. *Natives and Academics: Research and Writing about American Indians.* Lincoln: University of Nebraska Press, 1998.

Mithun, Marianne. "Untangling the Huron and the Iroquois." *International Journal of American Linguistics* 51, 4 (October 1985): 504-7.

Moore, Brian. *Black Robe: A Novel.* Toronto: McClelland and Stewart, 1985.

Moore, James T. *Indian and Jesuit: A Seventeenth-Century Encounter.* Chicago: Loyola University Press, 1982.

Morgan, Lewis Henry. *League of the Ho-deno-sau-nee, or Iroquois.* New York: M.H. Newman, 1851.

Morgan, Philip D., and Nicholas Canny, eds. *Oxford Handbook on the Atlantic World, c.1450-1840.* Oxford: Oxford University Press, 2011.

Morrison, Kenneth M. "Discourse and the Accommodation of Values: Toward a Revision of Mission History." *Journal of the American Academy of Religion* 53, 3 (September 1985): 365-82.

Müller-Schwarze, Dietland. *Hands-on Chemical Ecology: Simple Field and Lab Exercises.* New York/London: Springer Science+Business Media, 2009.

Munck, Thomas. *Seventeenth-Century Europe: State, Conflict, and the Social Order in Europe, 1598-1700.* Malaysia: Palgrave Publishing, 1989.

Murphy, Lucy Eldersveld, and Rebecca Kugel, eds. *Native Women's History in Eastern North America before 1900.* Lincoln: University of Nebraska Press, 2007.

Nichol, James. *Sainte-Marie Among the Hurons: A Play.* Vancouver: Talonbooks, 1980.

O'Brien, Jean. "'Divorced' from the Land: Resistance and Survival of Indian Women in Eighteenth-Century New England." In Murphy and Kugel, 333-67.

Otterbein, Keith F. "Huron vs. Iroquois: A Case Study in Inter-Tribal Warfare." *Ethnohistory* 26, 2 (Spring 1979): 141-52.

–. "Why the Iroquois Won: An Analysis of Iroquois Military Tactics." *Ethnohistory* 11, 1 (Winter 1964): 56-63.

Parker, Arthur. *The History of the Seneca Indians.* Port Washington: I.J. Friedman, 1967.

Parkman, Francis. *The Jesuits in North America in the Seventeenth Century.* Boston: Little, Brown and Company, 1867.

Parmenter, Jon. *The Edge of the Woods: Iroquoia, 1534-1701.* East Lansing: Michigan State University Press, 2010.

Peers, Laura. *Playing Ourselves: Interpreting Native Histories at Historical Reconstructions.* Lanham, MD: AltaMira Press, 2007.

Perdue, Theda. "Cherokee Women and the Trail of Tears." In Murphy and Kugel, 277-302.

–. *Cherokee Women: Gender and Culture Change, 1700-1835.* Lincoln: University of Nebraska Press, 1998.

Perrot, Nicholas. *Mémoire sur les mœurs, coutumes et religion des sauvages de l'Amérique septentrionale.* Montreal: Éditions Élysée, 1973.

Peyser, Joseph L., and José António Brandão, eds. *Edge of Empire: Documents of Michilimackinac, 1671-1716.* East Lansing: University of Michigan Press, 2008.

Podruchny, Carolyn, and Kathryn Magee Labelle. "Jean de Brébeuf and the Wendat Voices of Seventeenth-Century New France." In "Relazioni / Relations," ed. Tom Cohen and Germaine Warkentin, special issue, *Renaissance and Reformation / Renaissance et Réforme* 34, 1-2 (Fall 2011-Winter 2012): 97-126.

Pomedli, Michael M. *Ethnophilosophical and Ethnolinguistic Perspectives on the Huron Indian Soul.* Lewiston: Edwin Mellen Press, 1991.

Pratt, Mary Louise. *Imperial Eyes: Travel Writing and Transculturation.* London and New York: Routledge, 1992.

Quen, Jean de. *Relation de ce qui s'est passé en la mission des pères de la Compagnie de Jésus, au pays de la Nouvelle France, lés années 1655 et 1656 envoyée au R.P. Louis Cellot, provincial de la Compagnie de Jésus, en la province de France.* Paris: Sebastien Cramoisy, 1657.

Radisson, Pierre-Esprit. *Voyages of Peter Radisson: Being an Account of his Travels and Experiences among the North American Indians from 1652-1684.* Boston: Prince Society, John Wilson and Son, 1885.

Richter, Daniel. *Facing East from Indian Country: A Native History of Early America.* Cambridge, MA: Harvard University Press, 2003.

–. *The Ordeal of the Longhouse.* Chapel Hill: University of North Carolina Press, 1992.

–. "War and Culture: The Iroquois Experience." *William and Mary Quarterly* 40, 4 (October 1983): 528-59.

Richter, Daniel, and James Merrell, eds. *Beyond the Covenant Chain: The Iroquois and Their Neighbors in Indian North America, 1600-1800.* University Park: Pennsylvania State University, 1987.

Rockman, Marcy, and James Steele, eds. *Colonization of Unfamiliar Landscapes: The Archaeology of Adaption.* New York: Routledge, 2003.

Roderick, Stewart, and Neil McLean. *L'histoire du Canada et des canadiens.* Toronto: Éditions Gage Limitée, 1980.

Rushforth, Brett. "Slavery, the Fox Wars, and the Limits of Alliance." *William and Mary Quarterly* 60, 4 (October 2003): 777-808.

Sagard, Gabriel. *The Long Journey to the Country of the Hurons.* [1632] Edited by George M. Wrong. Toronto: Champlain Society, 1939.

Said, Edward. "The Mind of Winter: Reflections on Life in Exile." *Harper's Magazine* (September 1984): 49-55.

Saint-Thomas, Mère. *Les Ursulines de Québec, depuis leur établissement jusqu'à nos jours.* Quebec, 1863.

Sale, K. *The Conquest of Paradise.* New York: Penguin, 1991.

Salisbury, Neil. "Religious Encounters in a Colonial Context: New England and New France in the Seventeenth Century." *American Indian Quarterly* 16, 4 (Autumn 1992): 501-9.

Sayre, Gordon Mitchell. *Les sauvages américains: Representations of Native Americans in French and English Colonial Literature.* Chapel Hill: University of North Carolina, 1997.

Schivelbusch, Wolfgang. *The Culture of Defeat: On National Trauma, Mourning and Recovery.* New York: Henry Holt and Company, 2003.

Schlesier, Karl H. "Epidemics and Indian Middlemen: Rethinking the Wars of the Iroquois, 1609-1653." *Ethnohistory* 23, 2 (Spring 1976): 129-45.

Schmitz, Neil. *White Robe's Dilemma: Tribal History in American Literature.* Amherst: University of Massachusetts Press, 2001.

Seeman, Erik R. *The Huron-Wendat Feast of the Dead: Indian-European Encounters in Early North America.* Baltimore: Johns Hopkins University Press, 2011.

Shuval, Judith T. "Diaspora Migration: Definitional Ambiguities and a Theoretical Paradigm." *International Migration* 38, 5 (December 2000): 41-56.

Sioui, George E. *For an Amerindian Autohistory.* Montreal: McGill-Queen's Press, 1992.

–. *Huron-Wendat: The Heritage of the Circle.* Vancouver: UBC Press, 1999.

Skinner, Claiborne A. *The Upper Country: French Enterprise in the Colonial Great Lakes.* Baltimore: Johns Hopkins University Press, 2008.

Sleeper-Smith, Susan. *Indian Women and French Men: Rethinking Cultural Encounter in the Western Great Lakes.* Amherst: University of Massachusetts Press, 2001.

Smith, Beverly Ann. *Systems of Subsistence and Networks of Exchange in the Terminal Woodland and Early Historic Period in the Upper Great Lakes.* PhD diss., Department of Anthropology, Michigan State University, 1996.

Snow, Dean R. *The Peoples of America: The Iroquois.* Malden: Blackwell Publishing, 1996.

Snow, Dean R., and Kim M. Lanphear. "European Contact and Indian Depopulation in the Northeast: The Timing of the First Epidemics." *Ethnohistory* 35 (1988): 15-33.

Snyderman, George Simon. "Behind the Tree of Peace: A Sociological Analysis of Iroquois Warfare." PhD diss., University of Pennsylvania, 1948.

Spiess, A.D., and B.D. Spiess. "New England Pandemic of 1616-1622." *Man in New England* 34 (1987): 71-83.

Stahle, David, Falko K. Fye, Edward R. Cook, and R. Daniel Griffin. "Tree-ring Reconstructed Megadroughts over North America since A.D. 1300." *Climate Change* 83, 1-2 (July 2007): 133-49.

Stannard, D.E. *The American Holocaust.* New York: Oxford University Press, 1992.

Starkey, Armstrong. *European-Native American Warfare, 1675-1815*. Norman: University of Oklahoma Press, 1998.

Starna, William. "The Biological Encounter: Disease and the Ideological Domain." *American Indian Quarterly* 16, 4 (Autumn 1992): 371-82.

Starna, William, and Ralph Watkins. "Northern Iroquoian Slavery." *Ethnohistory* 38, 1 (Winter 1991): 34-53.

Steckley, John, ed. *The First French-Huron Dictionary, by Father Jean de Brébeuf and His Jesuit Brethren*. New York: Edwin Mellen Press, 2010.

–. "The 1747 Wyandot Elders Council." *Northeastern Anthropology* 75-76 (Spring-Fall 2008): 93-111.

–. *Untold Tales: Three 17th Century Huron*. Ajax, ON: R. Kerton Printing Ltd, 1981.

–. "Wendat Dialects and the Development of the Huron Alliance." *Northeast Anthropology* 54, 2 (1997): 23-36.

–. *Words of the Huron*. Waterloo, ON: Wilfred Laurier University Press, 2007.

Steele, Ian. *Warpaths: The Invasion of North America*. New York: Oxford University Press, 1994.

Sturgis, Amy H. *The Trail of Tears and Indian Removal*. Westport, CT: Greenwood Press, 2006.

Sulte, Benjamin. *Pierre Boucher et son livre*. Ottawa: J. Durie, 1896.

Sundstrom, Linea. "Small Pox Used Them Up: References to Epidemic Disease in Northern Plains Winter Camps, 1714-1920." *Ethnohistory* 44, 2 (Spring 1997): 305-43.

Taylor, Alan. *The Divided Ground: Indians, Settlers, and the Northern Borderland of the American Revolution*. New York: Knopf, 2006.

Thornton, Russell. "Aboriginal North American Population and Rates of Decline, ca. A.D. 1500-1900." *Current Anthropology* 38, 2 (April 1997): 310-15.

Thwaites, Reuben G., ed. *The Jesuit Relations and Allied Documents, 1600-1791*. 73 vols. Cleveland: Burrows, 1896-1901.

Tooker, Elizabeth. *An Ethnography of the Huron Indians 1615-1649*. Syracuse, NY: Syracuse University Press, 1964.

–, ed. *An Iroquois Source Book*. New York: Garland Publishing, 1985.

–. "Northern Iroquoian Sociopolitical Organization." *American Anthropologist* 72,1 (February 1970): 93-95.

Toupin, Robert, ed. *Les Écrits de Pierre Potier*. Ottawa: Les Presses de l'Université d'Ottawa, 1996.

Trautmann, Thomas R. "Lewis Henry Morgan and the Invention of Kinship." *Ethnohistory* 36, 3 (Summer 1989): 267-83.

Trelease, Allen W. *Indian Affairs in Colonial New York: The Seventeenth Century*. Ithaca, NY: Cornell University Press, 1960.

Trigger, Bruce. *Children of Aataentsic: A History of the Huron People to 1660*. Montreal: McGill-Queen's University Press, 1976.

–. "The French Presence in Huronia: The Structure of Franco-Huron Relations in the First Half of the Seventeenth Century." *Canadian Historical Review* 49, 2 (June 1968): 107-41.

–. ed., *Handbook of North American Indians*. 15 vols. Washington, DC: Smithsonian Institution, 1978.

–. *The Huron: Farmers of the North*. New York: Holt, Rinehart and Winston, 1969.

–. *Natives and Newcomers: Canada's "Heroic Age" Reconsidered*. Kingston: McGill-Queen's University Press, 1985.

Vachon, André. "L'affaire du Long-Sault: valeur de la source huronne." *Revue de l'Université Laval* 18 (1963-64): 495-515.

Vaugeois, Denis, ed. *Les Hurons de Lorette.* Sillery, QC: Septentrion, 1996.

Verano, J.W., and D.H. Ubelaker, eds. *Disease and Demography in the Americas.* Washington, DC: Smithsonian Institution Press, 1992.

Vogel, Virgil J. *Indian Names in Michigan.* Ann Arbor: University of Michigan Press, 1986.

Wallace, Anthony F.C. *The Death and Rebirth of the Seneca.* New York: Knopf, 1976.

Wallace, Stewart W., ed. *The Encyclopedia of Canada.* 4 vols. Toronto: University Associates of Canada, 1948.

Warrick, Gary. "A Population History of the Huron-Petun, A.D. 900-1650." PhD diss., Department of Anthropology, McGill University, 1990.

–. *A Population History of the Huron-Petun, A.D. 900-1650.* Cambridge: Cambridge University Press, 2008.

–. "European Infectious Disease and Depopulation of the Wendat-Tionontate (Huron-Petun)." *World Archaeology* 35, 2 (October 2003): 258-75.

Weaver, Emily. *A Canadian History for Boys and Girls.* Toronto: W. Briggs, 1900.

White, Randall. *Ontario 1610-1985: A Political Economic History.* Toronto: Dundurn Press, 1985.

White, Richard. *The Middle Ground: Indians, Empires, and Republics in the Great Lakes Region, 1650-1815.* New York: Cambridge University Press, 1991.

Wilson, Daniel. *The Lost Atlantis and other Ethnographic Studies.* Edinburgh: D. Douglas, 1892.

Zedeno, Maria Nieves, and Richard W. Stoffle, "Tracking the Role of Pathways in the Evolution of Human Landscape," in Rockman and Steele, 59-80.

Index